MOVING MOUNTAINS

Lt. General William G. Pagonis
with Jeffrey L. Cruikshank

MOVING MOUNTAINS
Lessons in Leadership
and Logistics
from the Gulf War

Harvard Business School Press
Boston, Massachusetts

Library of Congress Cataloging-in-Publication Data

Pagonis, William G., 1941-
    Moving mountains : lessons in leadership and logistics from the Gulf War /
William G. Pagonis with Jeffrey L. Cruikshank.
      p.   cm.
    Includes bibliographical references and index.
    ISBN 0-87584-508-8 (pbk: acid-free paper)
    1. Persian Gulf War, 1991—Logistics—United States. 2. Pagonis, William
G., 1941-   . 3. United States—Armed Forces—Management. I. Cruik-
shank, Jeffrey L. II. Title.
DS79.72.P34 1992
956.704'3—dc20   92-15641
                                                    CIP

Originally published in hardcover by the Harvard Business School Press

04 03 02 01   10 9 8 7 6 5

Unless otherwise noted, all photographs were furnished by the Department of
the Army.

The paper used in this publication meets the requirements
of the American National Standard for Permanence of Paper for
Printed Library Materials Z39.49-1984.

To my best friend, confidante, honest critic, and greatest supporter, regardless of the circumstances— Cheri. I am convinced that after 28 years of service to our nation, I couldn't have made it without you.

Gus

Also, to all the service members of our Armed Forces and their civilian counterparts who served in Southwest Asia, and especially to those who made the supreme sacrifice in the service of their grateful nation.

Contents

Preface

I am setting out in the following pages to record my observations on leadership, management, and logistics in the context of the Gulf War. The reader is forewarned that I am, first and foremost, a professional soldier. I don't like to write a great deal. The more you write, I've learned, the less likely it is that your subordinates will ever read anything that you write. For much the same reason—that is, protecting the currency from inflation—I rarely place my signature on anything. I hope that when I do sign something, it gets read.

When I write, I try to keep a few basic goals in mind. I aim for simplicity, brevity, and clarity. I am not optimistic, however, about achieving either simplicity or brevity here. The Army is a complex organization. It sometimes mystifies even those of us who have spent decades working within it. Major changes in the U.S. Armed Forces over the past quarter-century have had a direct impact on the outcome of the Gulf War, and these changes need some explanation. Similarly, the Middle East has bewildered some of the brightest minds of this century. The logistical aspects of the Gulf War in its several distinct phases—Desert Shield, Desert Storm, and Desert Farewell—were extremely complicated. Introducing and explaining these themes and their interrelationships, even in summary form, will surely fill many, many pages.

The lessons of the Gulf War, I feel, warrant careful examination.

We have seen the restatement of some of the oldest lessons of military history. I'm convinced, for example, that our side knew more about Alexander the Great's approach to logistics, and also about his principles of leadership, than Saddam Hussein's lieutenants did. We benefited; Saddam and the Iraqi army did not. At the same time, the unexpected outcomes of the Gulf War suggest that we can anticipate modifications to military doctrine. Some of these revisions have already occurred, and more are sure to follow.

The outcome of the war may also have implications for private industry. A number of observers have suggested that business leaders should pay close attention to the lessons of the Gulf War.[1] I did earn an MBA, but that was many years ago. Except to the extent that the Army is a business, I haven't been in business, and I certainly don't think of myself as an expert in private-sector logistics. But to those logisticians in business who are looking to our example to provide their company's next competitive advantage—and I think they can, in many cases—I will try to provide a clear roadmap: how we moved unprecedented numbers of people and quantities of material on a battlefield on the other side of the world, under staggering constraints.

Logistics is traditionally an unglamorous and underappreciated activity. To generalize, when the battle is going well, the strategist and tactician are lionized; it is only when the tanks run out of gas that people go head-hunting for the logisticians. Field Marshall Rommel, the leading figure in the first desert war between two mechanized armies,[2] was asked by the German Chief of Staff how he planned to supply and feed the two additional panzer corps that he was then demanding from Berlin, for an offensive that few in Berlin wanted him to mount. "That's quite immaterial to me," Rommel replied coolly. "That's your pigeon."[3]

Contrast Rommel's attitude with that of General H. Norman Schwarzkopf. During one of our many Desert Shield planning sessions, General Schwarzkopf commented that if hostilities broke out, they would represent the beginning of what he called "the first come-as-you-are war." And at his now-famous press conference—dubbed the "mother of all briefings" by one journalist[4]—on February 27, 1991, he specifically praised the thousands of men and women who had built and run his logistical operation, and thereby made the celebrated "end run" possible. "It was an absolutely gigantic accomplishment," General Schwarzkopf told the assembled reporters, "and I can't give credit enough to the logisticians and the transporters who were able to pull this off."[5]

There *was* leadership exercised in the 22d Support Command, at every level. To some extent, my troops drew upon the good lessons that they had learned from me, and that I in turn had learned from others. Equally important, I drew on what I had learned from them. Today's Army, including its remarkable logistics reserve units, has a lot to teach its generals.

This book is about all of those lessons. I hope it will be of interest to students and practitioners of business, as well as to soldiers: old, new, and in the making. And although I've given up on brevity and simplicity, I will still shoot for clarity.

One last point: like most of my colleagues in the military, I try to avoid the word "I" whenever possible. In my trade, as in most other interesting professions, real and sustained success comes only through teamwork. Ask any athlete who has played for the Boston Celtics since Red Auerbach first arrived on the scene. Or ask those athletes, like Wilt Chamberlain, who so often outclassed the Celtics in terms of personal talent but still couldn't bring home the championship.

But I can't think of a good way to avoid the first person singular in this assignment. To my colleagues who may read these pages, I do make a promise in advance. Wherever possible, you will get due credit from me for our shared accomplishments.

Acknowledgments

I'm told that this is the section of a book where the author thanks those who made the book happen. I intend to do that in due course; but first I'd like to expand the territory, and thank publicly some of those people who have done larger things.

By now, everyone who has followed the story of the Gulf War is aware of the contributions of the high-profile leaders of that effort. President Bush and Secretary Cheney have earned well-deserved praise for two key contributions: first, they defined our military objectives clearly; and second, once those military objectives were defined, they allowed the professionals to do their jobs. I had some extensive personal contact with Mr. Cheney and wound up very much impressed with his intellect, powers of logic, and skill at extracting the key issues from a briefing. His questions to me were uniformly penetrating, fair, and on point.

General Colin Powell, too, deserves great credit for forging these effective lines of communication, which ensured that ideas could flow in both directions. He took the weight of political considerations off General Schwarzkopf's shoulders, allowing Schwarzkopf to focus primarily on events in the theater. Powell also made a point of serving as the leader of *all* the services, embodying the notion of "jointness" which the Pentagon has tried so hard to foster in recent decades. He also had a feel for the common soldier, having served in the field; and was accepted by those in the military as a soldier rather than a politician.

Some of Norman Schwarzkopf's special talents are known to all who watched his celebrated briefings on television. He is, without question, a forceful and self-confident leader, tenaciously protective of his troops. For me, a highlight of his February 27, 1991, press briefing came when a reporter introduced a particular line of questioning by saying, "General, not to take anything away from the Army and the Marines on the breaching maneuvers—" and Schwarzkopf interjected, "Thank you, sir. I hope you don't!" And of course many other dimensions of Schwarzkopf emerged during these briefings. I'm sure many Americans were surprised and pleased to discover that our vigorous commanding general was not only a soldier but also an intellectual: witty, well read, well traveled, and articulate. No doubt it was these broad perspectives that led him to decisions that were correct and critical, from a logistical standpoint, including the key decision (made with General John Yeosock's strong encouragement) to centralize logistical support for all the services under a single, unified command.

But Schwarzkopf also has many other talents and strengths which were probably not obvious to the television audience. For one thing, in the context of the Gulf War, he understood and was consistently sensitive to the cultures of the Middle East. Truth be told, few observers thought that a half-million American troops could deploy into Saudi Arabia without major cultural conflicts. There were certainly frictions and misunderstandings, but there was not one single incident—not one—in which an American service man or woman was involved in deliberate misconduct. Much of the credit for this achievement goes to General Schwarzkopf, as well as to the general officers in the theater who understood and implemented his policies.

Schwarzkopf also deserves credit for being one of the first to perceive that the major threat to our national interests in the Persian Gulf was likely to come from Iraq, rather than hostile and hostage-taking Iran. In the late 1980s, he redirected U.S. Central Command's (CENTCOM's) planning and training activities accordingly. At his urging, in fact, our armed forces participated in a comprehensive computer simulation of an Iraqi invasion of Kuwait. This exercise was completed in July 1990, only a month before the real invasion, and it contributed mightily to our success.

Finally, as suggested above, Schwarzkopf put the safety and morale of his troops above all other considerations. Because he and I agreed absolutely eye to eye on this point, as did the rest of the general officers in the Gulf, our disagreements seemed trivial by comparison.

Bush, Cheney, Powell, and Schwarzkopf: these are the public heroes of the Gulf War. But there are thousands of other individuals, soldiers and civilians, who in their own ways helped win the war. Few of them received much public notice, and all of them deserve it. Let me acknowledge a few of them here.

First, General Carl E. Vuono. Recently retired as the Army Chief of Staff, General Vuono headed the Army throughout the Gulf War. Even more important than his wartime efforts, in my opinion, were Vuono's many contributions in the years before the war, when he relentlessly focused the Army on the importance of realistic training. There is no doubt in my mind that our desert training exercises at Fort Irwin, California—which, because of the incorporation of some of the most up-to-date technologies, were uncannily realistic—helped make the successes of Desert Storm possible.

General Vuono's successor as Chief of Staff was Gordon Sullivan. General Sullivan ran interference for me when I couldn't get something out of the bureaucracy, for which I'm eternally grateful. He was Chief of Staff during the Desert Farewell build-down phase, and maintained his intense interest in our operations even after the spotlight of public attention had moved on.

General John J. Yeosock, head of the Army Central Command, deserves high praise. Like me, John Yeosock is from Pennsylvania coal and steel mill country. He's tough, practical, an intensely hard worker, and (except for his fondness for those cigars) an excellent role model for and inspiration to his troops. He had great foresight which sustained us throughout the war. Although Yeosock was my direct superior, he had the wisdom and self-confidence to insist that I also deal directly with General Schwarzkopf on key logistical issues. It caused him no heartburn to give up his own assets, such as his transportation and petroleum groups and his MP brigade, in order to let my command develop into a strong echelon-above-corps organization. Yeosock also taught me more about the local culture than anyone else, having done a previous tour of duty in Saudi Arabia. Finally, he played an invaluable role in building links between my command and our counterparts in the Pentagon.

In addition to Yeosock, there were a number of extremely able corps and division commanders on the ground in Saudi Arabia, Iraq, and Kuwait, all of whom pulled together in support of our larger goals. I'm thinking, for example, of Gary E. Luck and Frederick M. Franks, Jr., who led the XVIII Corps and the VII Corps, respectively; and of the talented leaders in charge of our divisions, including Barry R. McCaffrey, James H. Johnson, Jr., J. H. Binford Peay III, Ronald H. Griffith, Paul E. Funk, Thomas G. Rhame, and John H. Tilelli, Jr. Last but not least, corps support commanders Robert P. McFarlane and John G. Zierdt, Jr., deserve special thanks from Americans in general, and from me in particular.

Desert Shield and Desert Storm could not have succeeded without the close cooperation of the Saudi Arabian royal family, political leaders, and our counterparts in the Saudi military, expressed in countless ways large and small. King Fahd showed great courage in allowing us into his country, and treated us with remarkable generosity throughout our stay. I also commend the king's son, Prince Mohammed bin Fahd bin Abdula Aziz, Governor of the Eastern Province where the logistical preparations for Desert Storm and Desert Shield took place. Prince Mohammed is both an astute businessman and a popular leader. In the venerable Arab tradition, his door is open to his people at any time.

Lt. General Prince Khalid bin Sultan was General Schwarzkopf's counterpart; he headed the Arab-Islamic Joint Forces Command, whose forces stared down Saddam Hussein's across the Kuwaiti border, and eventually acquitted themselves admirably in the field. My own closest Saudi contacts were Brigadier General (Prince) Turki bin Nasser bin Abdul Aziz and Major General Saleh Al Mohayah. General Turki, commander of the Saudi Air Force in the Eastern Region and as such the "landlord" for our Dhahran headquarters, was not only a strong commander but also a sophisticated intermediary and interpreter between the American forces and his government. For example, before we enlisted his aid, clearing our many tons of supplies through Saudi customs was extremely difficult. General Turki made it work. I confess that I sometimes took advantage of my friendship with General Turki, who was also a prince. When local vendors would try to give me a particularly hard time with prices, I would finally say, "Well, maybe I should go speak to Prince Turki." With that, the pace of even the most long drawn out negotiations magically picked up.

General Saleh, the Eastern Province's military commander, also served his country well. In the rare instance when a U.S. soldier acted in ways that could have been misunderstood by our hosts, General Saleh could be counted upon to make a quick and cool judgment. I should not fail to mention Major General Mohammad Al Alkami, who was the military commander at King Khalid Military Center (KKMC) in the Northern Province. His willingness to lend us the use of his facilities was absolutely critical to our shared success.

Back to our own ranks: I can't be objective about Dane Starling, who was recently promoted to lieutenant general. He is an old friend. He may also be the best logistical planner the Army has ever produced. Serving on General Schwarzkopf's staff, Starling was in constant contact with me throughout the Gulf War, making communications flow almost flawlessly between my staff and Schwarzkopf's headquarters.

In a very different field of endeavor was Warrant Officer Wesley Wolf, who was one of the early arrivals to my staff in Dhahran. At one critical meeting in August, Wolf said he had had a pretty good amount of experience in food service. I told him, "O.K., you're it. Go find food, contract for it, get it checked by the vets, get it delivered to the troops, and feed 'em." The whole string of innovations that resulted, including our in-theater truckstops and the justly celebrated "Wolfburger," went a long way toward making the harsh desert environment less oppressive to our troops.

Wes Wolf is only one of hundreds of such examples—a specialist who helped me, and more important, helped win the war. Throughout the book, I try to find opportunities to bring more of them into the spotlight.

I would be remiss if I didn't mention other members of my team who did outstanding jobs—Warrant Officer Mark Otterstatter and his replacement, Mark Boyer; my top enlisted soldier, Sergeant Major Ken Bridges set the example for all; my secretaries, Specialist Tracy Vanderham and Sergeant Suzan Eaton; my personal security team—like Warrant Officer Tom Murray, Sergeant Frist Class Don Bell, Specialist Vic Velazquez, Sergeant John Balcon, and Specialist J. J. Massey; Sergeant Ray Wohl, my indispensable driver; George Adonis and Saudi Arabian Morrison who provided our soldiers with the best meals possible—a superb effort. A truly unsung hero was Chaplain (Father Vince) Inghilterra. By a superb personal effort, Father Vince coordinated with the Saudi religious leaders to ensure that all religious services for our troops were conducted in a land where the only official religion was the Muslim faith.

I should not overlook the 12,000 members of the American business community in Saudi Arabia who made some very special contributions. First, they invited soldiers into their homes, thirty or forty at a time, throughout the course of the conflict. By my estimate, more than 100,000 soldiers were fed, had their clothes washed, and were given access to phones to call home. Another group, known locally as the "Desert Dogs," packed up four-wheel-drive vehicles with all kinds of food and drove hundreds of miles out into the desert to sponsor picnics for the troops. Two dedicated and tireless point people in all these efforts were the American Consul-General in Dhahran, Kenneth A. Stammerman, and his wife, Patty.

There are additional unsung heroes who, unfortunately, must also be recognized as groups. In this category, I'd put the Department of Defense (DoD) military and civilian personnel, our soldiers' family members, and our strong supporters in the American public. I'm thinking of DoD civilian workers not only in the Pentagon, but all over the United States: in Virginia, California, Nevada, and dozens of other places. Our soldiers' spouses and parents also pitched in, with child care, financial sacrifice, moral support, and the thousand other ways they found to boost morale and keep the home fires burning. The American public overwhelmingly supported our efforts in the Gulf.

Books don't come together easily. I'd like to thank a number of people who made this project work. First there was Paula Barker Duffy, Director of the Harvard Business School Press, who sent me the 3 × 5 card in Saudi Arabia that kicked things off. (More on 3 × 5's later.) The next indispensable person to come on board was Jeffrey L. Cruikshank. He learned more than he ever expected to about stand-ups and sit-downs—not to mention piers, dumps, and washracks—and spent many months helping me shape this manuscript. His colleague Patricia Toland kept him honest. Judy Kohn, another of Jeff's colleagues, designed our distinctive cover and photo sections. And finally, Carol Franco, senior editor with the press, took our rough product and made it ready to go to market.

Finally, I'd like to single out for praise the great contributions and undying patience of my wife, Cheri. Throughout twenty-eight years of marriage in the military, up to and including a sometimes trying book-writing process, she has been unfailingly supportive.

When General Schwarzkopf discussed my pending 3-star promotion with me, early in 1991, he said that he planned to leave me in the theater to conduct the retrograde operation. Before the beginning of the ground war, in other words, he was making long-range plans for the retrograde phase. And, being a committed family man, he generously suggested that I ask Cheri to come over and join me. I placed an immediate transatlantic call to her.

Cheri and I have made twenty-eight moves in twenty-eight years, and eight moves in the last four years. Given all that practice, we've worked out a pattern. The first time I call with a new assignment, she responds by saying, flatly, "No way." I say, "O.K., well, we'll work something out." The second time I call, she tells me what she would hope to get accomplished in the new posting. And the third time, almost without fail, she says, "This will be a great adventure!" This was the dialogue that we started early in 1991, and when she finally agreed to join me—despite her aversion to hot climates—I was greatly relieved. If I was to remain in Saudi Arabia for another year, I would need my great friend and confidante at my side.

The quality of my life improved immeasurably the instant she arrived, as did the lives of the many soldiers she subsequently brought into our home. Every other week, we had one of two groups to dinner. In the first week, she'd invite in twenty or more female soldiers to discuss problems they might be encountering—a tremendous assistance both to them and to me, in a country where they might otherwise feel isolated and excluded. And in the following week, she'd throw a lasagna party, assisted by my able enlisted aide Sergeant First Class Doug Cobb; together they'd feed thirty to forty-five soldiers who had signed up to eat at the general's house.

During her six months in-country, she welcomed more than 2,000 soldiers into our home—evenings that generated some of my fondest and most cherished memories of that tour of duty. Our service members are great human beings and remarkable Americans; and Cheri helped me get to know them. Maybe the first lesson in leadership that this book can offer is, "Marry well." Marry someone who has the ability to give you unique perspectives on your people, and who wants to be part of your career. I did, and I'm forever glad of it.

MOVING MOUNTAINS

Chapter One

Come As You Are

RUNNING LOGISTICS for the Gulf War has been compared to transporting the entire population of Alaska, along with their personal belongings, to the other side of the world, on short notice. It has been likened to relocating the city of Richmond, Virginia.[1]

Armies eat. In the year between August 1990 and August 1991— that is, before, during, and in the wake of the Gulf War—the logisticians of the U.S. Armed Forces in Southwest Asia, in an effort headed by the 22d Support Command and the 1st and 2d COSCOMS, planned, moved, and served more than 122 million meals. This can be compared to feeding all the residents of Wyoming and Vermont three meals a day for forty days.

Armies drive. Between August 1990 and August 1991, those same supply units pumped 1.3 billion gallons of fuel. This was seven times the fuel consumption of Washington, D.C. in the same period—and roughly equal to the 12-month fuel consumption of the District of Columbia, Montana, and North Dakota combined.

In that same one-year span, those supply units and their contracted drivers drove almost 52 million miles in the war theater. This is the equivalent of more than 100 round-trips to the moon; or more than 2,000 trips around the world; or more than 10,000 round-trips from Los Angeles to New York.

Armies are a constellation of needs. These needs are always numerous and complex, and sometimes contradictory. Armies need well-trained, mobile, flexible fighting forces (their "tooth," in military terminology); but they also need extensive support services (their "tail"). They need tanks, planes, and ammunition; they also need bakers and bureaucrats (yes, bureaucrats can be helpful), carpenters and cashiers, morticians and social counselors.

They need directions. During the war, almost 500 new traffic signs were erected along the Saudi Arabian road network, helping U.S. soldiers and third-country nationals find their destinations in a relatively featureless landscape.[2]

And, without a doubt, they need postal workers. For half a year, from November 1990 through April 1991, the suppliers and transporters of the Gulf War moved 500 short tons of mail per day. All told, they handled over 31,800 tons of mail—an amount that would cover twenty-eight football fields in mail six feet deep.

These tasks—and a myriad of others—are accomplished by logisticians. Logistics is the careful integration of transportation, supply, warehousing, maintenance, procurement, contracting, and automation into a coherent functional area; in a way that prevents suboptimization in any of these activities; and in a way that permits and enhances the accomplishment of a given goal, objective, or mission.

Logisticians deal with unknowns. They attempt to eliminate unknowns, one by one, until they are confident that they have done away with the possibility of paralyzing surprises. This is what we did in the Gulf.

PRELUDE TO A WAR

To many Americans, comfortably far from the battleground, the war in Southwest Asia came as a sudden and unexpected development. But for Iraq and Kuwait, the roots of conflict can be traced back decades, even centuries. Kuwait's name—a diminutive form of the word *kut,* or "small fort"[3]—suggests the region's turbulent past.

Of the two countries, Kuwait has long been the more stable. The Al Sabah dynasty, rulers for two centuries, has earned a reputation for benign leadership and a relatively high tolerance of dissent (at least by Middle Eastern standards). But Kuwait was never strong enough to stand alone in its "covetous neighborhood."[4] In the 1800s, while the Ottoman Empire was still the dominant regional power, Kuwait was a semiautonomous region within that empire, and was administered as part of the *wilayat,* or province, of Basra, which is today an Iraqi city. This relationship with Basra, which ended in 1919, has served as the basis for most of Iraq's subsequent legal claims on Kuwait. At the turn of the twentieth century, the ruling Sheikh Mubarek signed an agreement with the British, which in effect established his country as a protectorate of Great Britain until Kuwait was granted full independence in 1961.

Iraq, by contrast, has experienced turmoil almost since its emergence as a modern state in the early 1920s. One clue to Iraq's difficulties can be found in a speech delivered to the British House of Commons by Winston Churchill in 1921. It was British policy, he explained, "to attempt to build up around the ancient city of Baghdad, in a form friendly to Britain and her allies, an Arab state which can revive and embody the old culture and glories of the Arab race."[5] This was a weak foundation. In the next thirty-seven years, Baghdad saw fifty-eight governments rise and fall.

Six days after Kuwait received her independence from Britain in June 1961, Iraq's General Qassim claimed Kuwait as Iraqi territory. A show of force by the British deterred Qassim from acting on his claims, but the Iraqi threat to Kuwait—sometimes explicit, always implicit—persisted over the next three decades. In 1981, for example, Iraqi President Saddam Hussein told a Kuwaiti newspaper that border adjustments between the two countries were necessary. Specifically, he asserted that Iraq needed better access to the Arabian Gulf, which might necessitate the transfer of the Kuwaiti islands of Warbah and Bubiyan to Iraqi sovereignty.[6]

More threats and hostile acts followed. Iraqi extremists were implicated, for example, in a 1983 series of bombings in Kuwait; in the hijacking of a Kuwaiti airliner a year later; and in a failed attempt to assassinate Kuwait's ruler in 1985.[7] Despite this history of Iraqi belligerence, Kuwait's rulers were inclined to turn a blind eye toward their neighbor's aggressions. The reason was simple: although they heartily disliked the regime of Saddam Hussein, they were even more concerned about the threat posed by the fundamentalist Islamic regime in Iran. Iraq was then at war with Iran, and as the timeless Arabic saying has it, "The enemy of my enemy is my friend." Because Iran was then perceived as the most significant threat in the region, Kuwait readily allowed the use of its ports, roads, and other facilities for the transshipment of war materials to Iraq, and contributed more than $8 billion to Iraq's war effort.

But as often proves to be the case, peace could not be purchased.

Greed and grievances ran too deep. Thanks to oil revenues, Kuwait during the 1980s enjoyed one of the world's highest standards of living. Iraq had ample oil revenues of its own, of course, but these were more than consumed by the futile and seemingly interminable war with Iran. And disparities of wealth were not the only issue of contention. Debriefings of Iraqi prisoners of war, especially among the officer class, have revealed a profound resentment of the Kuwaitis. The Kuwaitis—according to the captured Iraqis—were arrogant and condescending toward Iraq. At least among those in the officer class, Kuwait was truly seen as a wayward province of Iraq. In their eyes, war was amply justified[8]—a conclusion with which I heartily disagree, on the strength of my interactions with hundreds of Kuwaitis.

By 1990, in any case, Saddam Hussein was eager and able to revive the military threat first posed to Kuwait decades earlier by his predecessors. He finally succeeded in ending the war with Iran, although after almost a decade of staggering losses he had won nothing for his people. Iraq, well armed but effectively bankrupt, needed increased oil revenues to pay her war debts—but the world oil glut had dramatically lowered the price of crude. Pumping more oil from Iraq's fields was likely to exacerbate the problem of diminishing returns.

At the May 1990 Arab League Summit in Baghdad, Saddam demanded an additional $27 billion from Kuwait, asserting that Kuwait had been stealing Iraqi oil from the Rumalia oil field underlying both countries. The following month, Saddam again demanded that Kuwait (as well as the United Arab Emirates, farther down the Gulf) cut production, a strategy by which he proposed to raise the price of crude from $14 to $25 per barrel. By July, Saddam was threatening military action against Kuwait, and—on July 24th—he deployed large numbers of troops on his southern border. The next day he sent U.S. President George Bush a letter underscoring his peaceful intentions; but his actions were already implying otherwise. By the end of the month, he had stationed 100,000 Iraqi troops directly adjacent to Kuwait.

The numbers were large and the threat was overwhelming. The Iraqi war machine was well seasoned after years of combat with Iran. Kuwait's armed forces were relatively inconsequential, and mostly defensive. They were certainly no match for what was then the world's fourth-largest army. These factors, as well as the modern road system between Baghdad, Basra, and Kuwait City, invited invasion.

That invasion came on August 2, 1990. It took less than a day for Iraq to overcome organized Kuwaiti resistance, although individual soldiers and armed civilians in the capital of Kuwait City continued to fight back for many days to come. The world community reacted with almost uniform outrage. The United Nations Security Council called for an immediate withdrawal. The U.S.S.R. and China, then Iraq's primary suppliers of advanced weaponry, announced an arms embargo. The United States, the United Kingdom, France, and Switzerland froze all Iraqi and Kuwaiti assets under their control. But Saddam responded with characteristically bombastic threats, aimed especially at those who might be contemplating a military response to Kuwait's conquest. "We will make Kuwait a graveyard," he announced defiantly, "for those who launch any aggression."

A LOGISTICAL WAR IN THREE PHASES

The Gulf War can be divided into three distinct phases: deployment, combat, and redeployment. The deployment phase, code-named "Desert Shield," officially began on August 7, 1990, six days after the Iraqi invasion of Kuwait. At that time, President George Bush announced to the American people that he had instructed the Army's 82d Airborne Division, as well as several key Air Force units, to take up defensive positions in Saudi Arabia. The deployment, Bush explained, was the result of consultations between the American government and King Fahd, and "reflected the longstanding friendship and security relationship" between the United States and Saudi Arabia.

> U.S. forces will work together with those of Saudi Arabia and other nations to preserve the integrity of Saudi Arabia and to deter further Iraqi aggression. Through their presence, as well as through training and exercises, these multinational forces will enhance the overall capability of Saudi armed forces to defend the kingdom.[9]

The immediate military goal of this "surge phase,"[10] therefore, was to discourage the Iraqi army—which by then included more than 100,000 troops in occupied Kuwait—from spilling over the border into Saudi Arabia. To this day it remains a mystery why

Saddam Hussein *didn't* continue his advance through Kuwait and on into Saudi Arabia. It is true that compared to Kuwait's military capabilities, Saudi Arabia's fighting forces were relatively large, well equipped, and well trained. Nevertheless, the Kingdom could not have resisted the Iraqis for long. And from the logistician's perspective, if Saddam had seized control of the major Saudi ports and airfields, any subsequent effort to retake the Arabian peninsula would have been immeasurably more difficult and costly.

As it was, our toehold in Saudi Arabia was extremely tenuous in the first week of August 1990. Long-standing Arab sensitivities had precluded any significant American presence on Saudi soil; only a small contingent of U.S. military personnel was then based in the Kingdom, mostly in an assortment of training and construction capacities.

One illustration should help make the point about our precarious position. My superior, General Yeosock, was one of the first to arrive in the Kingdom as part of the Coalition build-up. At an early in-theater strategy session, the Air Force's General Horner asked Yeosock what kind of protection the Army was prepared to provide to the Air Force. Yeosock, an honest man with a sense of humor, reached into his pocket and pulled out a small penknife.[11]

The Coalition's challenge for at least the first month of Desert Shield, therefore, was to rush enough troops and equipment into the theater to deter or resist the anticipated Iraqi onslaught against Saudi Arabia. This was a major logistical challenge in and of itself. Moreover, combat presence had to be built up quickly, which meant that the logisticians had to compete for space on incoming planes to get experts in-theater, and create a support structure for a deployment that was already well under way.

As Table 1-1 illustrates, that task was performed at a remarkable rate. In the first thirty days of Desert Shield, we landed and processed over 38,000 troops and 163,581 tons of equipment. This was significantly larger than the deployments that accompanied the initial phases of World War II, Korea, and Vietnam.

For example, we processed an average of 35 planes and 2.1 vessels per day. Over the full course of the deployment, we off-loaded 12,435 tracked combat vehicles and 117,157 wheeled vehicles. This is roughly equal to the number of trucks and buses registered in the state of Alaska; or those registered in Delaware and the District of Columbia combined. We off-loaded 33,100 containers, which, if laid end to end, would have stretched 188 miles.

Table 1-1

ARMY DEPLOYMENT COMPARISONS

	WWII 7 Dec 41	Korea 1950	Vietnam 1965	Saudi Arabia 1990
FIRST 30 DAYS		−	−	−
Passengers Shipped To Theater	29,839 Most by ship			
Passengers Airlifted To Theater		11,990 Aug	16,300	38,083
Tons of Supplies & Equipment Shipped	−	76,965 July	−	123,590
Tons of Supplies & Equipment Airlifted	−	−	−	39,991
FIRST 60 DAYS				
Passengers Shipped To Theater	91,045 Most by ship	−	−	1,039
Passengers Airlifted To Theater		22,716	85,563	106,000
Tons of Supplies & Equipment Shipped	560,160 Most by ship	400,437	1.2 million	400,000
Tons of Supplies & Equipment Airlifted		−	38,564	106,000
FIRST 90 DAYS				
Passengers Shipped To Theater	138,424 Most by ship	−	82,800	1,453
Passengers Airlifted To Theater		32,357	85,562	183,030
Tons of Supplies & Equipment Shipped	836,060	979,833	1.3 million	1,071,317
Tons of Supplies & Equipment Airlifted	−	−	38,564	175,668

Source: Headquarters, Department of the Army, Community Relations Office.

U.S. logisticians had no direct responsibility for supplying or transporting our Coalition allies. (For the most part, the armed forces of the individual nations opposing the Iraqis used their separate logistical infrastructures.) Cooperation and coordination among these many forces were vital, however. Common items such as fuel were shared and swapped among the Coalition forces. The vast movements of personnel and material during the ground war had to be carefully orchestrated between U.S. forces and our Coalition allies to ensure a totally integrated movement plan on the battlefield; and on an informal basis, we helped each other out wherever possible. At one point, for example, we provided minesweeping rakes to the Egyptians for use on their tanks.

The Army's VII Corps began arriving in Saudi Arabia from Germany in November—a development that those in the know took as a clear signal that the Coalition forces intended to go on the offensive if Iraq did not leave Kuwait voluntarily. But the VII Corps' M1A1 Abrams tanks were forest green, painted for concealment in the forests of northern Europe. With VII Corps' assistance, my 22d Support Command repainted the tanks desert brown. Most of my soldiers were aware that a layer of oil, covered with a mixture of sand and water, would have concealed the green paint almost as effectively, but we saw and took an opportunity to give our combat troops—our customers—an important psychological boost.

Issues of morale, welfare, and recreation, abbreviated in the military as "MWR," were a primary focus in the 22d Support Command. There was a second modification to the tanks, which I consider half tactically inspired and half MWR inspired. Many tanks came into the theater equipped with 105mm guns, whereas the new M1A1 tank has a 120mm gun. We huddled with our counterparts Stateside in the Army Materiel Command (AMC), and together worked out a plan to replace the 105mm tanks with 120mm tanks. AMC found several hundred civilian volunteers from their depots in the United States who were willing to set up and work on a "tank swapout line" in the port of Ad Dammam. These were men and women of all ages, who came in and worked day and night, seven days a week, twenty-four hours a day. They cut the anticipated swapout time by 25 percent below estimates, and delivered workmanship of the highest quality.

This was no accident. When the AMC volunteer civilian team arrived in-country, I met with them and discussed the need for total quality control. The tanks that were being swapped out had to be

100 percent fully operational, without fail. I mentioned to them that when I was a youngster my father always said, "Never buy a car that was built on a Friday." I told them that there were no Fridays in this theater, and that each worker had to be his or her own quality-control expert. The last of 948 tanks were retrofitted and repainted just two days before the ground war began; and to my knowledge, not a single gun misfired in the war that followed. In my opinion, this was American quality control in its finest hour.

Deployment continued through to the second phase of the war: Desert Storm. The war between Coalition forces and Iraq began at 2:30 a.m. on January 17, 1991, when our planes bombed targets in Kuwait and Iraq. Those planes dropped 2,500 tons of bombs in the first twenty-four hours of the air campaign. Within a week, they had flown more than 12,000 sorties; and by February 22d, more than 91,000 sorties. Meanwhile, preparations for the anticipated Coalition ground offensive accelerated. The month of intensive bombing had left the Iraqi military blind, and without effective command, control, communications, or intelligence capabilities. Coalition forces took full advantage of this fact to gear up for the now-famous "end run" around the western flank of the Iraqi border defenses.

For the logisticians in the theater and their colleagues back in the United States, this flanking movement represented an enormous challenge. Simply put, the two Army corps and all their equipment had to be trucked westward and northward to their jumping-off points for the assault. VII Corps was trucked 330 miles across the desert, and XVIII Airborne Corps leapfrogged more than 500 miles west and north. This required us to assemble a fleet of nearly 4,000 heavy vehicles of all types, many of which had to be contracted for, and for which drivers had to be hired. During Desert Shield and Desert Storm, my command drew up, executed, and monitored over 70,000 contracts. More than 2,700 miles of main supply routes were used. Just before the ground assault began, peak traffic at a key checkpoint on the northernmost of these supply routes approached eighteen vehicles per minute, seven days a week, twenty-four hours a day.[12] This volume of traffic was sustained for almost six weeks.

The ground war, which began on February 24th, lasted exactly 100 hours. Given the assessments of the heavy damage inflicted by the bombing campaign, we were expecting a relatively speedy collapse of the Iraqi forces—perhaps within a month. Instead, the Iraqis lasted four days.

Like all Americans, of course, we celebrated the quick end to the war and the low numbers of Coalition casualties. As logisticians, we further celebrated the fact that there would now be no need to set up the additional logistical bases that had been planned for deep inside Iraq, and that the ceasefire meant that there was now no chance of shortages of fuel, food, ammunition, water, or medical facilities. We coped with the massive burden of caring for and transporting over 60,000 enemy prisoners of war (EPWs)—many more than expected, and within a greatly compressed time frame.

Large logistical challenges normally consist of hundreds or thousands of small ones. The EPW situation provides a good illustration of this.

I like to play basketball, in part because as a general officer I get to shoot all the time without getting yelled at. But because I'm a basketball player, a swimmer, and a runner, I am (as one of my officers refers to me) also an antismoking nut, and I make my opinions known on this. How does this tie in to the logistics of EPWs? The Geneva Convention, which among other things defines how prisoners of war are to be treated, was hammered out back in an era when people were more or less unaware of the health risks of smoking. As a result, one section of the convention stipulates that EPWs be given a daily allocation of cigarettes, or, as an alternative, that they be provided the opportunity to make a small amount of money to buy cigarettes from their captors. Representatives of the International Red Cross came into my office one day to hold my feet to the fire on that point. I had already decided that this was a foolish way to spend the scarce time of my soldiers, not to mention the taxpayers' money. I told the Red Cross that as far as I was concerned, cigarettes weren't just a low priority, they were a no-priority. Rules were cited and voices were raised, but I was comfortable being stubborn on this particular issue.

A few days later, my chief contracting officer, Dan Bartlett, came into my office with a military lawyer in tow. "Boss," Bartlett announced, "this guy tells me that if you don't agree to buy cigarettes for the EPWs, *I'm* going to jail."

The battle was lost; it was time to cut our losses. "O.K.," I told him. "Go out and buy the worst cigarettes you can find in the whole world. Buy enough to last thirty days, and make it clear that we aren't buying any more of the damn things."

I'm told that the cigarettes were bad—very bad, in fact. But they obviously weren't bad enough. Within three weeks, Bartlett was back with more grim news: the Iraqis had gone through $80,000 worth of cigarettes in twenty days and were now demanding more, but fortunately the king paid for them.

Meanwhile, of course, larger issues were bearing down on us. Planning for the third phase of the war, redeployment, had been underway for months. Due to the sudden and unexpected ceasefire, redeployment had to be accelerated dramatically. In the United States, public sentiment to bring the troops home began to mount, and visiting members of Congress (among others) effectively conveyed that message to us. And I sympathized. About 75 percent of the personnel in my command—which peaked at about 81,000 soldiers, counting the MP brigades—were reservists, whose civilian lives had been interrupted by the war, in many cases for long periods of time. Obviously, they had to resume those lives as soon as possible.

The Saudis, too, were eager to see us decamp. I should emphasize as forcefully as possible that the Saudis were both strong allies and generous hosts throughout the Gulf hostilities. I believe that this degree of hospitality and cooperation is unprecedented in the recent history of U.S.–Arab relations. To cite just one uncelebrated example: King Fahd personally paid for the vast amounts of fresh fruit and soda that our troops consumed. I invite the reader to imagine supplying fruit and soft drinks for a half-million guests, for upwards of a year—a commitment which in King Fahd's case approached a billion dollars.

But from the start, Islamic fundamentalist factions within the Kingdom had opposed the introduction of large numbers of people whom they considered to be "infidels" into their country. One of the first directives given to me by General Schwarzkopf addressed this point. At the outset of Desert Shield, he said to me, "Gus, I don't want to win the war and lose the peace." I knew what he meant, and took that direction to heart. And although no Saudi ever complained to me about our willingness to help them defend their country, it was a shock to the Saudis when they began to realize just how huge and disruptive the Coalition presence in their country would necessarily be.

The comparisons are telling. Saudi Arabia, the nation most at risk after August 2, 1990, understandably committed its entire defense structure to the Coalition effort. That Saudi commitment was substantial for a country of only 7 million, amounting to some 110,000 troops, 550 tanks, 180 combat aircraft, and 8 frigates. But the United States, by contrast, sent some 560,000 troops through the theater, and deployed some 1,200 tanks, 1,800 warplanes, and 100 warships. Saudi Arabia is a relatively large country, with a land mass roughly equal to the United States east of the Mississippi River; but its population is concentrated along its coasts and in its major cities, which is where the great majority of the Coalition forces disembarked and where many of them remained throughout the war. There's no doubt in my mind that our presence, even though it was welcomed by most Saudis, created substantial social and political strains.

"Desert Farewell," as the redeployment was eventually nicknamed, was therefore under time pressures not typical of a retrograde action. And if anything, the redeployment task was even bigger than the deployment phase.

Most people, including some of my soldiers, found this last fact difficult to fathom. The question was, if we consumed huge amounts of material here, shouldn't we be taking less home than we came with? The answer, in a word, was "no." First of all, given the short duration of the war, many of the supplies brought into the theater, such as our huge stockpiles of ammunition, were never used. But other factors contribute to the challenge of redeployment. The analogy I make is to the family camping trip. It takes a lot of time to pack the station wagon (though happy anticipation makes this task seem the smaller). And it takes almost no time to unpack at the campsite. But eventually the weekend is over, and it's always a revelation to discover how much time it takes to clean up the campsite and repack the car. Yes, there's a psychological letdown at the end of a trip that complicates the calculation; but the important fact is that it does take more time to pack up.

This is even more true in a military theater of operations, where supplies often arrive in the form of bulk shipments and are then broken up into smaller quantities for in-theater distribution. If those supplies aren't used, they must then be reassembled—either in the field or in the port—before they can be loaded into ships or planes. On average, it took us three days to unload a ship, but up to five full days to load one.

This message was learned and transmitted in many ways. On my orders, most of the 22d Support Command's briefings of visiting dignitaries were conducted by soldiers of relatively low rank. This technique helped create the sense of "ownership" advocated above. It was also a great motivational tool. I'm convinced that our young privates listened to my own briefings much more carefully, knowing that they might be called upon to explain something to Defense

Secretary Cheney on his next visit. I recall one pertinent redeployment-phase exchange, between a young private and a congressman, that went something as follows:

Congressman: What's the hang-up here? The war's been over for quite a while. Why can't we get all of the troops home within a month or two?

Private: Well, sir, that's a good question, and the answer's not an obvious one. Look at it this way—have you ever thought about how much an aircraft carrier weighs?

Congressman (not quite seeing the point): No, I can't say that I have.

Private: Sir, I'm told by our Navy friends that an aircraft carrier like the *Abraham Lincoln,* which is the newest in the fleet, weighs something like 100,000 tons. And at last count, we had something like 250,000 tons of ammunition sitting out there in the desert, waiting to be packed up and sent home. Now, the Saudis have told us for sure that they want us to get all that stuff out of their desert. And since that ammunition has a replacement value of approximately $4 billion—or more than the aircraft carrier, pound for pound—and since that material is difficult and sometimes even dangerous to move, we think it's extremely important to do a safe and thorough job.

I think the congressman saw things in a new light after that briefing. (Among other things, he learned something about the quality and caliber of our soldiers.) But I don't mean to single out civilians on this score. Even Army people could not understand why redeployment had to take so long and occupy the attention of so many. My own perspective, of course, was 180 degrees different. I sometimes wondered, as I watched 5,000 to 6,000 troops leave Saudi Arabia each day following the end of the ground war,[13] whether the logisticians would soon be the only soldiers left to pack up all the camping gear. There are two general points to make here.

First, there was an infinite variety of tasks that had to be attended to. Many of these are not obvious, at least on first blush. Take, for example, the task of washing up.

When a force is redeployed to the States from overseas, the Department of Agriculture insists that all equipment be thoroughly cleaned to prevent the importation of crop-infesting insects. (This can also be done upon arrival in the U.S. ports, but that's the tougher and more costly way to do it since the Environmental Protection Agency then gets involved, with its own complicated sets of rules.) This is not an idle threat. The white fly that devastated California's Imperial Valley in the fall and winter of 1991–1992 is thought to have been brought to the United States on a cargo ship from the Middle East.[14]

Of course, we had been planning for the cleaning process during the ground war—purchasing steam cleaners Stateside, getting the first shipments of them airlifted to Saudi Arabia, and so on—but with the sudden ending of the war, we now had three full weeks taken out of our already tight schedule. Now, with almost every single American eager to go home, and with a host nation that was eager to see both them and their equipment depart, things got tougher. The cleaners had to be pulled together much more quickly; huge volumes of water had to be procured (in the desert) within a much tighter time frame; hard-stand macadamized "wash-racks"—akin to oversized carwashes—had to be built in five different places; and a 4.8-million-square-foot sterile staging area had to be completed to protect the sterilized equipment until it could be transported. (Keep in mind, too, the other tasks that were going on simultaneously: for example, transporting VII Corps and XVIII Airborne Corps back across the desert in 4,000 trucks.)

Second, the sheer scope of the overall redeployment task defied easy comprehension, even to those of us who had hoisted, counted, bar-coded, shipped, tracked, and unpacked the more than 1.2 million tons of material that arrived in the theater during the first ninety days of Desert Shield. Looking again at the equipment example: in August 1991, almost half a year after the ceasefire, one Pentagon-based general with a solid expertise in logistics came to Dhahran to see our operation for himself. I don't doubt that he came, in part, to see why things were taking so long. Our briefings in Washington evidently hadn't done the job; and now—as it soon became clear—our Dhahran briefings weren't doing the job. All that was left was for us to take him out to our main depot at King Khalid Military City (KKMC) and show him what was still out there.

There was a *lot* still out there. I've been told that this was the largest collection of military equipment ever assembled in one place, and I believe it. We took our visitor up in a Blackhawk helicopter and flew him around the perimeter of the KKMC supply depot, a trip which took over an hour. Even at touring speed, a Blackhawk can cover a lot of ground in an hour. As billions of dollars' worth of equipment flowed by beneath us, I knew that our visitor was drawing on his extensive experience to make all the right calculations: "Hey—they're going to need about a zillion ammo guys to pack, guard, and move this stuff; they're going to need truck drivers and truck fuelers and truck-repair guys; they're going to need MPs to watch the roads and the ports and the airports; and firemen to put out the fires; and cooks and bakers to feed everybody," and so on, and so on.

At least to this extent, Desert Farewell spoke for itself: no one ever asked for a second helicopter tour. And, for the record, the logisticians who remained behind completed the redeployment almost six months ahead of schedule.

Chapter 2

Basic Training

EVERYTHING MAKES pretty good sense after the fact. In retrospect, even something as complicated as a life can be made to hang together. This is especially true after enough time has gone by. The stray twists and turns, the accidents of fate, and the abrupt departures in our life stories tend to meet one of two fates. Either they wind up with enough meaning invested in them, and thereby earn a place in the narrative of our memories; or they get washed out. "Where I am is where I was meant to be," we eventually conclude.

So now that I've identified this trap, I'll jump right into it. I'm convinced that all of my experience before the Gulf War added up to a unique and highly specialized sort of training; and that it was only this training that allowed me to accomplish a series of very complex logistical tasks in Saudi Arabia. From my days as a newspaper boy and a delivery boy in a hardware store during high school, where I first learned some fundamentals of effective distribution, to my experiences leading troops out of ambush north of Can Tho in Vietnam, to staff positions in the Pentagon, to pick-up basketball games with some of the world's most competitive troops—it's as if these experiences had been lined up, one after another, to prepare me for the challenges we faced during the Gulf conflict.

A little modesty is in order here. From almost every vantage point,

I would argue that my life story isn't one that cries out to be told. But sometimes, as the historians say, we have to steer by our wake. Those readers who want to discover why the Allied effort in the Gulf succeeded need to understand the breadth and depth of experiences that the Army had already provided to me. And those who find my leadership style admirable, or objectionable, or something else, probably want to know about the person who takes responsibility for it.

JUMPING SHIP

I'll begin with my father. Throughout my childhood, my father drummed it into me that I should never ask how much a job paid. "Just get the job, go in, and do the best work you're capable of," he'd say in his forceful way, with the Greek accent and inflections he never lost, "and you'll get paid what you're worth. If you're aggressive and you're not lazy, you'll get your money." Maybe that notion sounds a little romantic or outdated in today's world, in which money serves as the first and final measure of so many things. But still, the fundamental idea of dedication to personal standards, and having enough confidence to believe that the world will seek out the particular variety of quality that you represent, has stuck with me.

People tell me that I'm a hard worker. That may be true, but few of them had the good fortune to know my Greek-American father, and therefore to know how he defined hard work. Constantinos Pagonis was, in more ways than I can recount, an incredible man. One of sixteen children of a fishing-boat skipper, he grew up on the Greek island of Chios. One night when young Costa was thirteen years old, he snuck down to the harbor in the town of Kardamyla, swam out to a ship that was at anchor there, and stowed himself away in a lifeboat. The ship was a Greek ship headed for America and was called the *Democracy*, appropriately enough. He had no passport and no money, but he did have one connection in the States: Ted Kukunas, who was married to his sister Penelope. Costa carried with him the clothes on his back, his high hopes, and precisely five days' worth of bread and water. Why five days? Because in his short lifetime of hanging around the waterfront he had learned that if a ship's crew didn't find him within five days, they couldn't afford to turn around and go back. In that case, he'd be guaranteed working passage to New York.

And that's what happened. After five days he presented himself for discovery and more supplies, at which point the crew made it clear that he would be shipped right back to Greece when they docked in New York. But my father had a plan for the western leg of the trip, too. As noted, he was a good swimmer. As soon as land was within his reach, he dove overboard. He swam to Ellis Island, somehow contacted his brother-in-law in Pennsylvania, who helped him talk his way past the bureaucrats—a group about whom I'll have more to say later—and set out to make his fortune in this country.

My father never told me that story himself; I only learned it from my aunt, who still lives in Kardamyla. But it rang true in all its details, because during my childhood everything my father did reflected those same qualities: courage, foresight, intelligence, and strength of will.

To make his fascinating story unfairly short, Costa moved to Pennsylvania, met his young bride-to-be in the small town of Swissville, near Pittsburgh, and together they made their way to Charleroi, also on the outskirts of Pittsburgh. There they opened the Pagonis Restaurant; and when the restaurant burned down (I was about ten years old), they purchased a small hotel, the Washington, also on the main street of Charleroi. Jennie Pagonis—who would eventually give birth to three children, of whom I was the first—worked alongside Costa, and together they did everything that needs to be done in a small hotel. They worked in the kitchen, tended bar, cleaned rooms, maintained the building, hired and fired staff, greeted the guests, and kept the books.

I suspect that in the midst of all that activity my own arrival on April 30, 1941, was small news. I also suspect that my father was glad to have a son presented to him, since a son might someday take on some of the burden of the family business. And in fact, as soon as I was old enough to make some kind of contribution, he put me to work. Each job he assigned me was an education, but just as important was the *way* he assigned it. Pretty early on, I recall, I was fascinated with the idea of being a waiter in the restaurant. They dressed well; they didn't wash dishes; and above all, they got tips. But my father would have none of that. He started me out at the bottom, cleaning the bathrooms.

Over the years, I moved up through the hotel's modest ranks: to busboy, then to dishwasher and pot-cleaner, then to short-order cook, then to waiter (no, it wasn't as glamorous as it had once looked), and eventually to a semimanagement position. Through it all, though, my father assigned me regular stints of latrine duty. I know it was partly to keep the boss's son humble. More important, though, as he told me, he was trying to make a point about organizations. You have to be involved in every aspect of an organization, he used to say, if you're really going to understand how it works: "If you think you can run a business from your office, you're crazy!" I know I heard that lecture more than once, and I can recall that it often ended with the caution, "Never forget how to get your hands dirty!"

LEARNING ABOUT MYSELF AND OTHER PEOPLE

As I recall, the entrepreneurial bug bit early. When I was about five or six years old I decided that it was time for me to do something to help out around the restaurant. I was mulling this notion over in my mind one day when a neighborhood shoe-shine boy came into the dining room, carrying his box of polish, brushes, and rags; and it was as if one of those cartoon lightbulbs lit up over my head. I went right out and got my own shoe-shine box, and—after a few lessons from my multifaceted dad, who had shined shoes when he first reached Pennsylvania—began shining shoes in the restaurant for a nickel a pair. My father looked over my shoulder from time to time, and always said that I should make a point of asking my customers if I'd done a good job. If I hadn't, my father advised me, I should reshine the shoes for free.

As I got older, I found I was working a variety of jobs in and around the hotel. We didn't get paid for the work we did in the family business—unless, of course, you counted food, clothing, and the roof over our heads as pay. (One day I asked my dad for $10 per week for helping out around the restaurant. He replied, "O.K., I'll do it. That is, I'll do it if you agree to pay me, say, $40 a week for the three meals a day you eat in here, and for all the sodas that you and your friends drink." This taught me that when you negotiate, you'd better know the other side's argument as well as you know your own.) If I wanted more spending money than shoe-shining was going to bring in, I had to get a job in addition to the ones I was already working at the hotel. And that is how, at the age of nine, I happened upon a job that introduced me to a new concept. The concept was turf—in the sense of territorial politics—and the context was newspaper distribution.

In those days, kids sold newspapers on street corners around town. For the most part, the paperboys were about fifteen or sixteen years old. Even though I was on the young side and small, I managed to sign up with the distributor of the *Charleroi Mail,* and soon staked out the corner of 5th and McKean as my beat. Things started going along pretty well for me there. I had regular customers, most of whom seemed to like this newest paperboy on the block, who could shout out the headlines with the best of them: "Korean armistice signed! Read all about it!"

I soon began to notice, though, that the real market for newspapers was in the restaurants and bars. I also observed that business was best around dinnertime, in the early evenings. At my little stand at 5th and McKean, I was averaging fifty copies per day. In the bars and restaurants, especially around dinnertime, you could sell fifty copies in two hours—and you got tips. The opportunity was obvious and irresistible.

So I decided to make a foray into the big time. My first step was to sign on another kid, whose job it would be to stand guard over my established corner. This would ensure that no one would pilfer papers from my stack, or worse, seize the location I had been assigned and was cultivating. Next, I gathered up my courage, stuck a dozen newspapers under my arm, and began making the rounds of the barrooms with my afternoon editions. It worked. I sold out the first armful, and went back for a second. And then a third.

Well, the word got back to me very fast that the older, bigger paperboys who normally sold papers downtown didn't appreciate my infringement on their turf. In fact, a group of them paid me a visit, gave me a few licks, and suggested that I stick to my quiet little corner and stay out of their restaurants. I tried negotiating with them, but they were more interested in making their own points than in listening to mine. On the street, possession was understood to be ten-tenths of the law.

So I stayed out of the restaurants—for a while. I let the heat subside and my bruises fade for a few days, and then I went right back to selling papers in those crowded barrooms again. Brash and foolhardy I was; dumb I wasn't. The opportunity was very good. And even then, I had a keen sense of justice. Why should those kids get to control the best territory, and push me around in the process, just because that was the way they had always done it? I didn't forget the thumps, but I kept coming back to the conclusion that the bars and restaurants were the place to be. If you're going to do business, you'd better do it in the right place.

We went a couple of rounds this way. Then, luckily for my aching bones, I was introduced to the notion of hierarchy. One day, the ringleader in charge of all the paperboys took me aside and gave me a rough-and-ready counseling session. First of all, he said, it was flat-out crazy for a little kid like me to be taking on the big guys. On the other hand, he told me, he liked my aggressiveness. He could see that I was a real hustler—which he obviously thought was a good thing to be—and he said that if I played by the rules, I could advance. Eventually, after I had paid my dues for a few months, he offered me a paper route. This was unqualified good news. It would guarantee me a certain number of sales per day, and would give me an inside track to power within the paperboy empire. I accepted, the deal was done, and the essentials of the paperboy power structure were preserved.

I stuck with paper delivery for quite a few years. The promises of my benefactor came true, and I gradually moved up to better routes, including those long-coveted bars downtown. Then another interesting thing began to happen. Even though I was still only a kid myself, I was aging, and thereby turning into the establishment, the impediment. Gus Pagonis was the obstacle—the one the young up-and-comers had to go up against. Well, I wasn't a saint, but neither did I want to spend my teenage years as a thug and an enforcer. So I called a meeting, and negotiated a schedule whereby the younger guys could sell in certain areas on the days when I wouldn't be around.

In retrospect, I can see that I had learned a lot about both entrepreneurship and frontier justice. I can also appreciate the wisdom of the young kingmaker and peacemaker who offered me that first paper route. John Winthrop, first governor of Massachusetts Bay Colony, was once criticized by the powerful clergy for being too lenient with troublemakers. "In the infancy of the plantation," he responded coolly, "justice should be administered with more leniency than in a settled state, because people [are] then more apt to transgress, partly of ignorance of new laws and orders, partly through oppression of business and other straits."[1] In other words, bending the law can lead to good things. I have kept this lesson in mind all through my days in the military, which has always had its share of bend-able rules.

Newspapers kept cash in my pocket well into junior high school, but they also helped make my crowded schedule even more dense. I went to school during the day, and when classes ended I was off to participate in all the extracurricular activities I could talk my way into. (By this time, I knew I was never going to be a seven-footer; still, basketball became a lifelong passion.) After school, I delivered my papers, worked as a hardware-store delivery boy in the late after-noon and early evening, ate dinner and did homework, and helped clean up in the restaurant and hotel at the end of the evening. By senior year, I was pounding through a string of 18-hour days, what with schoolwork, after-school jobs, regular work as lifeguard at the local pool, participation in the school play, and the weekend after-hours gigs playing drums with my rock-and-roll band. And no matter how I'd spent the day—whether as a scholar, actor, businessman, or rock star—I'd invariably wrap up the evening on the end of a mop or a broom.

So even if I wasn't the greatest scholar in town, by the end of my high school days I must have been Charleroi's best time manager. This meant setting schedules and deadlines for myself, and sticking to them. But it also led me to think about managing other people's time, too. After all, I couldn't play a dance by myself. (Gene Krupa wasn't afraid of my drumming, and Elvis wasn't afraid of my voice.) The rest of the band had to show up on time, ready to play, if everything was going to click and we were going to get paid.

And being dependent on other people, at least to this extent, led me to think a lot about human nature, values, and strengths and weaknesses. Popularity is everything in high school. Quite a few of the activities I jumped into were not particularly popular with the "in" crowd—for example, the school play. But like Rhett Butler, I didn't give a damn. I had a sense of being different. Since as far back as I could remember, certain kinds of kids had given me a hard time: because I was short and dark, because my father was an immigrant with an accent, because we ran a hotel and bar.

The older I got, the less I worried about the teasing. And on the positive side, all that teasing taught me tolerance. Intolerant kids in my home town taught me all about bullies and underdogs, and I've defended underdogs ever since. In fact, if I'm tough about anything, I'm tough about that. Although I'm still a jock at heart, I'll admit that I feel more than vindicated when I meet up with those old friends—the studious, academic types I got to know, who were taunted by the popular jocks all through high school—and I learn that they're now successful businessmen, doctors, and lawyers.

The key is to be open to different experiences and perspectives. If you can't tolerate different kinds of people, you're not likely to learn from different kinds of perspectives. "Effective leaders encourage contrary opinions, an important source of vitality," as Max De Pree, former CEO of Herman Miller, writes.[2] This is especially true in the military, where good ideas come in an incredible variety of packages. If you're a prejudiced soldier, and especially if you're a prejudiced officer, you hurt yourself first and worst.

FALLING IN

Grade school and high school were periods when I discovered a great deal about my social self. College was a time when, belatedly, I began to learn more about my academic self. It was in my first semester of college at Penn State that I made a shocking discovery: I was not a very good student. In fact, I was a terrible student. This brutal fact was pretty hard to overlook by the end of that semester, since I was flunking four out of five courses.

I was prepared to pack it in. My dad grabbed me by the scruff of the neck, almost but not quite literally, and told me to get serious about my education. At his forceful recommendation, I went out and hired four tutors and somehow muddled through. This painful process led to a related discovery, which was that I had an almost insurmountable aversion to textbooks. I just couldn't read them. I still can't. By contrast, I find it simple to listen to and assimilate information from a lecture. I can take information that is presented to me verbally and turn it into an effective visual presentation, a skill that comes in handy every day in the context of briefings. But unless I am absolutely fascinated by a subject, textbooks leave me cold.

I *did* get excited about one aspect of my college career: Reserve Officer Training Corps (ROTC). Penn State was a land-grant college, which at that time meant that all male students were required to participate in ROTC. By serving two years in school we got academic credits for military training classes. I think that was what kept me going when I hit the academic skids halfway through my freshman year. I didn't look forward to much during that long, cold winter, but I did look forward to getting up mornings and attending the drills. It was just about the only thing I had under control.

I'm sure that generals aren't supposed to admit this, but I fell into the Army entirely by default. Back in 1960, each ROTC student had his choice of which service he wanted to affiliate with, and there was no question about which one I wanted: Air Force. At that time, relatively early in the space race, the Air Force was actively recruiting for astronauts. There was a problem, though. I couldn't see well out of my left eye, and I knew that my eyesight wouldn't meet the exacting standards for astronauts. But I was so fascinated with the idea of astronaut training—the first step toward outer space!—that desperate measures were called for. I memorized the eye chart, and squeaked by.

Crime doesn't pay. After I had completed my two full years of Air Force ROTC training, the Air Force found me out. They used some high-tech equipment in a set of comprehensive physical exams, and I failed the eye tests so badly that they wouldn't even consider me for an administrative position. Astronaut Pagonis would not be flying to the moon.

I defaulted immediately to the Navy, figuring that the Greek fisherman's blood in my veins might count for something. The Navy threw up their own obstacles, wanting me to serve an extra year to compensate for lost Navy training time. Steering me toward an extra year of school was something like suggesting to Napoleon that he swing through Waterloo for a second look. At long last I approached the Army, which accepted me on the condition that I join their newly formed Ranger outfit. Having run out of services, I was not in a position to negotiate. On that inauspicious note, I began three decades of service to a complex and fascinating institution.

At first, I suppose, I loved ROTC because it represented a relief from academic problems. But over time, and especially in my junior and senior years, I came to enjoy and respect military training on its own merits. For the first time I was part of a (nonfamily) team, and I ate it up. It was by no means all easy sledding. For one thing, I was pretty far behind my peers in terms of Army training, having spent those two years in the Air Force ROTC program. And some of my peers and officers, who know about the haphazard way I had fallen into the Army, suspected the depth of my commitment. But there were others, peers and officers alike, with whom I really clicked. I can honestly say that I never looked back at the other services.

During summer camp before my senior year, I finally closed the training and credibility gaps, and started coming into my own. It was then that one of the sergeants of the ROTC department, a Sergeant First Class Fairchild, took me under his wing. This is a key aspect of military life that few outsiders can really understand. I've heard people in the business world talk about the importance of mentoring; I'll always be convinced that the Army invented it. Sergeant Fairchild spent a great deal of extra time with me, above and beyond any conceivable definition of his assignment. One day I asked him why he was going to all this trouble. He simply said that he felt I had the qualities it took to be an officer, and that if I did, he wanted to make sure I got there.

Sergeant Fairchild taught me what the military was all about. By his example, I learned about noncommissioned officers (NCOs) like himself, who are truly the heart and soul of the military. Three decades later on the other side of the world, when I wanted to make a big change in a hurry, I was at least smart enough to call in my sergeant majors.

Senior year rolled around. I met my future wife, Cheryl Miller, and at her insistence began working hard enough to be a credible student. Even more important, Cheri somehow looked past my faults and agreed to marry me, and we began to work out our plans together. We would get married and move to New York, where I would take a job working in my cousin's shipping company. Hazily, I had the idea that I would meet my obligations to the military by putting in the expected six months' active duty, and then serving in the reserves. This was the pattern that almost everyone else was following at the time, and I'm sure it was just about what the Army expected of me.

That spring, though, we went through a sequence of events that wiped out almost all of our careful planning. People tell me today that I must have been born for the Army. Maybe not; maybe I was born for my cousin's shipping company. That we'll never know, though, because the company went belly-up. I was left without definite prospects of work.

The marriage went ahead on schedule, and I know that at least one person in that church felt a lot of pressure to prove himself. I decided that I would go for a Regular Army commission. But that was only half of the story: now that Gus wanted the Army, did the Army want Gus?

With Sergeant Fairchild's help, I had done well in ROTC camp the summer before, which in terms of training brought me to within striking distance of a commission; but I was nowhere near the top 10 percent of my class, and this was the exclusive neighborhood within which the Army expected to do most of its recruiting. Once again, though, Sergeant Fairchild was watching over me. Somehow he persuaded the professor of military science who was making the assignments to take a chance and offer me a Regular Army commission. I received a transportation officer's commission with a two-year detail in the infantry.

I wed, graduated, and was commissioned on the same day, probably my all-time greatest feat of time management. But now I had reinforcements. Not only was the remarkable Cheri now at my side, but also Marjorie Miller Stuchul, Cheri's mother—a wonderful woman who was to me a friend, ally, and surrogate for the mother I had lost at an early age. I was doubly lucky, as I set out to seek my fortune in the Army.

EARLY MILITARY

We arrived at Fort Knox, Kentucky, in June 1964, and I was ready to jump in with both feet. Unfortunately, the Army hadn't structured things to my exact specifications. For my first job I was designated the company mail officer, in charge of two soldiers and several sacks of mail a day. And although there was lots of room for improvement in the way the company sorted and delivered its mail, serving as a minor-league postmaster was not quite the level of challenge I had anticipated when I signed up with the Army.

Then an interesting thing happened. Gradually, as the other lieutenants in my group began to depart for basic training, I picked up their responsibilities in addition to my own. (Normally, lieutenants go directly from college to their basic officer course, but if their course is filled, they are diverted for a few months to an Army unit.) First, I volunteered to be the mess officer. With my restaurant background, this was like falling off a log. Then I took over for the officer who had been overseeing the motor pool. Like the mail-delivery system, each of these service units had its problems. At the same time, the means were at hand to fix those problems. I began to realize that this was a type of challenge I really enjoyed—looking at a less-than-optimal situation and figuring out the best way to improve it. In each operation, I implemented what I considered to be commonsense changes, and I pushed people hard to understand the level of service and quality we had to achieve. In short order, all three of these organizations, which had formerly been thought of as weak and disorganized, were being praised as the best run and most improved in the company.

The company commander, Lt. Marty Brown, and I hit it off pretty early in my stay at Fort Knox, and he soon put me in charge of a platoon along with my other duties. For a young and relatively untested lieutenant, this was certainly an honor. You couldn't call it a plum, though, since on the strength of my organizational successes I was assigned the ten worst soldiers—that is, the biggest troublemakers—in the company. This was my first big challenge in the military, and I'm still proud of the results that I got. I spent a lot of time with those men, training them, teaching them respect for authority, rewarding their good behavior and punishing their bad behavior. I batted .900: nine of those ten soldiers I finally got through to and turned around. The tenth ultimately confessed to burglarizing our house. (I guess if you're determined to go out, you may as well go out with a bang. Don't rob just anybody's house; rob your lieutenant's house.) Overall, the assignment was very gratifying, and I began to think that maybe I was in the right line of work after all.

Meanwhile, miracles were occurring on another front. While we were at Fort Knox, our first son, Gust, was born—one of the great moments of my life.

Following my ten months at Fort Knox, we were sent off to the Infantry Officers' Basic Course at Fort Benning, Georgia. I could feel some of that old academic dread coming back as we pulled into the drab installation in western Georgia, near the Chattahoochee River. At Fort Knox I had had the chance to lead people and redesign systems, but now I was back to the books.

This was the flip side of going to basic after active duty. Of the several hundred officers in my group, I was one of the few who had already struggled with the realities of leading a unit. I concluded pretty quickly that the introduction to active duty being provided by the basic course was at best inaccurate. There was a tremendous gap between what they were teaching and what I had already experienced. In my opinion, at least, the course didn't concentrate enough on how to take care of soldiers, or on the critical importance of effective leadership to the success of a unit. This problem has since been fixed by the Army leadership, which in the 1970s and 1980s resolved to make our military schools the best in the world.

In any case, I didn't intend to run afoul of academia again. I studied hard and hung in there, and worked to get everything I could out of the course. My training even extended to parachuting, which for many was the highlight of the training program. For my part, I couldn't wait to get back to leading troops. But to do so, I would have to leap another major hurdle.

INVENTION, BULLETS, AND THE HIGH LIFE

In April 1965, I was offered a chance to go to Munich, Germany. Cheri and I wanted to see the world, and we had been hoping for a tour in Germany, then one of the most desirable postings in the U.S. military. The Germans were genuinely friendly, and the greenback went a long way. I jumped at the chance.

Like so many things, the German posting didn't turn out quite the way we had planned it. We arrived in Munich on June 9, 1965, and I reported for duty. The first thing I heard from the commanding officer, Lt. Col. Elmer Pendleton—a highly decorated veteran of the Korean War—was that it might be wise for me to send my wife back to the States. His rationale was that our unit was going into the field shortly, and would then be off on a rotation assignment to Berlin. It was abundantly clear that Colonel Pendleton anticipated long work hours and a tight housing situation. Cheri and I decided to ignore the colonel's suggestion, and she and Gust stayed on with me in Munich.

Life soon settled into a routine. I was the mortar platoon leader, tasked with overseeing a unit that operated several "tracks," or armored personnel carriers with 4.2mm mortars mounted inside. Among my other roles, I had to keep Colonel Pendleton informed on the status of these tracks. Truth be told, updating Colonel Pendleton was not the high point of the week for a young lieutenant. When I received the call, I would enter the headquarters building and wait outside his office, with a group of equally apprehensive superiors and peers, for what seemed like forever, until my name was finally called. Then I'd go in and report on how many of my tracks were operational, how long it would be before the broken ones became operational again, what other problems I was dealing with, and so on. That was it. A seemingly endless wait in the colonel's outer office, five minutes in his presence with not much information being exchanged, and then I'd be gone again for another week.

People have criticized me in lots of ways, but I can't recall anybody ever telling me that I was too patient. On one particularly endless day, I spent four hours in a chair outside Colonel Pendleton's office while just about every captain and first lieutenant in the company walked by me to give their report. To me, at that moment, it seemed crazy to be wasting so much time. On an impulse, I grabbed a 3 × 5 index card that I had in my pocket and dashed off a status report. "Subject: vehicle status," I wrote. "Three tracks down. I've taken steps x, y, and z to ensure that they will be operational by the middle of the week. If you need further information, I'll be happy to see you." I handed the card to the NCO at the desk, Sergeant Major Murray, and started to walk out the door.

The sergeant major brought me up short. "Sir," he said to my departing back, "you're going to be in deep trouble for this." I walked back to his desk. "Look," I said, "I just can't stand wasting this much time sitting here. If he wants to see me, I'll be downstairs in my office working."

The sergeant major liked me and thought I had a lot of spunk. And who knows? Maybe he relished the prospect of watching Colonel Pendleton hit the ceiling. In any case, he agreed to pass the card along. I went down to my office and waited for the explosion.

Later that afternoon there was a knock on the door. A private came in and handed me my 3 × 5 card. On the back of it Pendleton had scrawled, "O.K. Keep up the good work. Thanks."

This was a revelation. From that day forward, I made all of my routine status reports to the colonel on 3 × 5 cards. I also set up a simple system of communication among my troops using 3 × 5's. After all, what was good enough for Colonel Pendleton had to be good enough for my platoon. And so it proved to be: a reliable and simple way to keep information moving, up and down the hierarchy. I've used it ever since. In fact, it was a cornerstone in our Gulf War logistical operation.

Our battalion was, as noted, based in Munich. But every four months, one of the battalions in our brigade was sent into Berlin to supplement the Berlin Brigade, the military organization that had overall responsibility for defending U.S. interests in West Berlin.

Prior to our departure, I was called into Colonel Pendleton's office. I knew exactly why he had called for me, and this was a call I was more than eager to get. I had wanted command of his reconnaissance platoon—a component of the rotating battalion—ever since my first day in Munich. However, I was continually being turned down for the job, in part because I wasn't Ranger-trained, and in part because I was a transportation officer, then simply serving a two-year detail in the infantry. Colonel Pendleton had always leaned toward assigning this type of unit to a Regular Army infantry officer, but he had finally run out of them, and I knew it.

In response to Pendleton's summons, I walked into his office. The first thing he said to me was, "I see you're smiling. Do you know why you're here?"

"You must be offering me the recon platoon," I responded, still smiling, "maybe because there's nobody else left."

He smiled back and said, "That's right. I'm putting you in charge of the reconnaissance platoon. Don't screw it up!"

Working with the reconnaissance platoon in Berlin was a revelation for me. It was a novel and sobering situation—for the first time, I commanded a group of soldiers who were carrying live ammunition. The rules of engagement were clear: if the East German guards opened fire on an escaping East German, and if their bullets hit West German soil, we were authorized to return fire. During my first ten weeks of command, we facilitated a couple of dramatic escapes, and these were exciting and gratifying episodes.

Berlin was pivotal in helping me understand an officer's responsibilities to his troops. It was the first time I confronted live action. It was the first time where my orders, and the actions that resulted from those orders, affected people's lives to the ultimate degree. Up until that point, I realized, I had thought of training primarily as a way to instill discipline. Now I knew better. I recognized that I had an overriding obligation to train my people exactingly, to make sure they understood their duties, and kept themselves and each other alive. This was a lesson that I carried forward with me to the Gulf War, almost three decades later—that bottom-line attention to detail could save lives.

In Berlin, we were in fact responsible for lives: civilian, as well as our own. We were front-line representatives of the U.S. Army in a very visible and politically charged locale. We had regular interactions with the Soviet checkpoint guards, and we were subjected to intense scrutiny from the press. Back then, Berlin was seen by many observers as the most likely tripwire for World War III. I was twenty-four years old. An error of commission or omission on my part, or on the part of a single soldier in my platoon, could have had terrible consequences.

I finished out my tour as a platoon leader in Berlin. By then, our unit had won praise from the leadership for its professionalism, and also had earned plaudits from the community for our leadership in organizing holiday parties for the kids at the Berlin orphanage. Like the other officers' wives, Cheri was a super ambassador, in this and so many other contexts. I'm sure that she is remembered, and remembered with great affection, by many more people in Berlin than is any soldier.

The end of my tour of duty as a recon platoon leader coincided with the completion of my two-year infantry detail. At this time, the Army prepared to send me back into my area of specialization—transportation. I soon received my first assignment, which was to serve as the household goods officer in the skiing village of Garmisch. I was stunned. After the excitement of commanding a recon platoon at the foot of the Berlin Wall, I wasn't ready to take a staff position monitoring household goods. I was too young and inexperienced at that point to realize that those goods were what made up households like my own, and therefore made it possible for soldiers like me to have their families at their sides. Simply put, I wasn't ready for household goods, even though a lot of officers I talked to thought I was crazy.

There was only one person I knew in Germany who might be able to help: then-Major General E. L. Rowny, commanding general of the 24th Infantry Division. Since our rotating battalion was assigned to the 24th, General Rowny had visited with us on several occasions. On one visit, I served as his escort officer; and on another, he presented awards to members of my platoon. I recalled that he had once said to me, "Young man, if you ever need anything, I want you to come and see me."

Nowadays, of course, I'd be far too savvy and seasoned to take a two-star general up on a casual offer like that. But when you're young, success sometimes grows out of brashness and ignorance as much as it does out of raw talent. The brash young Lieutenant Pagonis called General Rowny's Chief of Staff and made an appointment.

When I told the general of my posting to Garmisch, he seemed almost as upset as I was. "Absolutely not," he said crisply, and telephoned the Pentagon while I was sitting there to see if he could get me transferred out of transportation. The Pentagon was not moved: no, he heard, that wasn't going to be possible; I had to serve in transportation for at least one year. At the time, facing the prospect of household goods, I thought that was a terrible outcome.

Again in retrospect, it would have gotten me started sooner in the field of logistics, where I would eventually prove most useful to the Army.

But in a last-ditch effort to help me out, General Rowny short-circuited the system by making me his junior aide. Beginning in April 1966, I worked for him for three months, at which point he decided that I would assist Brigadier General Herron N. Maples, then arriving as the new Assistant Division Commander for Support. Maples took me on a trial basis, and after about thirty days told me I had earned the job. I entered upon an exciting period of my life, during which I learned from a great mentor.

For one thing, the job afforded me an invaluable chance to examine a whole range of management styles. This was the military equivalent of a control experiment, in the sense that all of the many battalion and company commanders in the division were working on the same mission. But each of them approached their assignment a little bit differently—the way they took care of their troops, how they briefed the results of their actions, how well they presented themselves. From company to company, what was really changing was leadership. Again, this allowed me to make comparisons, and broaden my perspective. When I saw things that worked, I took note. Conversely, when I encountered management techniques that were out-and-out flops, I made a mental note of that, too.

Another thing that I got comfortable with during this period was a vastly increased scope of operation. As Assistant Division Commander, General Maples was involved in the logistical aspect of the 24th Division. This was an enormous operation, and I learned all kinds of things. From my bird's-eye perspective, I learned about transportation, supply, maintenance, the respective needs of infantry and armored divisions—in short, about all of the functional aspects of a division command.

I also learned, to my surprise, that combat arms officers, rather than logisticians, were then filling all the top logistical assignments. This was bad policy, any way I looked at it. First, we weren't grooming logisticians for division support commands. Second, and as a result, we were sending a clear signal to competent leaders who wanted real authority: stay out of division support! Again, this was changed in the mid-1970s, but in the 1960s it was still a serious problem.

At the same time, I got a very useful overview of the interconnections among all these functions, and how the levers of authority could be applied. In the parlance of the business schools, this was the "general management" view. I watched with interest as General Maples and other capable senior officers made the system bend to their will. Sometimes they issued orders, but more often, they planted a good idea in someone else's head and let them think of it. Leadership, as General Eisenhower once defined it, is "the ability to decide what is to be done, and then to get others to want to do it."[3]

Even then, I knew I was enjoying a unique learning experience for a relatively junior officer. Some of this exposure came through a soldier who was then a young major, and is now Under Secretary of the Army: John W. Shannon. Shannon was the G4 (Assistant Chief of Staff, Logistics) for the division, and he served brilliantly as the teammate and counterweight to General Maples. It was my first exposure to how logistics can and should work in a combat division.

Last but not least, the aide position forced me to analyze and improve my personal style. It turned out that even someone as stubborn as myself can pick up some stylistic tips. Grudgingly, I acknowledged that, in addition to the substance of an idea, the packaging of the idea also counted. Aides interact with people at all levels, including some extremely high ranking officials. In that rarified atmosphere, the best solutions weren't worth anything if one's personal style got in the way of communicating the message. I had to learn, for example, when to interrupt and when not to interrupt. I had to develop a more professional demeanor. Because people's time was so valuable, I had to learn to size up people quickly, figure out what they needed, and determine whose job it was to respond to a given request.

In other words, I was learning to think on my feet and solve problems, all the while making that unnatural process look effortless. My next assignment, in the jungles of Southeast Asia, fully tested this ability.

VIETNAM: FIRST TOUR

In April 1967, after nine months as General Maples' aide and a promotion to captain, my request for assignment to Vietnam was finally honored. I was assigned to Cam Ranh Bay as a transportation officer.

The assignment that awaited me upon my arrival at the huge depot was not quite what I had expected. I had been told when

I volunteered that I would be placed in command of a boat company—in other words, that I would finally be getting back in direct contact with soldiers, under my command. But when I reported to the in-processing area, I was informed that I had been named operations officer for the port. Once again, I was behind a desk.

I asked to see the colonel in charge. From the beginning to the end of the interview, he turned down all my requests to lead the boat company I had been promised. I'm sure he thought that was the end of it. But once again I was stubborn, figuring that I hadn't left my family and traveled halfway around the world to sit behind a desk tallying up incoming supply containers.

That night I received a phone call from the first sergeant of the 1097th Boat Company. He told me that his commander had left and that they were without a captain to command the unit. If I was willing to take command, he said, he was willing to come over and pick me up. I decided that that was good enough for me; I met him at the gate, drove to the company area at the port, and assumed command.

When I returned to pick up my official records, I was told to report to the colonel immediately. Needless to say, he was none too happy. He looked me in the eye and said, "Captain, I'm sure you know that the rules of this Army *will* be observed. And you know that you're not to leave this in-processing station until you're directed to do so."

"Yes, sir," I replied. "But the boat company needs a company commander." Their unit commander had already departed the theater.

He stared at me for a very long minute while I watched my future evaporate before my eyes. Finally, he said, "O.K., Captain. You'd better do a good job." I grabbed my papers and *ran* back down to that company before he could change his mind again.

Now that I had my command—of the 1097th Transportation Company (Medium Boat)—I had to learn a new job. From a logistical standpoint, as well as from many other perspectives, the infrastructural resources of Vietnam were a major challenge. Deepwater ports were plentiful, but the piers were small and congested. As a result, large, ocean-going ships arriving with supplies would generally approach the entrance of Cam Ranh Bay, anchor there, and get unloaded and reloaded by means of small "LOTS" (logistics over the shore) vessels. Our mission was to shuttle material back and forth between these large vessels and the shore, using small "landing craft mediums" (LCM-8's) that could land at many points along the shoreline. The trick, of course, was to develop effective teamwork in the loading and unloading processes; and I took that (along with maintenance of the vessels) as my first assignment. Within a few weeks, I felt the company was working well as a team.

About a month into my command, the assignment changed. I got orders to move the entire outfit to the Mekong Delta, about eighty miles southwest, down the coast from Saigon. I had 30 boats and 350 soldiers. The directive we received was vague, at best. All I was told was that we would be "moving artillery." As I recall, the commanding officer, Lt. Colonel Tom Eustis, said something like, "Just get down there, figure it out, and I'm sure you'll do a good job."

This was the kind of order I liked to get. I assembled my outfit for a pep talk before we left. We had learned to work hard and well together, I said, and now we were going to use our skills to help our fellow soldiers. Even then, I had a feeling that the pep talk was as much for my benefit as it was for theirs. Nobody, including me, knew what was awaiting us outside the relatively secure confines of Cam Ranh Bay.

It took us three days to sail down to the Delta. That gave us an opportunity to get in some important combat drill time. A few of the men hadn't been trained properly in how to fire their weapons, and almost everyone (including me) needed a refresher course; but we came up to speed in transit.

When we got to Dong Tam in the Mekong I reported to the colonel in charge, who had very little information to add to what I had already been given. He said that we were to mount 105mm howitzers belonging to the 3d Battalion, 34th Artillery, on a fleet of barges, and use our LCM-8's to move that firepower up and down the rivers of the Mekong Delta. The barges, which were huge, flat-bottomed affairs, weren't armed; and as far as the colonel knew, they weren't equipped to carry mounted howitzers or to support artillery fire. But our orders were to get it done in a hurry. Out in the jungle were soldiers—members of the 2d Brigade, 9th Infantry Division, as I later learned—who might die if that artillery wasn't available to support them.

The first order of business, therefore, was to figure out how to mount these guns on the barges. I leafed through the available manuals and found no guidance there. But having dabbled in military history during my several academic jaunts, I figured that in the long history of warfare, *somebody* must have tried to do something similar. I put in a call to the Office of the Chief of Military History, who dug around a bit and finally came up with a Civil War manual that depicted some Union barges on which guns had been mounted. He sent us copies of the relevant pages; and in short order, my sergeants were retooling our barges, mounting our own howitzers based on plans developed a century earlier. History, once again, proved to be very helpful.

We then went on to build quarters for our troops on the back of the LCM-8's, a POW compound, a first-aid station, a helicopter platform, and a recreational area in the well decks of the landing craft. Our notion was that the crews would live aboard the vessels, and that the gun crews would live on the barges. The barges were no longer seen simply as carrying capacity or floating surfaces; instead, they were fighting platforms. Along with our LCM-8's, they were building blocks in a coordinated mix of logistics and tactics, which came to be known as the "Riverine Operation" in the Mekong Delta.

Modification of the boats was an ongoing process, since we constantly faced new challenges in our mission. Almost from our first day on the Mekong Delta we were being ambushed by enemies, often unseen, on both sides of the several rivers on which we traveled. We almost always moved at night, in order to be in position for dawn landing attacks by infantry soldiers from Navy landing craft. Our challenge was somehow to maintain visual contact from boat to boat, up and down the length of the blacked-out convoy, and still remain invisible to the enemy. Given today's high-tech Army, it's hard to believe, but even as recently as 1967 our boats on the Mekong had no radar or sonar equipment—in fact, we had no advanced technology of any kind. So we devised a homespun solution: we mounted flashlights inside soda cans and fastened them onto the backs of our boats. The lights shone only directly behind, allowing us to keep track of each other and move single-file as a unit while maintaining a near-complete blackout. We moved like cat burglars up and down our rivers, learning and improvising, figuring out what we had to do and how to do it.

By now, the 1097th had been traversing the Delta for several months, learning to live with the ever-present dangers and discomforts and still get the job done. In the process, we were building crucial bonds of loyalty and camaraderie—bonds that were severely tested during a hair-raising incident in the second half of December.

In fact, it was December 19, 1967: my older son's birthday. We had received word that a tugboat had been hauling an ammunition barge. During that run, the weather had gotten bad and the lines had had to be cut, and now the ammunition barge was aground on a sandbar at the mouth of the Mekong River. We were dispatched, with a few of our LCM-8's and some accompanying Navy vessels, to go up and hook on to the barge when the tide came in, after which we would return it to our Dong Tam station.

When we arrived, we hooked up to the barge, but not quite fast enough. The tide went out again, and all of our vessels—including the Navy's—were high and dry. (The tidal flows on the Mekong were notoriously fast, and the river could empty itself out in a half hour. Our escorts were extremely embarrassed, since in the Navy, to get yourself grounded is the sin of all sins.) While we sat there, we received a call from an Australian observer who advised us that there was a Viet Cong company on its way toward us, apparently intending to capture the ammunition.

This was the beginning of a long wait. Which would arrive first: the incoming tide, or the VC company? We had taken a few infantry squads with us, and I placed them out in a little perimeter north of the barge. Just as the water started rising again around our boats, the VC company encountered our perimeter defenses. A sustained firefight broke out, and confusion mounted. We managed to get the barge hooked up, and soon all the vessels came free of the mud with the rising tide, but our communication link with our troops ashore broke down. Someone had to go in to the jungle and get them.

I jumped in to the waist-deep water and slogged ashore. Bullets popped into the water around me, which only made me hit the shore that much faster. I pulled the squads together, got them out of the jungle and back onto the boat, and we hightailed it out of there.

Two months later, a second drama took place against a similar backdrop. We had set up our operations on a small river north of Can Tho. This was during the Tet Offensive, when the enemy was launching their most concerted attack of the war. We got word that a Catholic orphanage was being burnt, that innocent civilians and nuns were being murdered, and that we needed to transport troops to the site as quickly as possible. The Navy refused to make this nighttime run, but I said we'd take it on. We left the artillery barges behind, took about thirty volunteers in the well decks of a half-dozen boats, and went downriver—about a five-mile journey.

Unknown to me, my outfit was directed to follow along behind us. They hooked up the artillery barges that we had left behind, and started off in our direction.

Meanwhile, we got to the mouth of the river and dropped off the infantry troops near the orphanage. At that point, I got a radio call that the barges coming up behind us were stopped dead in the water. The first barge had come under fire, had "crabbed"—gone sideway to the river—and two dozen boats were immobilized behind it. It was a moonless night, and looking upriver, you could see tracers burning across the river where our boats were stuck. The radio came on again. It was the battalion commander, ordering us *not* to go back to help them. I faked a broken radio—a time-honored military gambit when the wrong orders are coming in—and addressed my boat crew. "We've gotta go back," I told them, "but I don't want to take anybody back who doesn't want to go." They all volunteered; we turned our boat around and went back. It was a hellish ride, with red tracer streaks flying horizontally across the pitch-black river, and bullets bouncing off the boat. When we reached the crabbed barge, I could see that the guy behind the steering wheel had frozen. I jumped from my ship onto the barge and shook him back into action. In short order, we got the boat turned around and headed home again, with the Army fleet close behind us.

We counted our blessings; and I didn't think much about the incident until the next day, when the commanding general flew in and decorated several of my soldiers for bravery. This was gratifying, of course, but as I thought about these two incidents in subsequent weeks, I reached two conclusions, neither of which had to do with medals or honors. First, I grew secure in the notion that I could assess a situation quickly and accurately, and could issue appropriate orders. That, it seemed, was half the battle. The other half was equally important: I learned that I could control a tense situation, and that soldiers would *take* my orders. Field Marshall Montgomery once wrote, "The good military leader will dominate the events which surround him; once he lets events get the better of him he will lose the confidence of his men, and when that happens he ceases to be of value as a leader."[4] I made a point of being in the thick of things with those soldiers, and when I told them to do something, they trusted me and did it. I didn't panic under fire, or ask them to do things that I wouldn't do myself, and they repaid me with great gallantry.

The 1097th was the most highly decorated transportation company in Vietnam. We had an unusual mission, and we accomplished it with distinction under sometimes arduous conditions. Many individuals in my command were singled out for honors and commendations. Maybe most gratifying to me, personally, was the fact that the 1097th was awarded the Army Meritorious Unit Citation for our work in devising and perfecting a new way to use waterborne artillery in riverine warfare. We had innovated together, fought together, and were honored together.

Chapter Three

Opportunities of a Lifetime

ONE WELCOME outcome of my modest celebrity, following my river tour in Vietnam, was the chance to pursue what once would have been an impossible dream: graduate school. It was clear, by the late 1960s, that a graduate degree was a critical prerequisite for advancement to higher rank in the Army. Many of my contemporaries had already completed their advanced degrees, and I knew that comparisons would one day be made. But most important, I felt I was finally ready to tackle school. Enough things in my life had come together, and I thought I could finally make a success of myself in academia.

Meanwhile, I was sent to the Transportation Officer Advanced Training Course at Fort Eustis. The posting had its advantages. For one thing, it was in my chosen discipline of transportation. For another, I got to spend lots of time with my family, which I hadn't been able to do since our days in Germany. We made many good friends, and for the first time felt settled in a community.

My personnel assignment officers were not very supportive of my continuing interest in graduate school. In fact, because my undergraduate grades were so flat-out dismal, they brushed off the idea completely. But the idea stuck in my mind. One afternoon, for example, I was pulled out of class to take a phone call. The voice on the other end of the line said, "Congratulations."

I had no doubt what that meant. "Great!" I immediately exclaimed. "You're sending me to graduate school!"

"Well, no," said the voice. "As a matter of fact, you've made major."

I went back to the class and plunked myself down next to my tablemate, a West Pointer who was very knowledgeable about the ins and outs of the Army.

"What's with you?" he asked, trying to size up my mood. "Somebody sick?"

"Oh, no," I replied, "Everybody's O.K. I just made major." By any measure, this was a strange response to a below-the-zone promotion. (Military promotions tend to come according to a schedule, and "below the zone" translates roughly to "ahead of schedule.") I have no doubt that my tablemate thought I had gone around the bend.

By this time—the summer of 1968—I had served about four years in the Army. The usual promotion path to major took about seven or eight years. I had served well, but I was also lucky. The Chief of Staff of the Army at that time, General Creighton Abrams, had recently given the Major Promotions Board a clear directive. As I heard the story, he told them, "I want you to select young captains who were field soldiers in Vietnam and got their boots muddy." My tour on the Mekong Delta certainly got my boots muddy, and brought me into the limelight at an opportune juncture.

The promotion, in turn, had an unexpected consequence: the powers-that-were turned out to be more impressed with Major Pagonis than they had been with Captain Pagonis, and decided to let the freshly minted major take a shot at grad school. "If you can get yourself into a graduate program," they told me, "we'll let you attend." Maybe they thought that would simply shift the burden of saying no to school admissions officers. In any case, their O.K. was all I needed. I approached my alma mater, Penn State, and got myself admitted to the MBA program, with a specialization in business logistics and operations research. My acceptance into the program involved a little finagling on two counts. First, I had to agree to an initial period of academic probation. Second, my old business logistics professor from college days, John J. Coyle, went to bat for me.

Dr. Coyle and his Penn State colleague Robert Pashek deserve special note here. In the 1960s, they were pioneers in developing an integrated approach to logistics. This was during an era when most theorists and practitioners were still talking about "physical distribution." My comprehensive approach to logistics is derived, in part, from Coyle's and Pashek's broad-gauge orientation.

I've been brutally honest about my academic shortcomings up to this point, so I'd just like to make the point that this time things went well. I took the Penn State MBA program by storm, getting As in every class but one. What had changed? Me. I had only been out of school four years, but I had picked up a vast store of information, both practical and theoretical, in the military. I also had a new measure of maturity and determination. I was *motivated*. No, I didn't overcome my aversion to textbooks, but I was a sponge, to an extent that surprised even me. I wanted to get my hands on knowledge. I wanted to stuff my head full of it. And through all of it, I got tremendous encouragement from my wife.

Those were eighteen wonderful months. They not only yielded me an MBA degree, but also fostered a happy and stable home life, and gave me a chance once again to enjoy the Pennsylvania countryside which we have always thought of as our home. That home was blessed by the arrival of our second son, Robert, and this second family miracle only added to our contentment and sense of well-being.

Everything changes, especially for a professional soldier. Just one month before receiving my degree, I was called back to Vietnam.

BACK TO VIETNAM

My second tour in Vietnam was vastly different from the first. To begin with, I had just spent a year and a half on a college campus. Even in the heart of patriotic Pennsylvania, the debate over Vietnam was raging. The war, never popular, was by that time the most divisive issue faced by our country since the McCarthy era. Perhaps we have to look back to the Civil War to find a war that so divided the nation, and its families, into angry and passionate camps. Vietnam had already brought down one president, and now his successor was assuring a skeptical nation, once again, that all was going well.

In this country, soldiers and armies are instruments of policy, but not shapers of policy. Upon induction, we take an oath to defend the Constitution of the United States against all enemies foreign and domestic. We pledge to obey the orders of the president and officers appointed over us in accordance to regulations and laws. To my knowledge, ours is the only army in the world that pledges allegiance to a document—that is, a set of ideals—rather than an individual or group.

Our personal opinions about an individual leader or a particular war are therefore irrelevant. Which is not to say that soldiers don't have opinions about policies—they do, especially when those policies may call for sacrifice. My opinion of the war, as I flew back into Vietnam in July 1970 for a second tour of duty, was that ours was a good cause badly executed. Old soldiers with whom I talked often compared it to the later months of the Korean War, when overriding political concerns kept the Army from prosecuting the war effectively. I think this is a lesson that the entire political and military structure carried forward from Vietnam into the Gulf War: don't go halfway into a war. If you go in, go in to win.

I had been told that I would be assigned to the 4th Infantry Division as the division transportation officer. But upon my arrival in Vietnam, I was diverted to the 101st Airborne Division, which had just recently come off airborne status and was now designated an "air mobile" division. This meant that it used helicopters to take the troops into battle—a concept that had been developed specifically for Vietnam, and had proved very effective. I was named division transportation officer for the 101st, reporting to the Assistant Chief of Staff (G4), who was based in Phu Bai, near the former colonial capital of Hue.

Throughout my Army days I've had an aversion to desk jobs. Only when I reached the later stages of my career did I realize how important desk assignments and staff positions are to the overall military effort. But back on the ground in Vietnam, I found this job particularly difficult. Perhaps it was because I knew more about myself. I knew—or thought I knew—how I could best contribute to the war effort. Of course, as division transportation officer, my work had a useful, even important, place in the bigger picture. And I was good at what I was doing, in part because I put my newly acquired operations-research background to work for a superb leader: Lt. Colonel Claude M. Kicklighter, who later became a general officer.

But the unreality and the inequity of the situation began to eat away at me. The fact was, I was far too comfortable while other people were dying. I was eating three meals a day in the General Officers' Mess. I was working in a comfortable air-conditioned office. And every day I watched through my window as they took the body bags out of the helicopters, moving them across the runways and preparing them for the final C-141 flight home.

This sat in my stomach like lead. The Vietnam War, as one of its most decorated participants has noted, was "fought almost solely at platoon, company, and battalion levels, and a staff officer at brigade, division, and above was nothing more than a manager's assistant, a small cog in a huge paper-shuffling machine."[1] My first tour in Vietnam taught me that soldiers need strong and competent leadership—without it, they die. It taught me that I could be such a leader. There were plenty of strong leaders out there in the jungle with the fighting units, but I felt I could also help. In any case, I couldn't stand not pulling my weight, which is how I saw myself.

After just a month in Vietnam, I wrote to Cheri and told her that I felt obligated to request a transfer back to a field combat unit. We set up an urgent rendezvous in Hawaii, and tried to talk our way through my predicament. Cheri wasn't at all happy about my plan; she knew all too well how high the casualty rates were running among officers in the field. We had long, sometimes painful discussions. She argued that I had responsibilities to my two young sons, as well as to my comrades in arms. This was all true, and needed to be confronted. But Cheri and I both knew that I couldn't stay in a situation that was intolerable to me at the gut level. She reluctantly acceded to my wishes and flew back to the States.

I volunteered for a transfer as soon as I returned, but there was no place on the front lines for a transportation officer. I cooled my heels for another two months, doing my best to assist in my staff role, and trying not to see those body bags outside my window.

One night in November 1970, four majors serving as executive officers (XOs) were killed in a major battle at Firebase Ripcord, near the Ashau Valley. It was a serious blow to the field leadership of the division. The Assistant Division Commander, Brigadier General Sidney Berry, returned to headquarters the next day and called a meeting of all the majors on the division staff. There were about thirty of us assembled in the room, shocked and saddened at this sudden gap in our ranks.

General Berry got right to the point. "O.K.," he said crisply, as if trying to dispel the gloom in the room, "if there's anybody here who wants to be an XO of a battalion, raise your hand. There will be no negotiating with your superiors; they won't be able to stop you by saying you're indispensable. So if you want to lead infantry troops, this is it." My hand went up immediately. I was the only person to volunteer.

That night I informed Colonel Kicklighter about my impending transfer. He let me know, first, that he didn't want to lose me. Second, he questioned the legitimacy of a transportation officer being assigned to an infantry unit, and suggested that I was probably ineligible to be an XO. In fact, he indicated that he wondered if I hadn't pulled off a little sleight of hand, since as a member of the general staff I wore a general staff insignia on my lapels rather than that of the transportation branch. There was no way General Berry could have known that I was a transportation officer, Kicklighter noted, when he authorized the move.

I claimed innocence of any skullduggery. In any case, I further argued, the Army had called for volunteers. Majors were desperately needed in the field. I was the only candidate who presented himself, and I really wanted to go. Finally, Colonel Kicklighter—a true professional soldier whose heart, like mine, was in the field—smiled and said, "O.K., Gus; go and do a good job for the both of us."

I reported to the 2d Battalion of the 501st Infantry on November 8, 1970, as its executive officer. The posting controversy didn't die down; apparently my transfer was seen as an attempt on my part to circumvent the military bureaucracy. After a month at the 501st, for example, I got a visit from General Berry, who told me straight off the bat that he had been under heavy fire from the personnel people for authorizing my move to infantry.

"Why didn't you tell me you were transportation?" he demanded.

After thinking for a minute, I responded, "Well, sir, you didn't ask."

Then he did something very unusual. He said, "Well, at least take off that transportation wheel and put on infantry brass." (Transportation insignia are a wheel with a wing superimposed in the center.) I took that as an order, and changed my branch insignia. But things still stayed fairly hot. I got a call shortly thereafter from a member of the personnel office, who told me, in effect, that I had overstepped my bounds and thereby killed my chance for future promotion. I should have stayed on the general staff where I was, he told me, and developed my transportation expertise. I decided not to worry about whether I was now a major for life. I focused instead on fighting the war, which on the most fundamental level meant supporting the troops, keeping them safe and healthy.

My second tour in Vietnam was invaluable in shaping my understanding of what is necessary for combat, both tactically and logistically. My job as battalion XO was twofold. First, I served as the commanding officer's (CO's) Chief of Staff, which involved administration and logistics of the unit. Second, I was second in command of the battalion. This meant that we had an opportunity and an obligation to divide up the battalion workload in ways that reflected our respective strengths. I had the great good fortune to be assigned to serve as XO under then–Lt. Colonel Mike Boos, who accepted me into the battalion even though I was a logistician. Later, I served under his replacement, Lt. Colonel Ken Leuer, who was considered by many to be the best tactician in the division. For both of these commanding officers, I was a little bit of a windfall: they were expecting an infantryman, and instead got someone with infantry experience who was also a trained logistician.

Leuer and I were an incredible team, with skills that were almost exactly complementary. I learned invaluable lessons just from watching the way his mind worked tactically, and then formulating a logistical plan to achieve the stated objectives. At that point in the war, the U.S. forces were having a hard time finding the enemy. Simply put, no one was capturing or killing hostile forces, and the war was effectively at a standstill. One reason was because after more than a half-decade of dealing with us, the Viet Cong understood our tactics and our structures all too well. For example, they knew that our battalion had four companies, and that one always stayed on the firebase. If you could account for three of our companies, they knew, you were in no danger of a surprise American maneuver.

Perhaps I should say a few words at this point about the firebase concept. The U.S. military strategy in Vietnam was built on the notion of delivering immense firepower against the enemy, using a wide variety of land-, air-, and water-based weapons. (Moshe Dayan, the former Chief of Staff of the Israeli Army, observed one U.S. Army action in Vietnam which resulted in 200 enemy dead, but involved the use of 20,000 artillery rounds. Dayan pointed out with amazement that this was more artillery than was employed during the entire Sinai campaign in the 1967 Six Day War.[2]) This heavy-firepower approach meant that huge stockpiles of armaments, spare parts, and other supplies had to be maintained in key strategic positions around the South Vietnamese countryside. These positions, the nerve centers of our field logistical system, were known as firebases.

At the same time, our control over any given piece of South Vietnamese territory was always more or less tenuous. As the 1968 Tet Offensive and subsequent enemy campaigns demonstrated, we simply couldn't call anyplace "secure" without stationing a huge garrison there permanently. This, in turn, meant that the firebases tended to balloon up into huge enterprises almost overnight. These tendencies were compounded by the fact that the jungle was nearly impenetrable. Once you established a firebase in a remote patch of jungle, you usually kept it there, even if the "front"—such as it was—moved tens or hundreds of miles away. Almost inevitably, the firebases were bloated, immobile, and inflexible, and at their worst, unresponsive to the needs of the troops. The bigger the firebase, the worse the problems. The huge depots at Long Binh and Cam Ranh were famously unresponsive, in part because the people in charge of those depots were never quite sure what was in the overwhelming tide of containers they received daily—a problem that continued in the Gulf War and that the Army plans to have corrected.

In Vietnam, all of these logistical problems were greatly compounded by both the draft and the 12-month rotation system. Many people involved in maintaining the firebases, as well as those out on maneuvers, just weren't committed to the cause. Some soldiers hit the ground with commitment, but began tuning out several months before their tour was scheduled to end. Predictably, some of the draftees were the least committed. They didn't want to be there, and were unwilling or unable to make a real contribution to the fight.

Down on the battalion level, suffering from some but not all of these constraints, Ken Leuer decided that we would have to be innovative. For example, we fought hard against our own predictability. At one point, we decided to defend the firebase solely with logistics soldiers (cooks, truckdrivers, supply personnel, and so forth), so that the fourth of our four companies could be sent into battle. We pulled off several surprise attacks, using that extra company as the anvil on which our other companies hammered, before the enemy caught on to the trick.

Another lesson that I had reinforced, working under Leuer, was a crucial one for a young logistician. Yes, boiled water, canned rations, ammo, and clothing are the bare essentials of a soldier's existence; and they're enough to sustain a fighter in the field. But it's astonishing to see the impact that pure water, fresh fruit and vegetables, a hot meal, and fresh-baked bread can have on soldiers in combat. It's one of those connections that they teach in logistics school, but which doesn't get made until you lead and live with soldiers in the field. But Leuer and I were absolutely convinced that a meal makes morale, and morale often means the difference in battle. This is a conviction that I've carried with me, in my gut, ever since. And it is a conviction that General Schwarzkopf expressed continually and forcefully to me throughout the Gulf War: "Take care of the troops."

Working with Leuer, I also got my first taste of host-nation contracting. The conditions of warfare in Vietnam made logistical doctrine either suspect or irrelevant in many cases. Most Army doctrine has its roots in the campaigns of World War II, which were characterized by definable fronts, serviced by reasonably dependable supply lines to the rear. Doctrine had it, for example, that the Army was supposed to move its goods on its own vehicles. But we were very short on trucks down at the battalion level. During this second tour, therefore, I began to draw upon local resources to support my battalion. I bartered with a Vietnamese officer for the use of fifteen trucks to transport supplies, swapping him food for trucks. This was irregular, but it worked; and as far as I know, we were the only battalion in the division that overcame its transportation shortfalls in this way.

Perhaps Vietnam was a lost cause from the start. Without a doubt, it was an immensely frustrating and demoralizing experience for our armed forces, it consumed a huge proportion of the nation's wealth, and it opened up a rift between our society and its military that took more than a decade to close. On the other hand, it provided us with some hard-won lessons. Whatever we did in the future, we would not recreate the ponderous firebases of Vietnam, or develop massive depots such as Cam Ranh Bay and Long Binh, where it was often impossible to determine which supplies were on hand, or even where they might be found.

DESK HOPPING

The Army consciously tries to groom well-rounded individuals, in part by creating a balance between administration and front-line service. And as it turns out, the system works—but only if you let it.

I returned from the Far East in August 1971, and took the first in a series of staff jobs that ultimately gave me a remarkable overview of the Army. Without really understanding it, I was being given the opportunity to analyze and make suggestions for constructive change in various aspects of the service. My first job was with the Combat Development Command (CDC), Transportation Agency, located at familiar old Fort Eustis.

For several years prior to my return from Vietnam, the Army had been studying the use of air-cushion vehicles in LOTS operations. At the time I was brought on board, there were mountains of raw data that had been gleaned from years of research on high-tech watercraft, such as vehicles that rode on jets of air above the water. Unfortunately, the data had yet to be analyzed. As an operations research analyst, I was assigned to a very capable team of civilian and military personnel to pull together findings from this mountain of information.

Nine months later, after a grueling period of intensive analysis and writing, the "TRANS-HYDRO Craft Study (1975–1985)" was released. Briefly stated, the study concluded that the Army's "lighter-age" fleet (vessels for moving materials from ship to shore) was rapidly becoming obsolete, in part because of the growth of container shipping. In the future, the report said, the LOTS mission should be performed by two specific types of amphibious vehicles, three types of landing craft, and one helicopter. Specifically, the report called for a fleet of landing craft large enough to move heavy equipment along the coast. I know that at least some of the report's recommendations were acted upon, because more than a decade and a half later, four of these larger LSVs (logistics supply vessels) were under my command, and were used to run ammunition up and down the coast of Saudi Arabia, allowing us to relieve congestion on a critical stretch of highway.

Once the study was published and presented, I moved on to Fort Leavenworth, Kansas, to attend the Command and General Staff College. This was an honor extended only to about half of the field-grade officers eligible to attend. (A "field-grade" officer is one who has reached the rank of major.) As its name implies, the college attempted to teach both command and staff skills. The pace was pretty leisurely by Army standards, requiring only about six hours of classwork a day. For me, it was a chance to dig more deeply into the mechanics of logistics, and to begin to study the ad hoc innovations we had developed in the field.

In 1974, I moved into a position with the Army's Military Personnel Center (MILPERCEN), based in Alexandria, Virginia. While there, I handled special group assignments, realignment and reassignment of personnel from overseas bases, and the coordination of personnel actions with the Office of the Deputy Chief of Staff for Personnel. Even more important, I was asked to evaluate the military promotion system, and make suggestions for changes to the system—an important job, in one of the world's largest organizations.

Truth be told, though, the early months of this assignment caused some soul-searching on my part. My position didn't involve leadership, and it didn't seem to have much to do with logistics. Cheri and I spent long hours talking through the problem, and for the first time I seriously considered calling it quits and getting out of the Army. As usual, Cheri took the long view, telling me that maybe I had to pay some dues at this stage in my career. I wasn't convinced, but I took her advice.

And then a very strange thing happened. I began to realize that, contrary to all my expectations, I was learning some of the most important lessons of my military career. Day after day, I was in there analyzing the guts of the bureaucracy—who it rewards, and how, and why. And I came to a very surprising conclusion: that bureaucracy is not a bad thing. I began with the obvious fact that some types of tasks can only be accomplished by huge, complex organizations. Mom-and-pop operations don't build transcontinental railroads, or fly to the moon, or develop Patriot missiles. Complex organizations need structure, which means bureaucracy. The bureaucracy is not there to impose limitations, as I began to realize; rather, it is there to create a basic framework, some kind of order, whereby a huge organization can function. When a bureaucratic system works well, I concluded, it encourages people of every rank to perform the best they can, and to contribute to the institution in ways that can be assimilated.

Napoleon knew this, and that's why he invented the bureaucracy. All the time I thought I was managing my career there were ranks of Army bureaucrats who were actually calling the shots, and doing it brilliantly. I thought that my consistent mentoring, my run of good breaks, my educational stints, had happened *despite* the Army's bureaucrats. The fact was, I was being carefully cultivated, along with tens of thousands of other people. In particular I should cite the dedication of my mentor, then-Colonel Buzz De Haven, who had been monitoring my career from the day I joined the Transportation Corps. He had ensured that my skills fit my assignments, and he placed me in slots where he knew I would be groomed for bigger and better things.

De Haven also had three superb young lieutenant colonels working for him: Bill Farmer, Jack Piatak, and T. Irby. Along with De Haven, these assignment officers went out of their way to make sure

I got positions in which I could grow and excel—just as they did for thousands of other young officers. These dedicated personnel officers were, in effect, grooming their own competition for the limited numbers of slots that would be available in the higher ranks. Nevertheless, they were more concerned about developing officers for the future Army than about their own prospects. I'm happy to report that the Army recognized their contributions, and all three became members of the general officer corps.

Humbled by and fortified with this newfound awareness that the bureaucracy did good things, I approached my work with new eyes. I focused on the importance of taking care of people—with a capital "p"—and applied this lesson for the rest of my career.

My next assignment was a real treat. In March 1975, I moved from Virginia into Washington, D.C., to serve as a congressional liaison officer. In my new job, I was responsible for coordinating the Army "track" (tracked vehicle) procurement budget request—which then totaled about $4 billion—with special emphasis on the Army Tank Program. When I took the position, Congress was debating the question of funding the then-experimental XM1 tank. Many members were determined to squelch the project, and I knew I had to make a compelling case for saving it. I first learned every single thing I could about the proposed tank programs, and then I made myself visible and available to answer questions or clarify points for members of Congress, pro and con. I'll never know for sure, of course, but I think my ability to take complex information and present it in a way that is comprehensible to a nontechnical person may have helped save the M1 tank—in conjunction, of course, with the work of many colleagues.

This was a suit-and-tie position; I never wore a uniform. I traveled quite a bit with senators and congressmen, one-on-one. I even had the opportunity during that time to brief the Army Chief of Staff on various aspects of the tank programs. (This is something like the parish priest briefing the Pope.) I worked on my interpersonal skills, and my powers of persuasion. And truth be told, I was absolutely mesmerized by Capitol Hill. I was Jimmy Stewart in *Mr. Smith Goes to Washington,* and loving it.

As my assignment in Washington drew to a close, I thought again about leaving the military. One of the Big Three automakers in Detroit was wooing me to be their lobbyist on Capitol Hill. They were offering what seemed to me an enormous amount of money, and also offered to throw in free cars for myself and Cheri.

Once again, we had to make a tough choice. This one took longer than most. At one point I drew up an elaborate chart of pros and cons. Certainly, the lifestyle and the money were enticing. Just when I had begun to lean toward Detroit, however, a little voice began to speak up in the back of my mind. "Hey, Gus," said the voice, "wait a minute. You'll be there visiting your friends in the Pentagon, wearing your nice new suit. They'll want to see you because you're a friend. You'll want to see them to sell them a contract." Once I framed the question that way, I realized that there was no way I could trade on old friendships. For her part, Cheri had no doubts. She knew I would stick with the Army.

The issue was finally resolved in the fall of 1976, when the new list of battalion commanders was published, and my name was on it. This was a complete surprise, and a thrill: I had been selected to lead a battalion as a lieutenant colonel. Now everything was put in perspective. So much for the military-industrial complex; I was going back to the soldiers. Leaving the Army would not come up again as a serious possibility; the Army would now have me as long as they wanted me. Detroit would have to find another man.

TWENTY-THREE MONTHS AT THE HELM

I arrived back in Fort Eustis in January 1977, ready to take command of the 10th Transportation Battalion. This position was one that would introduce me to logistics on an entirely new scale. I had always had large companies, perhaps because I had earned a reputation as someone who was happy to take on big jobs. But this new battalion under my command was unusually large. Whereas an average battalion consists of between 600 and 700 soldiers, the 10th Transportation had about 1,300.

But in addition to numbers, there was a new breadth of tasks and responsibilities. The 10th Transportation Battalion comprised two Terminal Service companies, which loaded and off-loaded supplies in port operations; two Medium Boat companies and two Heavy Boat companies, which transported goods and personnel up and down the coast, on inland waterways, and in LOTS operations; two support detachments which were earmarked for use in REFORGER (REturn of FORces to GERmany) exercises; and a Headquarters Company to handle administrative details.

The new experience for me in this context was learning about port operations, and learning firsthand about LOTS operations. But once again my previous experiences all came together and helped me in ways I couldn't have anticipated. I had already been involved in transporting goods by boat; now my boat companies would be interacting directly with the off-loading stevedores, once they arrived in port. I knew all about asking for supplies; now I was keeping precise inventories of what was being packed and shipped, and making decisions about priorities to ensure that soldiers entering a new theater would be adequately supplied to fulfill their mission.

Even my research positions, which always seemed a little otherworldly while I held them, began to pay off in unexpected ways. We were the only LOTS battalion in that Army at that time. I trained my seven companies in a LOTS exercise, drawing heavily on the knowledge I acquired through the TRANS-HYDRO Craft Study years earlier.

This was a diffuse and dispersed command, and it brought into sharp focus the importance of a clear and accessible information flow. I had been using 3 × 5's throughout my career, but the system really got formalized in the context of the 10th Battalion. The index cards moved information quickly up and down the chain of command, and across the individual companies. It was clear that the system worked on a much larger scale than I had previously tested it.

There were new inventions needed, though. Despite the fact that all of my companies were supposed to be working in concert to accomplish shared goals, the reality was sometimes different. Sometimes the ball got dropped, and the bad part was that it wasn't clear who dropped it. I decided that we needed some additional communication channels through which all involved parties would receive joint instructions, emphasizing the context of the wider mission.

With this objective in mind, I established a schedule of meetings, regular open-office hours, and impromptu visits among the troops to hear their feedback. These were reinforced by a series of bulletins, which I issued when the need arose. My goal, as stated, was to make sure that everyone who contributed to a particular mission had a clear and compelling sense of the whole. Seen in this light, little things were big things. Seen in this light, the piece of fruit served with lunch in the jungles of Vietnam could represent the difference between success and failure.

Total investment in a mission isn't bought, or commanded; it is built. I knew I had to make contact directly with the soldiers if I wanted to get that level of investment. This meant 3 × 5 cards and accessible office hours for my staff; it also meant going out to see the troops as often as possible. Communication had to flow both ways. I had to get a true sense of whether or not people were truly happy, motivated, productive, and invested in their work. Just as important, my troops had to know that I was motivated and invested in my own work.

Just short of two years in my role as battalion leader, I was selected to attend a War College. This was an unusual turn of events, since I had only fourteen years in the Army at that point, as opposed to the conventional sixteen to eighteen years of experience usually required for selection to a War College. Moreover, I had not been in the 10th Battalion long enough to have received an evaluation in that position. Still, my file was strong, and all my previous ERs (Evaluation Report, a yearly report card of sorts) recommended enthusiastically that I be trained as a general officer. My work to date had won me some powerful supporters in the system.

I was admitted to the Naval War College in July 1979. (In the spirit of "jointness" among the services, officers from one service regularly attend another service's War College.) And put simply, this was one of the great experiences of my life. The instructors were fantastic, and the subject matter uniformly absorbing. We were immersed, for example, in military history. We studied the Peloponnesian Wars, the campaigns of Napoleon, the strategies of Bismarck, the writings of Clausewitz; we steeped ourselves in the tactics of Alexander the Great and Rommel.

Just before I attended the War College, I was promoted to colonel; and once I finished the course, I was selected for a command. The problem was that I was named an alternate, rather than the primary choice, and I didn't get the command. That was a disappointment; but the fallback position I received turned out to be a blessing in disguise. Now-General De Haven was looking out for me, once again.

JUNGLES, DESERTS, AND GERMANY

To my great surprise, I found I was being sent to Panama to serve as G4 and Director of Industrial Operations (DIO) for the 193d Infantry Brigade.

Truth be told, I didn't know much about Panama, but I had always heard that it was a posting where colonels would go to wrap up the last years of their career. G4/DIO in Panama, in the U.S. Southern Command, didn't sound like much of a challenge. My interest picked up substantially, though, when I found out that my old commanding officer in Vietnam, now-Brigadier General Ken Leuer, had negotiated my assignment to Panama.

Ken Leuer had given me an extraordinary degree of responsibility in Vietnam, and he did so again in Panama. In fact, he gave me an opportunity that most logisticians only dream about: I became the single point of contact for all logistics in-theater. In addition to monitoring the port operations for the command, an area in which I had lots of recent experience, I also ran the railroad and truck operations, automation systems, a bakery, a mortuary, a laundry, and supply services. The position encompassed everything from housing to food and clothing to training to administration. It meant that I was setting up automation and warehousing systems; securing contracts from regional sources for goods, services, and vehicles; negotiating customs and trade details; projecting supply and uniform needs for the brigade; and formulating and implementing staff operating policies. We also estimated possible contingencies and disaster relief operations for Central and South America, and prepositioned war reserve and disaster relief supplies in Panama in anticipation of such events.

In April 1981, after about eight months as G4/DIO, I was promoted to the position of Chief of Staff of the U.S. Army Forces in Panama, and in July was named Commander of Logistics Support Command—a command created out of General Leuer's efforts to bring all logistical operations under one commander serving as single point of contact. That was my role: I orchestrated the interface with SOUTHCOM (U.S. Southern Command); FORSCOM (U.S. Forces Command); the Panama Canal Commission (PCC); Navy, Air Force, and Army elements in Panama; and third-country nationals.

On April 7, 1982, I relinquished command of the Logistics Support Command in a ceremony at Corozal, Panama. I was then moved back to the States to head up a Division Support Command (DISCOM) at Fort Carson, Colorado. The DISCOM provided logistical support to the 4th Infantry Division (Mechanized), which comprised about 6,000 personnel and included a Medical Battalion, a DS (Direct Support) Maintenance Battalion, a Supply and Transportation Battalion, a Division Materiel Management Center (DMMC), and five separate companies: Adjutant General, Finance, two Chemical companies, and a Headquarters Company. Our mission included the logistical support of two mechanized brigades, an armor brigade, division artillery (DIVARTY), and seven separate battalions.

A key lesson that I learned at Fort Carson involved the use of provisional units—that is, temporary organizations that are not a part of the force structure but are formed to provide an interim service while conventional forces are being brought on board. For example, I organized forward-area support coordinators who would become provisional commanders, pulling a Medical, Maintenance, and Truck Company together as needed to function in the field. This was a direct forerunner to the forward support battalions that were used in the Gulf War. Also, I insisted that all my separate companies be placed beneath a battalion commander for guidance. Again, during the Gulf War, tailoring provisional organizations to meet the needs of the mission at hand became a way of life. Flexibility was the watchword, and this was the way to do it.

Like the 3 × 5 card and the bulletin information system, in other words, the provisional unit became one of my informal trademarks. A young sergeant once told me that if he dropped into a new theater and heard talk about 3 × 5 cards, or heard that provisional units were being formed, he began looking for Gus Pagonis behind the bushes.

At Fort Carson, we were preparing the troops for combat. The focus was far forward, on the field of battle—how to get troops to the front; how to anticipate what they'd need in the trenches; where and how to fill a tank for combat; field maintenance; and a host of related concerns. I stayed in Colorado for three and a half years, constantly expanding the scope of my logistical experience. I also got the chance to receive some more training, which turned out to have interesting, long-term implications. My units went to the National Training Center, located in the middle of the Mohave Desert, about a dozen times during my tenure at Fort Carson. This gave me a thorough understanding of how things operated in the desert, and of how the desert challenges soldiers and their equipment.

While commanding the DISCOM at Fort Carson, we also helped deploy a winter REFORGER. It was a pretty complex exercise, looked at from end to end. I packed up my troops onto planes; packed their equipment onto trains that then off-loaded onto a ship; flew my soldiers to Germany, where they married up again with their equipment; and then supplied our division's maneuvers in Germany. This was one of the largest REFORGERs up to that time, and it was held during some of the coldest weather experienced since World War II.

It was a time of tremendous adversity, but it was a great learning experience, both for me and my troops. Speed was of the essence— despite our large numbers, despite the complications presented by the frigid weather. Quickly, and without accidents, we had to off-load ships, draw prepositioned equipment out of warehouses in the host country, and mobilize troops and vehicles efficiently. That monumental REFORGER was invaluable for me, especially in that it helped me run an exercise on the largest possible peacetime scale, with a myriad of complex logistical elements.

In the Army, as in any large organization, there are always whispers in the wind. The whispers I was hearing then told me that I had finally peaked—that I would never make another promotion, mainly because, for a transportation officer, I had spent too much time with combat arms. O.K., I told myself; I'll do what the Army tells me to do, and I'll train young officers and NCOs whenever I get the chance. But the list of colonels promotable to brigadier general released in July 1985 proved the whisperers wrong. Gus Pagonis found himself on the list, and was moved up and out.

My new assignment landed me in Kaiserslautern, Germany, in the 21st Support Command (SUPCOM). The 21st is the Army's largest logistics force deployed overseas. Comprising about 35,000 personnel, the 21st is located in outposts across the European continent: in Belgium, the Netherlands, Luxembourg, Germany, and the United Kingdom. It is an enormous enterprise.

During my three-year stint in Germany—the first year as Special Assistant to the DCG, and the following two years serving as DCG of the 21st—I was involved in running several REFORGER exercises, this time on the receiving end. For the most part, we worked with supplies and resources sent from the States or stored in warehouses in Europe, but I also gained formal experience in the use of host-nation resources. I negotiated with service organizations in Belgium, the Netherlands, Luxembourg, and Germany to establish contracts for the procurement of food, vehicles, and other supplies for REFORGERs, mostly through the use of "dormant contracts" that would be activated when an exercise began.

In retrospect, that experience was invaluable for an understanding of what should come from where: which items had to be shipped in, for example; and which items might be better acquired locally. This involved a painstaking analysis of storage space, timing, and the availability of resources in a particular locale.

PUTTING IT ALL TOGETHER

By 1988, I had had direct experience in Europe, Asia, Central America, and the United States. My assignments had encompassed a broad range of functions, operations, locations, and objectives. In June 1988, I was selected for major general—a two-star—which was again a high honor and a new level of responsibility.

Now I was returning to Washington, where I was to serve as the Director of Plans and Operations, Office of the Deputy Chief of Staff for Logistics (ODCSLOG). The position entailed contingency planning exercises, projecting logistical needs should a conflict arise in various parts of the world. In simple terms, we were answering the question, "If war broke out in X-country today, what logistical supplies would we need to fight effectively, and how would we secure such supplies in that location most efficiently?"

This was a great assignment, in part because I was working directly for Lt. General Jimmy Ross. General Ross had provided me excellent guidance over the years, and now I had the chance to observe his leadership style firsthand. But because we were preparing contingency plans for potential conflicts, it was also an unusual opportunity for me to bring all of my experience to bear. By this time, I knew how soldiers experienced combat. I'd seen how different terrains and host-nation resources affected logistical operations. I understood the down-and-dirty mechanics of logistics, such as transportation, off-loading, and warehousing. It was like taking batting practice, but having the home runs count.

In the year I spent in Planning and Operations, we spent some time considering potential conflicts in Southwest Asia and drawing up operational plans. We never considered the exact scenario that was to play itself out in August 1990, but I had carefully considered the potential for conflict in the region, and had become acquainted with the political, social, and economic profiles of the various countries involved. It was formal training, but it was also fast-paced and comprehensive. All of my interests were converging, and I ate it up.

My next position gave me a chance to anticipate the needs of our forces during peacetime. Still located in ODCSLOG, I served as

Director for Transportation, Energy, and Troop Support. Here I approached logistics on a truly grand scale, overseeing everything from strategic airlifts to T-shirts. As my title implied, I had reponsibilities in three basic categories: transportation, energy, and troop support. I developed strategic mobility policies for the movement of soldiers throughout the world, and also formulated plans to accommodate the movement of Army dependents, freight, and household goods. (Yes, many years later, my household-goods job had caught up with me.) This wasn't just theory, though; my group managed all water and petroleum logistics worldwide, and coordinated and implemented a formal Energy Conservation Program for the Department of the Army, which also included research and development and new-product procurement.

Troop support, one of my three responsibilities, encompassed a wide range of details. For example, we oversaw and supervised the Army commissary system. I also was involved in field feeding—that is, learning how "MREs" (meals, ready to eat) and other prepackaged resources might fit into an integrated food service picture, both in peacetime and in combat. My group was responsible for ordering, distributing, and developing uniforms, boots, and clothing of all types.

I recall having some interactions with a very forceful general, a big fellow named H. Norman Schwarzkopf, who was working on a redesign of the lightweight uniform and boot that our troops were supposed to wear in the desert. General Schwarzkopf wasn't happy with what was then available, and he let the system know about it. Months later—and only minutes before General Schwarzkopf promoted me to three stars in the desert during the Gulf War—the CINC had his ace logistician, Major General Dane Starling, ask me to make a report to Schwarzkopf regarding his long-awaited redesign of the lightweight desert uniform and boot. As I entered Schwarzkopf's aircraft to escort him to the promotion ceremony, I had to report to him regretfully that the study had not yet been completed. He looked at me deadpan, with a slightly arched eyebrow, and said, "Well, then, maybe we shouldn't go through with this promotion." Then he smiled that broad smile of his and let me off the hook.

After two years in the Pentagon, it was time for me to get back out into the real world again. I pinned on my second star in October 1989, and both the Army and I felt that I was ready for a new challenge. At this point, I was sent to Fort McPherson, Georgia, where I was to serve as J4 (Director of Logistics) of Headquarters, Forces Command (FORSCOM), in charge of all logistics in the continental United States (CONUS).

This job once again increased the scale and scope of my responsibilities. At that time, FORSCOM provided for the logistical readiness of eleven active-duty divisions and six separate brigades, comprising in excess of 510,000 soldiers. In addition to providing resources and policy guidance to support troops, FORSCOM implements modernization planning and new systems programs, and formulates logistics plans for global deployment contingencies. I supervised contract management in excess of $1.2 billion, as well as serving as Program Director for the FORSCOM Stock Fund of over $1 billion and managing the $640 million logistics portion of the FORSCOM Command Operating Budget.

The FORSCOM position allowed me to exercise all of my skills, and call upon all of my knowledge: about military logistics in particular, and about the Army in general. I knew soldiers, and I knew countries. Through twenty-six years I had been given logistical command positions of increasing responsibility, depth, and breadth. By the time I took over at FORSCOM, I was absolutely focused on the big picture. And once again, I give Gus Pagonis only a little bit of credit for that accomplishment, and I give the Army a great deal of credit.

And I was by no means perfect, despite our best efforts. I had no idea, for example, that there was a much bigger picture coming into focus on the other side of the world.

Chapter Four

I Get the Call

AFTER MORE than a quarter of a century in the military, I've become accustomed to enormous changes at the last moment. Geopolitical fault lines fracture and shift overnight, and the life of a soldier (and sometimes a nation) must change along with them. For a certain kind of person—like myself, for example—this isn't all bad. In fact, I'm the first to admit that I relish the challenge of adjusting quickly to murky, ill-defined, unprecedented situations.

Still, there's always that initial jolt.

As I recall it, the fourth of August 1990 was a particularly hot, humid, and gritty day in Georgia. It was Saturday; Cheri and I spent the morning and most of the afternoon unpacking the last of our boxes into our new home at Fort McPherson. Twenty-six moves in twenty-six years had taught us how to move, but we still had to spend the better part of a month getting our personal effects sorted out and settling in.

Even though this move proved to be time-consuming, it still represented a small but satisfying step forward. I had devised a method of color-coding the rooms of our new home and our various boxes and crates. The dining room had yellow dots over the door; the basement was blue; the attic red; and so on. Each household good or box coming out of the truck also sported a colored dot, signaling to the movers its ultimate destination. For the first time, the boys'

weight-lifting apparatus ended up in the basement, the kitchen uten-
sils wound up in the kitchen, and my files and books made their way
to the attic office space. I recall taking a break out on the porch, a
Diet Pepsi in hand, congratulating myself that this time things had
mostly wound up in the right place.

Maybe this was a good omen, I thought, since getting the right
thing in the right place, on the grand scale, was my new professional
assignment. I had been sent to Fort McPherson as the Director of
Logistics, Forces Command—in Army lingo, the J4 FORSCOM. In
this new job I would be responsible for all logistical support for
FORSCOM.

The designation "4" in J4 deserves decoding. Consistently across
most of the world's armies, there are seven functional areas designated by numbers. They are: 1, personnel; 2, intelligence; 3, operations; 4, logistics; 5, host-nation liaison/foreign area officer; 6, communications and command control; and 7, foreign military sales/
foreign affairs. As I sat on my porch, celebrating the success of my
color-coding system, I had been J4 (head of logistics) of FORSCOM
for about a month.

That night, as Cheri and I relaxed after a celebratory dinner out,
the phone rang. It was Major General Pete Taylor, Chief of Staff for
FORSCOM, instructing me to get myself over to Lt. General John
Yeosock's quarters ASAP to attend an emergency meeting. Given the
Iraqi invasion of Kuwait two days earlier and the continuing threat
to Saudi Arabia, I suspected that the situation in the Middle East
might be on the agenda. But whatever this was, it was not business
as usual; and General Taylor wasn't providing any details over my
unsecured phone line. I grabbed my tennis shoes and, without taking
the time to tie them, jogged to Yeosock's quarters, just a few houses
up the street.

THE SITUATION AND THE MEETING

It was sometime after 10:00 p.m. when I arrived at Yeosock's quarters. General Yeosock, a fellow Penn State graduate whom I had
known and admired for half a decade, greeted me at the door and
quickly filled me in on the state of affairs. The subject was, indeed,
the Middle East. President Bush had spent the day in conference with
his advisers at Camp David, and had reached the decision to offer
military aid to Saudi Arabia's King Fahd. General Yeosock, as Com-

mander of Army Central Command (ARCENT), had immediately been informed of the president's decision. It was now Yeosock's urgent task to describe our logistical needs to the Saudi officials in Riyadh, in the event that American troops were deployed to Saudi Arabia.

It was no sure thing that the king would agree with President Bush's assessment of the situation. Nor was it necessarily the case that, even granting the fact of a threat to his country, he would accept American military assistance; and it was obvious that we would only intervene if invited to do so by the king. As General Yeosock informed me, several high ranking U.S. civilian and military officials were leaving for Saudi Arabia the next day to discuss Saddam Hussein's threat and the range of responses that might be made to it. The delegation was to include Secretary of Defense Dick Cheney; General Norman Schwarzkopf, Commander of Army Central Command; and Yeosock himself. They were scheduled to meet with King Fahd and Crown Prince Abdullah, half-brother to the king and head of the Saudi National Guard, to determine whether the two countries could reach agreement on a joint strategy. It was obvious that the American delegation had to be prepared to list its immediate strategic and logistical needs—such as access to ports and airports, exemption from customs and immigration, and so on—and this was General Yeosock's formidable task.

But Yeosock was by no means starting from scratch. For several years in the 1980s, for example, he had served in Saudi Arabia as project manager for the Saudi Arabian National Guard Modernization Programs. During this tour of duty he made the acquaintance of the crown prince and others, and as a result, he had a small network of personal relationships, the foundation of so much in the Middle East, to call upon. Equally important, Yeosock was a member of the group that just a month earlier had completed INTERNAL LOOK 90. This was a Central Command war-game exercise, initiated at the urging of General Schwarzkopf, in which members of the Army command had worked through the details of a hypothetical armed conflict in Iraq. So while the time frame for Yeosock's new challenge was greatly compressed, he was well prepared for the job. He knew from firsthand experience a great deal about the political and social relationships, customs, and military capabilities of the nations in the Middle East. And what he didn't know, as of August 4th, he arranged to have assembled in his living room.

The atmosphere in Yeosock's home was one of controlled urgency. He had pulled together about fifteen experts in various disciplines who might contribute components of the plan. When I arrived, these assembled experts, whose ranks swelled throughout the evening, were working in small groups scattered around the downstairs rooms. Several of these groups stuck together for the duration; others finished a specific task and broke up, with members then attaching themselves to new working groups.

My role, I learned, was to serve as a sounding board for any logistical questions that might arise. I'd worked with General Yeosock earlier in the late 1980s on a series of REFORGER exercises. He knew that I understood the complex challenges inherent in moving large numbers of personnel and material from one place to another quickly, but still in an orderly way.

REFORGERs were, indeed, a good background—maybe the best background that any army could have provided—but I knew immediately that the deployment of large numbers of troops to Saudi Arabia would be a challenge of a different order of magnitude. In Europe, the basic infrastructure within which REFORGER participants were transported, processed, fed, and housed was well established. Lines of supply, including host-nation support, were defined by dormant contracts, which automatically kicked in at the beginning of the maneuver. I had worked on these contracts in an early assignment as the DCG, 21st SUPCOM, and knew the procedure well. In addition, huge stockpiles of supplies and equipment were already in the theater, available to be drawn upon by incoming soldiers.

There were no such logistical advantages in Saudi Arabia. In fact, we had no formal bases anywhere in the Middle East, and except for limited depots in Oman and Bahrain, relatively few prepositioned stocks. Existing military infrastructure was limited, and based on past experience, military facilities in Saudi Arabia were not likely to be available to us. REFORGER exercises forced us to answer the questions of who and when. A Saudi Arabian deployment would require that we address these same questions, while also addressing the much tougher issues of what, where, and how.

General Yeosock took me over to a corner of the dining room and introduced me to several harried-looking officers. This group consisted of logistics experts with ARCENT, and many of them had participated in the INTERNAL LOOK 90 exercise. Several had a great deal of experience in constructing contingency plans for conflicts in the Middle East. "What I need," Yeosock told us, after brief introductions were completed, "is for you guys to put your heads together and come up with a list of requirements and assistance we will need from Saudi Arabia in order for us to deploy forces into the Kingdom. I have to tell the king what we will need logistically—in other words, a shopping list fit for a king."

Hatching the METT–T

While we worked in our corner, General Yeosock established himself as the overall quarterback. He circulated constantly from group to group, asking and answering questions, all the while draining mugs of black coffee and dispatching cigars. The phone rang constantly. Sometimes the phone demanded his personal attention; most of the time the incoming calls were dealt with by an aide.

In military terminology, Yeosock's responsibility was to perform a "METT–T" assessment of the situation. As he has described it, a METT–T is "the framework to assess key organizational parameters and the catalyst to transform doctrine into theater-specific solutions."[1] The METT–T consists of analyses in five basic categories: mission, enemy, terrain, troops, and time available. As such, it serves as a helpful guide to organizing the constantly changing flow of information in-theater. On the other hand, the METT–T is anything but rigid. It is altered constantly, according to changing circumstances: troops entering a theater, supplies becoming available, new allies pledging support, battles won or lost. The METT–T is the military equivalent of a business plan, providing a structure whereby information can be processed, and change can be assessed. It allows everyone to become focused, and not vacilate.

As of the evening of August 4th, details in each of the five METT–T categories were necessarily sketchy, but they did provide some jumping-off points for planning.

The *mission*, as far as was known at that juncture, was to deploy American troops and weaponry into Saudi Arabia to establish a defensive posture and deter an invasion of the Kingdom by the Iraqi forces occupying Kuwait.

The *enemy* had an impressive military machine, and was thought to possess a vast arsenal of weapons, including devices for nuclear and chemical warfare. It was a fighting force that was certainly experienced, based on its conflict with Iran, but which was thought to be fragmented by internal divisions, including ethnic tensions and hierarchical difficulties (e.g., the "elite" Republican Guard versus the "nonelite" Regular Army units).

The desert *terrain* and environment would pose major challenges to both troops and machinery if war broke out. At the same time, a flat and featureless terrain also presents some potential for exploitation, by both the tactician and the logistician.

The lack of U.S. *troops* in the theater would necessitate the creation of a military presence, including infrastructure, from scratch; although the (potential) host nation's excellent ports and airbases would offset some of these challenges.

Time available was almost completely undefined, but it was assumed to be scarce. Saddam Hussein's troops could attack Saudi Arabia at any time, and in that early stage of the game, the Kingdom was extremely vulnerable.

Armed with this very basic information, and drawing upon our own experiences, we set to work. We decided that the most reasonable way to think through a large-scale deployment, such as was contemplated, would be to start with the REFORGER model and work our way backward. This turned out to be a very productive approach. For my part, I had run port operations and managed large-scale transport of troops; I therefore knew what was necessary to get the job done in terms of airfields, ports, transport equipment, food and water, fuel lines, lodging, and sanitation. Others in the group were invaluable sources of theater-specific information, some having worked for years on the development of highly detailed plans for the Southwest Asia region. These plans had focused mainly on Iran, but also encompassed Bahrain, Saudi Arabia, and several other neighboring countries. As a result, these planners knew the general physical capacities of all major in-theater ports, airfields, road networks, and other transportation routes. They were fairly familiar with the usable and "contractible" resources of the various Middle Eastern nations.

RECEPTION, ONWARD MOVEMENT, AND SUSTAINMENT

As a group, we started assembling a logistical plan. Again, the structure was that of a REFORGER, and those exercises have a sequence of three basic components: *reception* of troops in-theater, during which they retrieve supplies and weapons that have been shipped from the home base; *onward movement* to a designated location to take up their defensive position; and *sustainment* of those troops for the duration of the mission. Reception, onward movement, and sustainment: these were the building blocks that had served well in Europe, and—to our satisfaction—were transplanted effectively to the Gulf, and continued to function throughout the several phases of the Gulf War.

By about 12:30 a.m., we were just beginning to fill in the details of our emerging logistical plan. At that point, General Yeosock returned with a change of orders. We were to pack up what we had up to that point, he told us, and get ready to relocate our little operation. Yeosock had just received orders to report to CENTCOM Headquarters at McDill Air Force Base in Tampa, Florida. From there, he said, it was likely he would have to grab a seat on Secretary Cheney's plane, along with Cheney, General Schwarzkopf, and others, and head directly for Saudi Arabia. Upon his arrival in the Kingdom, he would be expected to have a list of requirements in hand to present to the king. Since most of the specifics of that list were still in our heads, our informal log team would be going along for the ride to Tampa to flesh it out in transit.

General Yeosock was obviously exhausted. The word was that he hadn't slept for days, probably since the Iraqi invasion of Kuwait. As soon as we boarded the C-12 headed for McDill, Yeosock dropped himself heavily into a seat, stuck a rolled-up blanket under his head, and was dead to the world in a matter of seconds. This, we knew, was an important nap. He would have to brief General Schwarzkopf and his staff on the plan in less than two hours, and then, most likely, proceed directly to the Middle East.

Taking care not to disturb our sleeping comrade in arms, we spread our notes out and picked up where we had left off. The first component of the plan, reception, presented an obvious requirement: an appropriate place to receive. "Appropriateness" is defined by the nature of the materials and personnel to be received, by the means of transport to be used, by the schedule that is being followed, and by proximity to the action. Since the deployment time frame was assumed to be extremely tight, it made sense to have most of our troops and a large proportion of their supplies airlifted to Saudi Arabia from various locations around the world. The existing airfield at Dhahran, in the northeast corner of the Kingdom, was an enormous and modern facility. In addition, there was a second airfield then under construction just a few miles north of Dhahran, which could provide even more extensive facilities. Both airfields were plenty close to the potential action—in fact, if we'd had a lot of other choices, one could have made the case that they were a little too close to Kuwait and Saddam's legions.

So we were confident that we had our airports. The next issue was port facilities. Some supplies and equipment, as noted, could come in by air. But the vast bulk of supplies and equipment needed by a large fighting force would have to arrive by water. One result of America's tenuous political relations with the Islamic nations of the Middle East was the lack of a land-based "platform" for the projection of military power. In the early 1980s, the Pentagon attempted to overcome this shortcoming by establishing floating stockpiles of military equipment and supplies, known as "maritime preposition ships" (MPS), or, in shorthand, "prepos." These ships are moored in several strategic locations for reasonably rapid deployment to military hot spots, especially where the United States has few other resources to draw upon. As it turned out, they were absolute lifesavers in the Gulf.

We knew that six prepos (two Air Force, primarily carrying ammunition; and four Army) had already been mobilized, and were on their way to the Gulf from their mooring at the island of Diego Garcia in the Indian Ocean. Most likely, these would constitute the first significant stock of supplies that we would receive in-theater— assuming Americans were indeed sent to the theater—and the ARCENT log team gave me a quick rundown of the contents of the ships then steaming toward the Gulf. Each ship contained at least the bare minimum of almost every imaginable item needed to support a "baseless" army in the field. These supplies included, for example: small arms ammunition and 32,550 hand grenades, 16 bread ovens and 3,000 land mines, and 5.5 million gallons of jet fuel. The prepos carried cranes, refrigerated vans, and forklifts. They carried machine guns, mortar rounds, 6,000 sleeping bags, uniforms and coveralls, and seven field laundry units; 124,000 Class-1 rations (MREs), and fuel bars for heating other kinds of food; medical supplies, cots, blankets, tents, stencil machines, microfiche viewers, file cabinets and radio units; and countless other items. As it turned out, one of the most important items on the prepos was lumber: some 450,000 board feet of lumber and 1,800 sheets of plywood. Within a few days of the arrival of U.S. forces in Saudi Arabia, most of the wood building materials in the country had been consumed by our construction units.

Saddam Hussein had no navy to speak of, and we were confident that the prepos would arrive safely in port—assuming, of course, that the Saudis would let them moor somewhere near the potential conflict. The prepos would give us breathing room, enabling us to arm and house our troops, feeding them and keeping them reasonably clean and healthy, meanwhile setting up a rudimentary system for continuing sustainment. This would be a prerequisite to any effective military command in-country.

There are three major ports in Saudi Arabia—at Ad Dammam and at Al Jubayl on the east coast, and at Jidda in the west—which comprise some of the largest and best-equipped port facilities in the world. As we sketched out the extensive resources already available in these ports, such as cranes and warehouses, it was clear to me that they would be more than sufficient for our purposes. The eastern ports, reasonably close to the Kuwaiti border, seemed ideal. If you had to have a war, we agreed among ourselves, this would be a great place to have it.

While General Yeosock napped, his list of requests to the king was steadily expanding. Reception, the first logistical challenge of the proposed deployment, would be feasible only if we had unlimited access to and use of the airfields and ports to receive personnel and supplies. It would also require an appropriate site or sites from which we could mount our operations. Although much of Saudi Arabia looks to the uninitiated observer like a trackless desert, in fact every parcel of land in the Kingdom is carefully controlled, usually by someone with close ties to the royal family. (This is not surprising, given that Ibn Saud, the first king of the country that took his name in 1932, had thirty-one sons.[2] Today, the royal family includes some 4,000 male members,[3] whose influence extends to almost every aspect of life in Saudi Arabia.) There was no doubt that the king and his relatives would be closely involved in the reception of our troops, again assuming a deployment took place.

The next phase of our emerging logistical plan, onward movement, was every bit as dependent on the goodwill of the Saudi royal family. How would we transport thousands of soldiers and millions of tons of supplies from the airfields and ports to our base locations? On the basis of my experience, I had developed a strict and unwavering policy: when a ship is unloaded, *nothing* sits on the dock. The linchpin to this policy, of course, is adequate transportation capacity to move material away from the waterfront. Almost from Day One, therefore, we would need a fleet of trucks, buses, and HETs (heavy equipment transporters) at our disposal. Equally important, those vehicles would have to have a priority access to the Kingdom's limited road network.

The final phase, sustainment, was the hardest to project, since it would depend in large part on the unfolding of events in the weeks and months ahead. Our sense was that the prepos could tide us over until our sea lines of supply to the United States and Europe were established. Once those sea lines were open, we could anticipate adequate supplies of nonperishable goods, including everything from bandages to batteries. Food would be another story. Soldiers can survive indefinitely on MREs, but if only for morale reasons, an endless diet of dehydrated/rehydrated MREs is not recommended. Doctrine says that whenever possible, the logistician should search out freshly prepared food. As it turned out, locally procured food was both better and cheaper than MREs, which cost about four dollars apiece, and for which our soldiers developed a number of colorful nicknames. At the bottom of our wish list, therefore, we suggested that General Yeosock secure permission from the king to procure fresh food and fruit, along with other critical goods and services, from the local economy.

OUT OF SIGHT, BUT NOT OUT OF MIND

This was the state of our logistical planning when our C-12 touched down at McDill Air Force Base. General Yeosock roused himself, thanked us for our work, and was immediately whisked off by members of the CENTCOM staff for command-level discussions. We were greeted by our logistical counterparts on the CENTCOM staff, and with them started reviewing our list.

The sudden silence that followed the shut-down of the C-12's engines, as well as the balmy breeze that was blowing steadily across the dark runway, brought me down out of my adrenaline overdrive. I glanced at my watch, discovered that it was well after 3 o'clock in the morning. It had been more than five hours since I left my house, and I realized that I hadn't even told Cheri how long I'd be gone. This was bad. She is extremely tolerant of my erratic work hours, but gets very nervous when I don't tell her where I am, or when I'm not where I've told her I'm going to be. I scouted up a telephone and said simply that I had been asked to work on a special mission, and that I would be back when I could.

Although I felt my concentration ebbing, my mind was still churning its way through a sea of questions. Many of these questions had to do with contracting, which I now took to be the key sustainment issue. Through several years of REFORGER work, I'd become very well acquainted with the complexities of negotiations with host nations. These negotiations are as much about political relations and diplomacy as they are about goods and services. For example, one deal that I facilitated among five NATO nations in the 1980s started out as a five-page document, but eventually boiled down to one, very carefully worded paragraph. The single most important issue dominating those negotiations—that is, residual resentments left over from World War II, and even earlier—never quite surfaced at the bargaining table. At the end of the discussions, I felt we were lucky to settle upon our one paragraph.

Relations between the United States and Saudi Arabia, let alone any other Middle Eastern nations that might become involved, promised to be at least as delicate and sensitive—and, as yet, none of us knew the magnitude of the demands we would be placing on Saudi Arabia. On the positive side, though, the threat of invasion makes for very cooperative bedfellows. Perhaps contracting for host-nation goods and services would run even more smoothly than they had in the peacetime REFORGER exercises.

Operating on that assumption, I sat by the edge of the now-quiet tarmac for about another hour, trying to flesh out the list of basics that we would require in order to get ourselves up and operating in Saudi Arabia. One of the hardest tasks, for logisticians and nonlogisticians alike, is to look at a list and spot what's not there. I soon became convinced that I was planning in a vacuum. This is always a recipe for bad planning. And finally, truth be told, gravity was starting to work on my eyelids. At 4:30 a.m. I decided that it was time for a nap.

I wandered around the CENTCOM headquarters, noted a familiar name on a nearby door, let myself in, and stretched out my tired bones on the couch inside the office. I had just about dozed off when Major General Dane Starling, J4 of CENTCOM (in other words, head logistics officer for United States Central Command, reporting to General Schwarzkopf) blew into his office to grab a stack of reports on the credenza and to pack out his desk. Dane and I had known each other for years. By any reckoning, these were unusual circumstances for a reunion, since I neither worked at CENTCOM nor served in any official capacity on General Yeosock's ARCENT staff. I explained my hired-gun status, and Starling reciprocated by filling me in on the developments of the past few hours. Among other things, Starling told me he would be accompanying Generals Schwarzkopf and Yeosock, as well as Secretary of Defense Cheney, to Saudi Arabia to help in the negotiations with the king.

At that moment, though, Starling was on his way to gather up the various logisticians who were still busily refining the reception–onward movement–sustainment list. I tagged along to learn how the plan had progressed since I last saw it. The planning team was just wrapping up, and they suggested that I review a copy of the list to see if I could spot any obvious gaps. I couldn't; all the subjects we had discussed on the flight down to Tampa were still there, along with a lot more detail. We discussed and agreed upon some final refinements.

General Yeosock then reappeared, looking like a man determined to make every minute count. He gave us three of those minutes, listening to what was on our list and why. "Great!" he exclaimed, ending the impromptu briefing by grabbing our list and heading back out to the runway, where a plane was revving up for an imminent flight to Washington to pick up Secretary Cheney, and a subsequent leg to Riyadh. A raggedy band of logisticians watched the plane take off, and then headed over to the snack bar for a cup of coffee and a donut. A few hours later we hopped a C-12 back to Georgia, and were home again well before a full day had passed.

The afternoon and evening of August 5th were uneventful. I didn't much enjoy my day off, though. Little details of the planning sessions kept coming to mind, uninvited, as I tried to attend to the mundane details of a Sunday. What had we forgotten? What had we overestimated, or underestimated? Of course, the mission was top secret, so I couldn't share my thoughts with anyone. In fact, I had already decided to carry on with my regularly scheduled Monday agenda, which included a long-scheduled visit to Fort Hood, Texas, to avoid arousing suspicions in anyone's mind that anything out of the ordinary was happening.

But I knew that the situation was far from resolved, and I had a strong hunch that I hadn't seen the last of that plan. So on Sunday evening, I sat down and rehashed the entire plan, step by step, point by point. Assuming a deployment actually took place, this would be time well spent, since I would certainly be supplying deployed troops in my capacity as J4 at FORSCOM. The mental review proved to be a reassuring exercise. After a few hours of testing and probing the assumptions our little band of logisticians had made during our five hours of intensive planning, I wound up confident that we hadn't neglected anything of critical importance. I packed up a bag for my trip out west, hit the sack, and slept like the dead.

The next morning was comfortably routine. I woke up, ran, showered, and got dressed. During my run, I had my Walkman radio tuned to a news station. President Bush had announced on the previous day that a puppet regime in Kuwait was unacceptable to the United States, and the news analysts were scrutinizing the significance of the speech. Right on schedule, I went to the office for a quick status report, then to the airfield to catch my flight to Texas.

I had gotten about two-thirds of the way through my schedule down at Fort Hood, on a trip designed to help me get to know the men and the operations at that installation, when I received an emergency telephone call. Once again it was Pete Taylor, ordering me to return to Fort McPherson on the double. Taylor himself was waiting for me as I stepped off the plane. He told me, in a very few words, that General Yeosock would not be returning as anticipated from Saudi Arabia to Fort McPherson, and that I should stand by for further instructions. Apparently, Yeosock had asked that I join him in Saudi Arabia.

In short order I was speaking to Yeosock on the phone. The negotiations had been successful, and there had been few major surprises. King Fahd had approved the deployment of American troops to Saudi Arabia, and had offered the full cooperation and resources of his country.

In retrospect, I suspect that few Americans can appreciate the courage that this decision by the king required. The reader might well ask: What ruler in his right mind would turn down military assistance? But to many in Saudi Arabia, the threat posed by Saddam Hussein was less troubling than the prospect of hundreds of thousands of American "infidel" soldiers on Saudi soil. The religious fundamentalists in particular were certain to criticize the king's decision, and perhaps even challenge his authority. According to reports after the war, there were influential members of the royal family who opposed an American intervention.[4] The king took a big risk, and deserves much credit for that decision.

Yeosock went on to confirm the story that Taylor had just sketched out, and filled in some of the details. Because of my RE-

FORGER experiences and my other logistical training, he told me, I had been selected to go to Saudi Arabia and head up host-nation support negotiations on behalf of our troops. Interestingly enough, this was the very subject that I had recently been concentrating on, and had identified in those mental reviews as the key to any Saudi Arabian deployment. The goal, Yeosock told me, was to establish a civilian infrastructure to support our now-definite intervention. It would be complicated: General Schwarzkopf had concluded that we had to deploy our combat forces as rapidly as possible, using our limited rapid sealift and airlift resources, so that we could get enough force on the ground to defend the Saudis. The military logistical forces would have to wait—and to fill the logistical void, we would have to use host-nation assets.

In effect, I would be doing a market survey, much as a corporation does when it contemplates opening a new facility. In many cases, subcontracting for facilities, personnel, and other resources is much more cost-effective than shipping all needed assets to the new site. That was my anticipated role, one greatly complicated by the urgent need to get fighters on the ground.

I stopped by the home of FORSCOM's Commander in Chief, General Edwin H. Burba, Jr., who had already signed off on my abrupt change of scenery. General Burba was thoroughly familiar with the scope of my logistical experience, which had included tours of duty on three continents, and in a wide variety of settings.

"Gus, I'd like to keep you here at FORSCOM," he told me, "but I honestly think you're the guy to whip this thing into shape."

"I'm just going over to serve as the host-nation consultant," I replied. "I'll be back soon enough."

He smiled wryly, and shook his head. "I won't bet on that. Right now you're an adviser for host-nation matters. But I know you. Once you get there, you'll throw yourself into the challenge, and they'll find more and more ways to put your talents to use."

While General Burba and I were sitting there, he received a call from the Chief of Staff of the Army, General Carl E. Vuono. After a few minutes of conversation, Burba handed me the phone, and I spoke directly to the Chief. Vuono was succinct. "Gus," he told me, "as soon as you figure out what you need over there, I want you to just ask for it."

I responded that I would like to take a few experts with me, people who had worked with me before and who understood my management style, and who were knowledgeable in reception, onward movement, and sustainment. The chief told me to send him a list of the twenty people I wanted, and he would "make it happen."

General Burba hung up the phone and we terminated our short but eventful session. He shook my hand and said, "So I don't expect to be seeing you back at FORSCOM. Good luck."

This was a typically selfless send-off from an officer who is not only a great leader and patriot, but also a gentleman. Many in the Army, and probably in the private sector as well, would have extracted concessions from the hierarchy before releasing someone on my level. Many would have worried first about their own needs, rather than the needs of the overriding mission. Not General Burba. And as it turned out, Burba had his own massive mission just over the horizon: mobilizing the reserves and the National Guard for deployment to Saudi Arabia, while also preparing the U.S.-based divisions for their Saudi Arabian missions.

There aren't too many votes of confidence that I would take more to heart than General Burba's. I thanked him for his support, and left. As I walked away from his house, I realized that I would soon be leaving my wife temporarily, and my old job permanently. At least I had no apprehensions about my wife, since General Burba had assured me that she could remain in government quarters indefinitely.

A DIFFERENT KIND OF LIST

The mood at home that evening was far different from the relaxed calm of the morning, just twelve hours earlier. In fact, domestic tensions were running high. The mission was still classified top secret, which means that no one talks to anyone outside the mission. All I could say was that I was working on a highly confidential operation, and that I would be gone for a while. I started packing my suitcase, putting in bare necessities.

Cheri watched these preparations with understandable apprehension and frustration. I had to turn away all of her questions, which wasn't particularly satisfying for either of us. I was going somewhere, but she couldn't know where, and she couldn't know for how long. I confess to being short with her—at one point, I told her to go turn on Cable News Network and see if she could figure things out for herself. This peevishness was out of character for me, and it did nothing to reassure Cheri.

What *did* reassure her, at least partially, was an opportunity to help me out in my preparations. While I continued to pack, Cheri riffled through my extensive filing system, in which I had records on most of the officers and NCOs with whom I had worked over the course of my twenty-six years in the military. She called out names, dates, and notations, and compiled a list of the people I chose. No, she couldn't know exactly why she was doing what she was doing, but it did her a world of good to contribute in some meaningful way.

Meanwhile, as I packed my clothes and worked up this list of candidates, the list's longer-term implications were becoming more and more clear to me. I needed to pull together a very particular team of soldiers, all of whom would be expected to hit the ground running. There would be no time for training or for cults of personality. The lack of an established in-country infrastructure would require that all our attention be focused on getting our host-nation logistical operations up and running, with minimal delays. There could be no distractions from the task at hand.

This influenced my responses to the names that Cheri was calling out. Over the years, I have developed a very distinctive leadership style. Gus Pagonis's command style, like everyone else's, is unique. This meant that I had choices to make. Would I rather have the world's best port operation officer, if he was someone who didn't already know my style? Or would I rather have the world's second-best port operation officer, who knew my style intimately and was comfortable with it? The answer was obvious: we couldn't waste time fighting our own systems. Equally important, we couldn't afford the time that would be wasted as a new person tried to impress me, or get on my good side. We needed an instant body of leaders, strengthened by a united front. We needed to know that we could depend on one another unconditionally. We needed confidence that the mission, and not personal advancement, would always be paramount in the mind of each participant.

With these thoughts in mind, and with Cheri's help, I sketched out my ideal command. It was an extremely talented group of soldiers, including specialists in all of the areas that I knew would be important: oil and fuel management, host-nation relations, port operations, food services management, transportation, and so on. There were no guarantees that I could get all of them. On the other hand, General Burba had told me that very few of my selected candidates would be excused from reporting to Saudi. With some excitement and satisfaction, I issued my first (informal) order of the campaign: I asked Cheri to forward the twenty-soldier list to my executive officer at Fort McPherson. He would in turn deliver it to Pete Taylor, who would pass it on to the Department of the Army.

In the meantime, I started making some phone calls of my own. I knew that I would have at least twelve hours, maybe as many as fifteen, on the flight over to Saudi Arabia. This seemed like an ideal opportunity to bring a few people up to speed on the plan, and to start making the initial arrangements to implement it.

Fortunately, three out of my list of twenty men were able to break away immediately from what they were doing, no questions asked, and meet me in Tampa. It reminded me of the opening scenes of a John Wayne cowboy movie, in which Wayne sends out gold coins in a silent summons to his key deputies. My deputies responded magnificently. None of us knew what lay ahead, but they knew I wouldn't have called unless the mission was of critical importance, and they responded. If they had not—if those three pros hadn't been willing to drop everything they were doing and help out—we would never have enjoyed the successes that followed. I owe them, and their spouses and families, a great debt.

My first gold coin—sent to my old friend and an outstanding logistician, Colonel Jim Ireland—almost didn't pay off. Jim had served as my executive officer when I was stationed at the Pentagon. He knew my management style inside and out, and could run any aspect of my administrative organization and information systems as well as I could. He was the logistician's equivalent of the all-star utility infielder—someone who could play any one of a number of roles, and at the highest level of proficiency. Having Ireland on board would guarantee that we could focus on the job at hand, rather than training for the job at hand. Jim was on temporary duty (TDY) visiting an Army post in New Jersey when I phoned, but on the off chance that he'd be checking in soon, I left a note on his answering machine. "Jim," I told the machine, "I need you. Pack a bag with a few uniforms in it, and meet me at Tampa."

The gods were smiling on me that day: Ireland got the message and hopped the next commercial flight to Tampa.

Jack Tier had worked for me as my operations officer when I was a battalion commander at Fort Eustis. We hadn't worked together since then, but his competence had left a lasting impression on me. He'd had a great deal of port operations experience; and on top of that is a superior planner and thinker. I put in a call to his boss at

Fort Lee, Virginia, and said, in effect, "I've been assigned to a top secret mission; I need Jack to help me out. We'll be leaving from McDill in a matter of hours." Tier was on his way immediately.

Steve Koons was the easiest of all to track down, since he was then stationed with me at FORSCOM. I first encountered Steve four years earlier during a REFORGER exercise, in which he ran airfield operations for me. As I got to know him, I learned that he had also served in the 101st Airborne Division—a nice plus, since he knew firsthand the logistics of airborne and airmobile (helicopter) interventions. Koons was extremely knowledgeable about running airfields; he knew exactly what was necessary to get people off planes and moving. He happened to walk by me in the hallway; I told him he had thirty minutes to pack up and meet me for a C-12 flight to Tampa.

I said goodbye to Cheri, forgetting my map of Saudi Arabia on the kitchen table in the flurry of activity. By the time I missed it, I realized that I could either go back for it, or make a planned stop at the Dairy Queen. I opted for the Dairy Queen, for what I suspected might be my last banana split for quite a while, and then headed to the airport where I rejoined Steve Koons. We reached McDill Air Force Base in the evening on August 6th. While we awaited the arrival of the rest of our party, I ran through an abridged version of the previous two-and-a-half days. We noticed other small pockets of people waiting around the airfield. Since there was no other compelling reason to be hanging around McDill that day, I assumed that they were waiting for the same C-141 as we were—the next flight to Riyadh.

The CENTCOM war room was handy to the runway, and I decided to stick my head in. I noticed some commotion on the other side of the room, and spotted the imposing figure of General Schwarzkopf. I decided I would go over and let him know we were there, and that I would be working as a part of his team.

After exchanging greetings, General Schwarzkopf confirmed that he was indeed surprised to run into me at McDill, especially since he assumed I was still working supply issues in Washington for the Department of the Army. As discussed earlier, this was the context in which, about seven months earlier, Schwarzkopf and I had first interacted professionally. I was then working in the Office of the Deputy Chief of Staff for Logistics at the Pentagon. As Director of Transportation, Energy, and Troop Support, I was responsible for supervising the procurement of Army goods, equipment, and services.

Naturally, my sphere of influence extended to Army uniforms. General Schwarzkopf, as Commander in Chief of CENTCOM, had contacted my office to complain about the shortcomings of our heavy desert uniform, and particularly about the desert boot that we were then distributing to our troops. The boots had been designed for combat in Vietnam, where buried booby traps had posed a serious threat to soldiers. In that era, therefore, a metal plate had been incorporated in the sole of the boot, providing nearly complete protection against pungi-stick traps. But what is a boon in the jungle may turn out to be a curse in the desert, where the extreme heat of the sand—say, at midday in August—would heat up the plate in the soldier's shoe, and consequently badly burn his or her feet.

General Schwarzkopf had spent much of his childhood in the Middle East. He knew firsthand why people wore loose-fitting clothes in that region, and why they avoided stepping on hot metal. I was also sympathetic: if you once picked up a metal tool on a hot tank under the blazing sun during a desert training exercise at California's Fort Irwin, you never did again. Schwarzkopf carried out a vigorous and ultimately successful lobbying campaign to get the boots redesigned.

We briefly discussed my impending host-nation responsibilities. In the course of our conversation, he essentially issued "mission orders" for the upcoming conflict—that is, a clear and concise statement of the "who, what, why, where, and how" on which my plan was to be based. Drawing again on his personal experience, Schwarzkopf offered me two pieces of advice, which turned out to be typical of his attitude throughout the war—and indeed, throughout his career.

"First and foremost," he told me, "take care of the troops; make sure they are getting everything they need. If you don't get that done, nothing else counts." I could only agree, wholeheartedly. This had always been the underlying premise and touchstone of my commands.

"And second," he continued, in the gruff, forceful voice the entire nation would soon come to recognize, "I don't want to win the war and lose the peace. The Saudi Arabian government has agreed to work with the United States through this conflict, and it's extremely important that we be sensitive to their laws, customs, and traditions. They will be our hosts, and we will be their guests. We can't afford to alienate them or abuse their hospitality in any way." I assured him that I understood and could work within these very clear guidelines. My subsequent experiences only underscored for me the wisdom of General Schwarzkopf's impromptu advice, which would serve us so well in the field.

I headed back to rejoin Steve Koons and greet the newly arrived Jim Ireland and Jack Tier. The C-141 had arrived and was nearly ready for boarding. The crowd had gradually grown, and there were about 100 people in line to board the craft. Among them were my logistics colleagues from ARCENT, who were to rejoin General Yeosock in Riyadh.

As we brought each other up to date, a message which had been wending its way by word of mouth through the crowd reached us. President Bush, according to the grapevine, had approved the deployment of troops to Saudi Arabia, and the XVIII ABN Corps was mobilizing even as we spoke. Even if this development didn't alter the basic structure of our plan, it would certainly compress its time frame into unrecognizable form: under this kind of time pressure, our angel food cake was in peril of turning into a pancake. If the deployment rumor was true, we now had a substantially different mission. Instead of landing, getting our bearings, and then organizing an operation for a sequence of steps—reception, onward movement, and sustainment—we would be setting up the organization at the same time we would be receiving and moving the troops. From a logistician's point of view, the stakes had been raised dramatically.

All of this put an interesting spin on our planning session during the 24-hour flight to Riyadh. Ireland, Tier, Koons, and I got down to work with a redoubled sense of urgency. They were soon fully familiar with the plan that had been roughed out by the ARCENT log team and me. During these discussions, and by lucky coincidence, we also attracted the attention of Lt. Colonel Tom Ehlinger, another member of General Yeosock's planning crew, and a crackerjack contracting specialist.

We quickly got to a joint understanding of what I took to be our role in the theater. Technically, we would serve as host-nation coordinators, obtaining goods and services not already established in-theater—which, in this particular situation, meant just about every type of goods and services. Sticking with the basic framework of reception–onward movement–sustainment, we sketched out a plan whereby we would set up an aerial port in Dhahran. We would receive troops there, moving them by bus as soon as possible to a forward location, where they could relax, catch up on their sleep, and await their assignments. We would purchase food locally to feed the incoming soldiers. And finally, in preparation for incoming supply vessels, we'd secure adequate amounts of contracted labor to run our port operations, at least until sufficient numbers of military stevedores could be brought into the theater. In all cases, our efforts would complement the work of the corps-level logisticians.

This in-transit brainstorming session allowed us to clarify our mission and define our respective responsibilities. As a rule, I'm skeptical of brainstorming, which in most cases seems to amount to earnest people sitting around and throwing out random ideas. Even the metaphor confuses me: Does a heavier storm lead to clearer vision? I feel that you must have a controlled session with clear objectives. Our session on the C-141 to Riyadh was very successful, mainly because from the outset we had a well-defined structure for invention. We worked toward several clearly expressed goals, and there was an imposed time limit to keep us on track. And finally, our various expertises were complementary. We needed each other, and we knew it. Tier knew port operations; Koons knew airfields; Ehlinger knew contracts; Ireland knew overall logistics and how to set up a staff; and I knew how to bring it together. And we benefited from the experience of senior logisticians Colonel Robert Klineman and Lt. Colonel Larry Grishom, who carefully reviewed our objectives. The plan took shape quickly.

Throughout the ensuing weeks and months, of course, our early thinking changed often, sometimes dramatically, reflecting the shifting political and theater situation. This demonstrates another advantage of our organization—a group admittedly tiny at the time of the C-141 flight, but which quickly grew to comprise 39,925 soldiers, or more than 80,000 individuals. That strength was flexibility, both as individuals and as a group. Organizations must be flexible enough to adjust and conform when their environments change. But flexibility can degenerate into chaos in the absence of well-established goals.

In my terminology, a goal is something that is nonquantifiable, purposely broad, and overarching. Once everyone in the organization understands the goals of the organization, then each person sets out several objectives by which to attain those goals at that given time, within his or her own sphere of activity. Concurrently, a wide variety of communication channels must be opened and cultivated, to ensure that these decentralized efforts add up to a coordinated whole. When it works, and in my experience it always does, cooperation and collegiality are enhanced, and in-fighting and suboptimization are minimized.

The goal of reception, for example, does not lend itself to quantification. But when faced with the prospect of receiving 5,000 troops per day—troops who will most likely arrive tired, hungry, thirsty, and aching for a shower—a good manager starts formulating a list of objectives to accomplish that goal as effectively as possible. If you are a transport specialist, for example, you begin looking for buses ASAP. If you are a fuel and water specialist, you start investigating pipelines, desalination plants, and bottled water. Control is centralized; execution is decentralized.

The punch line is productivity. I have found, time and time again in commands around the world, that my troops are more invested in their work and better motivated when they understand and buy into the ultimate goals of the operation. Reason counts for far more than rank, when it comes to motivation. And motivation is the root of all organizational progress. Motivation begets success, success begets confidence, confidence begets risk taking, and risk taking begets innovation.

ON THE GROUND

We arrived mid-morning on August 8th and reported directly to General Yeosock, who had already established his planning unit in Riyadh. It was this operation to which the ARCENT logisticians were assigned almost immediately, and it was from this post that they continued to help shape ARCENT's logistical activities in subsequent weeks.

Those of us without an obvious unit to latch on to—in other words, Gus Pagonis and his three aces—set up shop in temporary office space in Riyadh, and then joined General Yeosock for a look at the city's resources. What we saw was a very modern looking city, baking under the desert sun, with a feel something like that of Washington, D.C. There was certainly no panic or war fever in the air; in fact, people were going about their business at a relaxed pace, appropriate to the very hot and bone-dry weather. It was clear from General Yeosock's commentary that CENTCOM would be based in Riyadh, in part because the Saudi Ministry of Defense and Aviation (MODA) was there, and close coordination between these two commands would be vital to the defensive effort.

As we explored, Yeosock mentioned that the 82d Airborne, commanded by Major General James H. Johnson, was already arriving in Dhahran. We had already picked the ports and airfields in the vicinity of Dhahran as most suitable for our purposes. We also knew that the country's major oil field and its desalinization plants were also in the Dhahran area, and that these represented major temptations for the Iraqis. Now there was added incentive to head for Dhahran: whoever was there on the ground, trying to deal with the arrival of the 82d Airborne, would almost certainly need our help. We packed up our ever-evolving plan and our paltry belongings and headed east.

About one hour later, we disembarked onto the King Abdul Aziz Airbase in Dhahran. The first thing that struck us as we stepped off the plane was a hot wall of humidity: given Dhahran's proximity to the Gulf, the desert air there is paradoxically waterlogged. The second thing that hit us was a state of swirling, overwhelming chaos on the ground. Our eyes took it all in the way the camera panned the outdoor hospital scene in *Gone with the Wind*: the more you looked, the more appalled you were by what you saw. There were already thousands of American troops on the ground, standing, sitting, or milling around. Every few minutes another transport plane would arrive, pouring hundreds more soldiers into ever-denser knots around the runway. Shelter from the blazing sun was almost impossible to find, and in the few places where a building or aircraft threw off some shade, soldiers jockeyed for position.

A lone American officer stood heroically in the midst of this cyclone, trying to impose order on chaos. Lt. Colonel Ed Lindbloom, Army Logistics Adviser with the U.S. Military Training Mission of Saudi Arabia (USMTM) in Riyadh, had flown over to Dhahran as soon as President Bush announced the decision to deploy troops in Southwest Asia. Against odds that were getting worse by the minute, he and a few overworked representatives of the Saudi military, led by Colonel Khalif al-Shahari, were trying to set up an impromptu structure for receiving the 82d Airborne.

Through the 1980s, USMTM was as close as the United States came to having a military presence on Saudi soil. USMTM serves a multipurpose educational function for joint services, including the armies and air forces of both the United States and Saudi Arabia. Located in both Riyadh and Dhahran, USMTM is technically not a military installation. The 300-or-so Americans serving there are soldiers and airmen, but they carry no weapons; they are funded, housed, and protected by the Saudi Arabian government through MODA. They aid the Saudi military with training techniques for large and small unit tactics; they make suggestions as to maintenance of machinery and weaponry; advise the Saudis as to which American weapons systems might be appropriate to purchase, and then serve as technical liaison between the Saudis and the U.S. Congress.

Despite the Herculean efforts of Lindbloom and the Saudi soldiers, the situation at the Dhahran airbase was bad and getting worse. There was no logistical structure in place to receive the incoming units. It was approximately 140 degrees. The troops were confused, tired, and irritable. They had been flying all night. They had not been told much about their mission, except that they were being deployed to the Gulf. Whatever else happened, they would need water, food, and shelter very soon.

Sanitation facilities were also an immediate priority. British military historian Bryan Perrett, a specialist in desert warfare, defines this logistical challenge in graphic and colorful terms:

> The desert may possess its own sterility, but this vanishes as soon as it is penetrated by armies which daily deposit hundreds of tons of human waste on its surface. Not for nothing was the name Beelzebub, meaning Lord of the Flies, conferred by the Israelites on the Devil, for these loathsome insects feed on excrement and breed by the millions, battening in food and open wounds to spread their filthy diseases. . . . In the days before the connection between hygiene and health were fully understood, armies venturing into the desert tended to sustain higher losses from dysentery and other diseases than they did at the hands of the enemy. . . . In the desert, the smallest scratch, let alone a major wound, is quickly infected by grit and flies, the result being the notorious desert sore which refuses to heal and often becomes ulcerated.[5]

In other words, all of our twenty-first-century military technologies could easily be undermined by prehistoric sanitation and health facilities. And—as General Schwarzkopf had already underscored for my benefit—we were guests in this country. We had responsibilities both to ourselves and to our Saudi hosts.

Steve Koons, our airfields expert, took the bit in his teeth immediately and started organizing the soldiers on and near the runways. I think it's safe to say that Colonel Lindbloom was relieved to have some competent help, and also to get some follow-up for the steps he had already taken. For example, he had hired a group of Saudi buses and drivers to get people off the airfield; but like the 82d

Airborne, they were now standing around waiting for Lindbloom's next directives.

I buttonholed the most impressive-looking of the bus drivers—a big guy—ascertained that he spoke English, and told him, "Congratulations. You've just been appointed bus company commander." There was no such title, of course, but he looked pleased. "Get your men organized so we can start shipping people out of here."

"Yes, sir!" he replied crisply. "And where shall we take them?"

This and other questions were answered with Lindbloom's help. Within a half hour, the first busloads of troops were on their way to a nearby barracks, about three miles from the airbase, which had formerly housed Saudi soldiers.

The next few days were a thorough test of our skills, patience, senses of humor, and stamina. The basic problem we were dealing with was that we were trying to set up a logistical structure for reception in the middle of a deployment. According to doctrine and common sense, you set up the structure first, and only then do you begin the deployment. But the reality of the military situation didn't allow us this luxury. As a result, we worked a grueling thirty-six hours on, four hours off schedule. Truth be told, we spent less of our time as logisticians, and more of our time as managers, fixers, firefighters, father confessors, and cheerleaders. There was simply nobody else around to play any of these roles.

The first night was probably the worst, during which we took turns grabbing catnaps on the side of the runway. Whoever was awake at any given moment continued to process incoming troops in as orderly a fashion as he could. Things improved slightly on the morning of August 10th, when we successfully commandeered an unclaimed four-door sedan. This was our first Dhahran headquarters: office space in the front seat and a relay-style sleeping area in the back. It wasn't until our third day in Saudi Arabia that we moved our operations into a room with a floor, walls, and a real bed. At that point, we secured a bachelor officers' quarters (BOQ)–style room, where we set up operations in the sitting room/kitchen area.

From our first day in-country, my group drew up and issued a daily situation report, or SITREP, which we forwarded both to ARCENT headquarters in Riyadh and directly to the Pentagon. This was a personal priority of mine. I made it clear to my four subordinates who were there at the outset, and to all key officers who arrived in-theater subsequently, that the SITREP would be the single official document to come out of my command each day. The SITREP is not new; in fact, it's probably as old as writing and warfare. On the other hand, I viewed it as a key communications tool in the Gulf context. If used correctly, it would not only fill in other commands (including ARCENT, CENTCOM, Army Materiel Command, and the Pentagon) as to our progress and needs, it would also serve as an internal benchmark and conscience. Taken together, these two communication channels met the overall goal of the SITREP—to make sure that everyone worldwide was working from the same sheet of music.

This practice ties in directly with my conviction about the need for a shared understanding of common goals. Keeping your subordinates, peers, and superiors abreast of your actions, as well as the rationale behind those actions, puts everybody on an equal information footing. I believe information is power, but only if it's shared. I had a pretty unique perspective on communication flow in the military. For example, I served a two-year stint as head of logistics in Panama, and then in the Pentagon during the Panama conflict. I could see the logistical demands of that conflict from both sides at once, and I never saw a difficult situation—not one—that wasn't improved by a straightforward communication of the facts.

Personality is also a factor. I've always been a cards-on-the-table individual. Maybe someone with a different personality from mine could succeed by throttling the information flow. I only know it wouldn't work for me.

Finally, in the chaos of those first few days of the Gulf conflict, any sort of organizational structure, no matter how thin or tenuous, was a welcome reassurance. Troops continued to arrive constantly throughout those first three days. It was like standing next to a water main that had burst open, with only a mop and bucket in hand. But we quickly got better with the mop. Thanks to Tom Ehlinger, we secured the use of 10,000 Bedouin tents, and hired dozens of third-country nationals to come in and put them up for us. As befitted their nomadic origins, these tents were simple and quick to erect, and did the key job of getting our soldiers in out of the sun. Solving the shelter problem freed us up to begin making other logistical arrangements. For example, we found and rented several refrigerated vans, and used them to start bringing in cold drinking water. (This wasn't just a luxury. Water left out in the sun actually boiled. It soon became obvious that cold water was to soldiers in the desert what dry socks and boots were to soldiers in Vietnam.) Meanwhile, we started purchasing food from a variety of Saudi companies. We quickly developed a taste for fresh pita bread, supplied by the local bakers; this taste long outlasted the war.

TWO TURNING POINTS

The lack of logisticians on the ground in Saudi Arabia during the second week of August 1990 was the result of two factors: doctrine and sheer necessity. These two forces set the stage for some early bureaucratic wrangling, in which I was involved, and which probably needs some explanation.

According to doctrine, it is only when more than one corps is stationed in a theater that a higher-level logistical organization is needed, in part to ensure that the two corps don't start competing for scarce resources. When a second corps arrives in a war theater, a Theater Army Area Command (TAACOM) support operation is established to handle these sorts of situations, and to deal with overarching logistical needs. The TAACOM exists as an echelon above corps (EAC) unit, and generally operates to the rear of the conflict, with the COSCOM concentrating on forward actions. So while combat personnel from the XVIII ABN Corps were arriving continually—not only the 82d Airborne, but also the 1st Tactical Fighter Wing, the 24th Mechanized Infantry, and the 3d Armored Cavalry— no extra logistical support was coming in to support those divisions.

In fact, very little logistical support at all was coming in. More important than doctrinal considerations were the tough and pragmatic choices then being made in Washington. During that murky stage of the conflict, Saddam Hussein's plans were unclear. It was conceivable, at that point, that the act of deployment would itself prompt Hussein to invade Saudi Arabia. In any case, the threat of invasion overshadowed all our decisions and actions. When the president approved the deployment of troops in the Middle East, Generals Powell and Schwarzkopf specifically ordered in the combat troops first to deter an Iraqi invasion. As a result, the standard order in which units are sent into combat was resequenced. The combat troops moved up the list, and the logisticians—even the logisticians who made up the XVIII ABN Corps' COSCOM—moved down.

The practical result, from my worm's-eye perspective, was that four people (my three officers and I) constituted the entire logistical operation in-theater. We had been recruited and sent in as host-

nation specialists, and now we were something else—something undefined, but bigger. General Vuono had generously allocated me my
twenty good men, but like the XVIII ABN Corps' COSCOM, most
of them were still stuck at Fort McPherson, getting bumped off each
departing plane in favor of desperately needed combat troops. Meanwhile, I was dying for logisticians. It was like inviting everyone to
dinner except the cooks. Our combat presence in the Kingdom was
expanding by thousands of people each day. We needed more people
to process the sheer bulk of administrative work associated with
buying bread, buying water, building latrines, setting up tents, and
so on. And very soon, we would have those vital prepo ships to
unload.

By our third day of trying to corral the airfields and temporary
sleeping quarters into some semblance of order, we were reaching
the limits of our collective abilities. I decided at that point to take a
look at the "Time-Phased Force Deployment List," or TPFDL (pro-
nounced "tipfiddle" in Army circles). This is the master list of units
being introduced into a theater of war, in their anticipated sequence
of deployment. It is now computer-based, of course, and is constantly adjusted to accommodate changing circumstances in the field.
What I wanted to see was when I could expect the 1st COSCOM,
which was the logistical corps support command of the XVIII ABN
Corps. The news was discouraging: they, too, had been displaced on
the list by more combat troops, and would not arrive for another
month.

Here I made a bad decision for good reasons. I petitioned the
Pentagon directly, asking my counterparts in Washington to revise
the TPFDL and get me some help. The next thing I knew, I was
getting my ears boxed by the tactical planners down in Riyadh, who
were in charge of sequencing the deployment and absolutely did not
appreciate my sending mixed signals out of the theater. They told
me in no uncertain terms that *they* would decide when the theater
had received enough "killers" (a common and nonderogatory scrap
of Army jargon), at which point the logisticians would get their seats
on the airplanes.

So by the afternoon of August 11th, I was at the end of my tether.
I needed some good news—and all of a sudden, I got some. Into my
office walked a closely cropped, barrel-chested colonel who introduced himself as Colonel David Whaley, commanding officer of the
7th Transportation Group from Fort Eustis, Virginia, reporting for
duty with 300 stevedores in tow. Whaley's timing was perfect: the

first of the six prepo ships from Diego Garcia was due in two days. The unloading of those ships would be an absolute priority, since they contained all the supplies necesssary for our survival as a military force.

"Welcome to Saudi Arabia, Colonel," I said. "I'll get right down to it. I need two-thirds of your people." I went on to explain that as of that moment, they were reassigned to serve—among other things—as military police, in which capacity they would patrol the roads and airports and try to keep the trucks and buses moving. The other 100 would go with Whaley to the port at Ad Dammam and prepare to unload the prepos that were expected. They would be working alongside the host-nation stevedores and crane operators who were already down there.

I admit in retrospect that this was the roughest of introductions. Even then I could see that Whaley was an intensely independent commander, the type who invested a lot of himself in his troops. Here he had come into the theater with 300 of his best people, fully expecting to be given an important mission and a lot of latitude; and the first thing I proposed to do was to steal two-thirds of his command. It's a credit to Whaley—now a general officer, and deservedly so—that he released those 200 men to me immediately and without complaint. It is also a credit to him that his men adjusted so well and so quickly, picking up tasks that were completely outside their training. In retrospect, I'm very glad that my relationship with Whaley survived that first, tough meeting. In short order, he proved to be the best field transporter in the U.S. Army.

This was the first turning point. I finally had enough people to start playing logistical catch-up. I divided up Whaley's men among the various areas needing immediate attention—for example, military police work, transportation (in which they were trained), contracting, engineering, and port and airport management. Stevedores became white-collar soldiers overnight, and did a hell of a job. Meanwhile, down at the port, Whaley and his depleted stevedores had something to prove. Working with host-nation stevedores, crane operators, and forklift operators, they proceeded to off-load the prepo ships in record-breaking time. Supplies were starting to flow.

In fact, the good news was coming in relative torrents. Just before midnight on August 12th, my missing deputies finally arrived in Riyadh. No one was there to greet them at the airstrip, so they headed over to the Marriott Hotel where most of the newly arrived officers were congregating. They enjoyed one night in the lap of luxury, for which they would more than pay on the following day. They learned through the grapevine that morning that I was head-quartered up in Dhahran, so they rented a wheezing old bus in order to report for duty. About two hours into the six-hour ride, their transmission seized up, and they had to turn back to Riyadh, with plenty of hours out in the noonday sun. They searched all afternoon for another bus; finally they found two mini-buses and headed out on their second trek east. They arrived in Dhahran at about midnight, tired and cranky but ready to work.

Most of the guys had become acquainted during their long and arduous trip from the States to Saudi Arabia, and a rapport was establishing itself among them. They rapidly discovered the common thread: almost all had worked for me at least once before, either directly or indirectly, during their previous military careers. Of my original list of twenty people, the Department of the Army had made four or five substitutions. Each of the replacements came with impressive experience, at least equal to that of the individual he had replaced. As for the rest, I knew them all, and was elated to see them. In some cases, we renewed friendships that had been put on hold for more than a decade.

This was the second turning point. This was when we would go from being reactive to being anticipatory—when we would stop being firemen and start being logisticians. I gathered my deputies together (the original twenty had been complemented by four specialists I had requested from Europe), and briefed them on developments to date. We were seated in a large circle around the room. I suggested that each person introduce himself, tell a bit about his former military assignments, and explain how he developed his expertise. This was both an exercise to let them get to know one another's strengths, and an opportunity for me to catch up on what these officers had been doing since I last worked with them.

Given the time pressures that were upon us, this first meeting quickly turned into a tasking session. This was when Chief Warrant Officer Wesley Wolf told the gathering that he had had lots of experience in food service. "O.K.," I told him, "you're it. Go find food and feed the troops."

I'll introduce other members of this stellar group in subsequent chapters. At this point, though, I'd like to single out one of those officers who was new to me: Colonel Roger W. Scearce. Scearce, a quiet and intellectual man with a sharp wit, had spent several years at USMTM in the early 1980s, both as a financial officer and a host-nation coordinator. He was an absolute gold mine for our bud-ding logistical enterprise. He had strong and ongoing relationships with key Saudi officials and businessmen in the Dhahran area, he knew the ropes, and he played an invaluable role in our initial ar-rangements with our hosts and third-country nationals.

Once everyone was acquainted and responsibilities had been as-signed, I asked for a show of hands of those who were on lists awaiting promotions. Nearly half had been designated "promot-able," approved by Congress for promotion. However, they were in the position of waiting until their "sequence number" came up. (In other words, when an opening for a major is created by a withdrawal from the service, a death, a retirement, or some other cause, major-promotable number one on the promotion list moves up.) But when a promotable officer is placed in a position of higher authority, he or she is allowed to be "frocked"—promoted to the higher rank without additional pay. Figuring that these were truly extenuating circumstances, and recognizing that my deputies would need plenty of clout as they went out to deal with both American officers and Saudi officials, I authorized mass frock promotions on the spot. It was a memorable moment, and one that I imagine a lot of grandchil-dren will someday hear about. Lieutenant colonels handed down their brass to now-frocked majors, and those lieutenant colonels assumed the eagles of colonel-promotables. Somehow, the lack of pomp and circumstance underscored the cooperative nature of our new enterprise.

We were on our way. I knew most of the officers who joined me in Saudi Arabia during that first week of what was now being called Desert Shield, and I had immense confidence in them. As for the newcomers, I've always had an ability to size up people quickly, and I was impressed by what I saw. We had the nucleus of an excellent team.

Equally important, most of them knew me. They already knew my management systems, and the rationale behind my techniques systems. They were skilled specialists who shared an overriding con-cern for the troops, and they knew that I shared that concern.

Chapter Five

Desert Shield

TRUTH BE TOLD, it was the flexibility and cooperation of the U.S. soldiers arriving in Saudi Arabia that saved us in the initial few weeks of the conflict. During mid- to late August we had to concern ourselves with establishing a bare-bones infrastructure, which could sustain life in the harsh desert environment during the brutal heat of late summer. In the midst of on-again, off-again chaos, we stuck doggedly to our basic, three-phase structure: reception, onward movement, and sustainment. But our initial arrangements were of necessity fragmented and disaggregated. The situation was simply too overwhelming to grasp fully and to structure in those early weeks. Army doctrine presumed a base on which to build a command, and no such base existed.

My group and I began referring to our mission in the first few weeks as "survival"—and that's essentially what it was. We worked with what we had available, our needs having been reduced to the lowest common denominator: food and water, shelter and sanitation, and as much of an organizational structure as we could muster.

Of course, there was basic doctrine that we could call upon as a starting point. And again, the patience of our soldiers, in the face of inevitable frustrations, was remarkable. Perhaps we benefited from a theaterwide sense of lowered expectations: in the desert, in August, anything we could do for the soldiers was a gift from heaven!

Bare Necessities

Our first priority was water. The heat hovered somewhere in the range of 120 degrees in the afternoons, and it didn't get much cooler at night. (That first summer, as it turned out, was much hotter than the one that followed, in part because in the summer of 1991 smoke from the Kuwaiti oil well fires blocked the sun.) But water alone would not be enough, as I knew from desert warfare exercises at the National Training Center. If water was left unattended and unrefrigerated in the desert sun, it would soon boil and be rendered virtually undrinkable. We moved into the local community immediately, with the invaluable help of Colonels Lindbloom and Scearce, in search of both bottled water and refrigerated vans.

These resources we procured quickly enough, although not without some lopsided bargaining. The merchant renting us the refrigerated vans demanded $1,000 per day for each of them. It was an exorbitant price, but there was no time to haggle—we had hundreds more people entering the country with each passing hour. We took the vans at the inflated price, and vowed that we would return to negotiate again. Right now, we decided, our time would be better spent tending to the troops.

There was no host-nation food contracting in position yet, nor could we see any hassle-free, dependable mechanism for setting one up on short notice. But we weren't going to starve, since we could lay our hands on an almost infinite supply of MREs. And now, with our vans under contract, we had something to wash the MREs down with. In terms of food and drink, survival was assured.

Housing remained a problem. The 10,000 Bedouin tents that Tom Ehlinger procured for us provided a bit of breathing room. But that respite was short lived and illusory. For reasons of safety and hygiene, we had to get our people away from the airfields and into reasonable accommodations. It was a situation that threatened to get out of hand quickly, since we were receiving thousands of new arrivals almost every day.

At one point, for example, there were more than 5,000 soldiers sleeping at Dragon Base, a Saudi facility designed to accommodate 200 personnel and their families. We had soldiers jammed into every single apartment—and many more sleeping in Saudi military tents, on the floor of the administration building, in the mess hall, and in the base laundromat. Another facility, nearby, designed for 100 people and occupied by 1,000, seemed spacious by comparison.

Throughout this "bare necessities" phase, our choices were basically two: we could either panic, or bite off little bits of the problem at a time. Naturally, we took the latter course. We focused on taking small steps each day to create a humane and livable environment. We started with whatever resources were available (empty buildings, water and refrigeration units, stacks of Bedouin tents) and threw them against the challenge of survival.

At the same time, we tried to identify additional urgent needs— sanitation, for example—that might lend themselves to innovative solutions. How can you make thousands of soldiers' lives bearable in the open desert? How do you help them keep clean, for example? With a visual memory of the Vietnam-era portable latrine and shower units depicted in the movie *Platoon,* one of my young captains made a prototype that solved a problem for hundreds of thousands of people.

One Head, Three Hats

During the first weeks and months in Saudi Arabia we knew very little about Hussein's ultimate plans. But we were continuously aware that he and his 100,000-man-strong Republican Guard forces could attack us at any minute, and we tried to come up with a logistical contingency plan that reflected this ever-present enemy threat. At the beginning and end of every day, the question we asked ourselves was, "What do we do if Saddam attacks *today?*" Every day, as the military balance shifted slightly more in our favor, the answer was a little different.

Concurrently, of course, our little band of twenty had to facilitate the front-line deployment of XVIII ABN Corps, a deployment that was directed by Generals Yeosock and Luck. (In other words, when we wore our "Host-Nation Support Coordinating Cell" hats, and I wore my "Director of Host-Nation Services" hat, we were working for ARCENT.) Joint progress toward the deployment of XVIII ABN Corps was critical because it made the Iraqis that much less likely to attack.

Almost as soon as we arrived in Saudi Arabia, Generals Schwarzkopf and Yeosock came to the shared conclusion that the only way they could operate successfully in the theater would be to establish a single point of contact for all logistical needs. I was it: the Deputy Commanding General for Logistics. This was my second hat. Responsibility for fuel, water, food, vehicles, ammunition, all classes of supply (except equipment repair parts) for the Marines,

Air Force, and the Army, as well as items common to all the services (T-shirts, socks, and such), was entirely mine.

With the active encouragement of General Yeosock, I kept General Schwarzkopf informed on all logistical matters. One way I did this was to check in weekly with the CINC. Often I joined him at the flight line at Dhahran, taking the opportunity to brief him on the status of logistics as he waited for transfer from his aircraft to a vehicle to go visit the troops. He listened carefully, tested my assumptions, approved or rejected ideas, offered guidance, and brought me up to speed on the tactical plan as it developed. During that time, I saw more of the CINC than the tactical commanders did; he understood, as have all great military leaders throughout history, the importance of good logistics to a successful mission.

The complexity of the arrangements being made in my command, and the problems inherent in its ad hoc nature, prompted General Yeosock on August 16th to designate my logistics operation as a command of ARCENT. Yeosock had very generously relinquished a part of his command to me, and in doing so guaranteed me the kind of autonomy necessary to operate a logistical command under highly unusual circumstances. The title of "Commander, ARCENT (Forward)" carried significantly more clout than Director of Host-Nation Services, particularly with the bureaucracy- and hierarchy-conscious Middle Eastern merchants and third-country nationals with whom we were signing contracts. Two days later, ARCENT formally established the ARCENT SUPCOM (Provisional), with me as commanding general.

Holding these multiple titles and responsibilities—acting as host-nation coordinator, overseeing logistics and supply for the theater at large, and serving as the commander of Army Central Command Support operations—required some mental juggling on my part. Quite often I found myself negotiating contracts in which I was my own largest client. As ARCENT Gus, for example, I needed supplies immediately, and was willing to pay any price. But Host-Nation Support Gus was obliged to consider budgets and bargaining. And DCG Gus had to be able to distance himself enough from the situation to determine whether that particular load of supplies was most needed by the 24th Mechanized Division, or whether it should be diverted instead to another Army command, or the Marines, or the Air Force.

I don't think I have too many unique talents, but I do seem to have an unusual ability to process information from several different vantage points. This capacity came in handy as I cycled through my three hats. I was careful not to confuse my various roles, and I took pains to make sure that my subordinates understood the missions and goals of the different outfits that "employed" us. As a result of the guidance (and the strong hand) of the CINC, all of the U.S. forces in the Gulf shared the same basic mission: to defend Saudi Arabia and liberate Kuwait. No matter which hat I was wearing, therefore, my responsibility was to assess how to best supply and outfit the various branches of the armed forces in the field to accomplish that overarching goal. It was like fitting together a puzzle—a puzzle made more challenging by the constant addition of new pieces.

Recruiting and Training

After two weeks in Southwest Asia, I had collected lots of hats but few helpers—our personnel base remained woefully thin. As noted earlier, General Yeosock gave up many of his assets to help me sort things out more quickly, including Dave Whaley's 7th Transportation Group, a military police brigade, and a POL (petroleum, oils, and lubricants) group. These teams were expert in their respective fields, but I needed logisticians, and the logisticians weren't arriving.

So I made up my own team. With supreme self-confidence, we began plundering incoming military outfits (as we had with the 7th Transportation Group's stevedores). Once enough bodies had been shanghaied, one or more of my two dozen logistical experts would take responsibility for retraining our new recruits on the spot. I've been told that this tactic became a running joke among arriving officers. At one point, my chaplain drew a mock chart depicting Beetle Bailey's General Halftrack—me, without a doubt—"collecting volunteers" at the port of entry. The general would greet the arriving CO with a "Hey, how many people you got there? Ten? Great, I'll keep five, and you can take the other five to your new assignment."

The cartoon version oversimplifies, but only by a bit. Borrowing bodies from incoming companies was an absolute necessity. We were in desperate need of soldiers to run logistical operations, especially in light of the enormous numbers of combat personnel arriving in the theater each day. In the two-week period between August 10th and August 25th, for example, we received more than 40,000 XVIII ABN Corps troops in Saudi Arabia, essentially without benefit of a prepositioned or predefined logistical structure.

To be fair to us hijackers, the cartoon doesn't tell the whole story. As I acquired new personnel from incoming units, I systematically (but slowly) released the people I had hijacked earlier, returning them to their original units and responsibilities. This borrow–train–return cycle had a hidden advantage which surfaced only after a while. Soldiers returning to their outfits after a stint with our provisional logistics team took with them an understanding of the management style and information flow within my operation. They understood how we communicated with each other, and how to get a message into our system most effectively. By an accident of circumstance, in other words, we achieved a sort of managerial cross-pollination across the units of the SUPCOM that would demonstrate its value in future operations.

On August 22d, President Bush signed an Executive Order which called 48,000 reservists to active duty by September 1st. This action had a significant and positive impact on our combat support (CS) and combat service support (CSS) outfits in the desert, and it is worth considering in some depth.

The story predates the Gulf War by some twenty years. Beginning about 1971, partly in response to our troubles in Vietnam, then–Army Chief of Staff General Creighton Abrams and others devised a plan which became known as the Total Force Concept. Among other things, the plan stipulated that the majority of slots in the Army's combat and infantry units would be filled by regular, active-duty soldiers; while slots for logistics personnel, whose many civilian skills such as forklift operation, truck driving, and so forth are directly related to the military support role, would be filled by reservists. Among other things, the Total Force Concept was seen as a way of forcing the political process to commit itself fully to a military engagement, rather than prosecuting a war halfheartedly. The logic was sound: if a war can't be fought without support personnel, and if most support personnel are in the reserve ranks, then the Army can't be asked to fight much of a war unless the politicians are willing to let the reserves get called up. That's precisely what happened in the Gulf War. Almost every single person in the United States was touched personally by the Gulf War—either a relative, or a friend, or a neighbor was called to service.

The Total Force Concept also recommitted the Army to training its personnel. Beginning in the early 1970s, the Army instituted an aggressive education and training program, which was available to members of both active-duty and reserve units. This emphasis had multiple benefits. Obviously, it helped existing personnel retool for a changing Army. But it also helped the Army recruit a higher caliber of soldier. Overall, education and training yielded a more capable, inventive, adaptive force. Smart weapons only work when smart, well-trained personnel are available to operate them.

I owe much of the success of my command to the talents of our flexible and well-trained reserve component (National Guard and reserve units). Those talents came to the Army as a direct result of the Total Force approach. At the height of the Gulf conflict, the 22d Support Command drew a full 70-plus percent of its personnel from reserve units; and we're lucky that we were able to do so. Reserve logisticians entering the theater thoroughly understood pertinent military doctrine, and also possessed the intellectual flexibility to use doctrine as a jumping-off point for innovation. They were fully confident in their ability as leaders—and in fact many had been leaders in the private sector—and they accepted broad responsibilities eagerly.

They were also eager to learn. So, from Day One, I held large, open classes where we discussed scenarios and potential solutions. I would pose a question to the group: "O.K., you have a ship that docked at Ad Dammam this morning. It's ready to be unloaded, and the onboard crane breaks. What's our response?" Collectively, the groups would work toward one of several possible solutions. (In that case, one good answer would be to get the ship back out of the dock and fix the crane at anchor, thereby freeing up the dock for another ship with a working crane.)

Logistics involves getting your hands dirty, and one of my goals was to get people to think in concrete terms. On one occasion, I posed the following hypothetical scenario: "Tomorrow, we find out we're receiving 15,000 troops rather than our usual 5,000. How are we going to adjust to the increase?" The group immediately focused on food, tents, water—the necessities—and came up with some good responses. I listened to the whole discussion, and then said, "That's good, but what about the buses? The water, food, and tents aren't going to do you much good if your people are stranded along the runways."

These group sessions served several useful purposes at once. Obviously, they brought potential challenges into the open so that people could better prepare for them. I constantly told my people that I wanted us to do our Monday-morning quarterbacking on Saturday afternoon—in other words, to use hindsight ahead of time. Equally important, they promoted collaborative discussion about problem solving and responsibilities across ranks and disciplines. In fact, there were occasions when we received as many as 15,000 troops in a single day, and our dry runs proved extremely helpful.

In mid-September, the reserve units we had been waiting for finally began to arrive, and a large contingent of CS and CSS troops entered the theater. In addition, the 1st COSCOM—the corps' logistical support for the XVIII ABN Corps—was deployed. In this same period, a second wave of logisticians, mostly reservists, arrived to assist our group with planning and implementation. The average age in my command jumped from twenty-one to twenty-six almost overnight. These new arrivals integrated themselves quickly and smoothly into our operations, and set to work with real enthusiasm. At the end of one month in the theater, I could see that we were about to move beyond simple survival, and assume a proactive planning stance. A word of caution to those who feel more positions can be transferred from the active force to the reserves to perform the logistical mission: the percentage of positions is now right, but to continue to switch more to the reserves will not allow the active forces, who can deploy immediately, to be able to support our active combat troops.

The LOC and the Log Cell

One evidence of that progress is that we were no longer working out of the backs of cars or on kitchen tables. In the last week of August, we set up our central planning unit in a small recreation center at Dhahran's USMTM locale, affectionately dubbed "Hotel California" after the Eagles' hit song from the 1970s. The room looked exactly like a church function room in any small town in the States: windows along the side walls, food service in the back, and a raised stage with heavy curtains in the front. I set myself up on the stage, with a huge map mounted on the wall which charted the movements of our divisions in-theater, and depicted the logistical supply network that supported them.

Everyone on the logistics staff at that time also worked in that one large room. There were desks and chairs gathered into informal nodes all over the former dance floor. This was the nerve center of our operation, and the activity was frenetic, twenty-four hours a day. Sometimes, as I surveyed the action from my perch up on the stage, the scene reminded me of the floor of the New York Stock Exchange: an anthill of people moving in some incomprehensible choreography, somehow getting things done.

It quickly became apparent that we were faced with two distinct types of tasks, and that these tasks needed to be handled by different types of structures. On the one hand, we needed a near-term, problem-solving element to address our immediate concerns. With the ever-increasing number of troops in-theater, answers had to be discovered quickly. But we couldn't focus solely on the torrent of day-to-day requests and needs, and thereby play only a firefighting role for the duration of the conflict. Instead, we needed a structured entity one step removed from crisis, which could use current numbers to project forward for any number of eventualities. The deployment was still at risk, and it seemed to me that without this capacity to look forward and plan, it would remain at risk.

We were already well on our way toward solving the problem of addressing near-term needs. The Logistics Operations Center, or LOC, had grown from my original twenty men into the group that was now sprawling across the dance floor at Hotel California. We had clusters of transportation experts on one side of the room, fuel people on the other, and nodes of food procurement specialists, airport, and port operations people filling in the middle tables. Working out of this one room was a great advantage, since people had the benefit of real-time reactions from experts in all pertinent specialties. If someone wondered whether their proposed action would have good or bad consequences elsewhere, they simply had to walk over and ask.

But the need for longer-term planning remained. After some thought and consultation, I decided to create a structure that would be entirely separate from the LOC, but would play a complementary role. This structure was the logistical cell, or "log cell," and it was one of the distinctive innovations of the 22d SUPCOM.

The log cell started out as a small, ad hoc think tank. I threw my famous net over Colonel John Carr—an officer I had worked with at the Pentagon, an expert on fuel, and one of our best field operations officers—and squirreled him off in a room with four other very talented logisticians. The group collected and analyzed operations-related information provided by the LOC, and constructed plans to address the contingencies I presented to them.

These were my men: they reported directly to me, and within reason had complete access to me at any time. I made it clear from the start that I wanted total honesty from them, and that they shouldn't worry about hurting my feelings, or jeopardizing their careers, or anything of the sort. Their job was to face facts, and confront me when they thought I was moving in the wrong direction on something. I told them that I would go after their assumptions with equal candor and vigor.

The log cell took over the task of asking the question, "What will we do if the Iraqis decide to attack today?" Each morning they presented a detailed plan showing proposed movements of vehicles, fuel, ammunition, food, and water that would most effectively stave off an attack. This scenario was updated continually, from hour to hour, as pertinent information became available. The 1700-hour version was sometimes very different from the 0800-hour version— and staying absolutely current was a constant priority, because we felt we might well have to answer this question in earnest.

But this was only one of many scenarios spun out by the log cell. Using the most up-to-date information developed by the LOC, and keying off of a scenario outlined by me, my logistical wizards would formulate contingency plans. They also maintained a centralized three-ring binder, known as the Red Book, which used charts and graphs to summarize all pertinent logistical information in the theater. The Red Book served as our bible of current capability, as well as a comprehensive historical record of the build-up. Members of the LOC and the log cell updated the Red Book as soon as new information became available. It became my traveling companion. Whenever I had a few minutes of free time (usually en route from one place to another in a car or plane), I flipped through its pages, keeping current on our dynamic and constantly evolving theater operations.

A STRUCTURE SPREADS OUTWARD

During our first month of operations, our strategy was to set up an organization that could function coherently and consistently. The focus was internal—at least to the extent that circumstances allowed. In this period, our arrangements with host-nation vendors were essentially spontaneous reactions to immediate needs. But gradually, as the command proved it could function as a cohesive unit, we turned our attention to forging, rationalizing, and strengthening our external relationships.

A top priority was to establish strong ties to both the Saudi Arabian military and the Kingdom's private sector. Nothing was certain, but it looked as if our deployment was going to be a lengthy one. This was the period in which many voices around the world were arguing for letting economic sanctions force Saddam Hussein out of Kuwait. Such an extended stay would require much more systematic logistical arrangements with our host nation.

With the benefit of regular updates from the CINC about our overall strategy and tactics, we developed a new approach to procuring goods and services. First, we introduced competitive bidding and pricing practices among vendors in the theater. Second, again with an eye toward competition, we created (and publicized) a three-legged supply stool: host-nation goods and services, contributions from allied nations supporting our cause, and supplies provided by the United States. Over time, as the crisis diminished and our logistical resources grew, we came into conformance with doctrinal guidelines governing bidding and purchasing. But it took time and great effort to reach that level of organization. For one thing, doctrine presupposed a host-nation logistical infrastructure. Until we had built such an infrastructure, doctrine had to stay flexible.

Arabian Rites

We made our share of mistakes. I was the prime mover behind one of those mistakes, which could conceivably have disrupted the harmonious working relationships that we were trying so hard to build with our Saudi hosts.

By late December, we had rented every car, truck, and bus that was rentable in Saudi Arabia, and we still didn't have enough transport. Several discussions we were having with vendors led me to suspect that there were more vehicles available, but that profiteers had conspired to limit the supply and keep prices high. At the same time, I began hearing rumblings through the grapevine that some of our people—both in my command and in the forward fighting units—were increasingly frustrated by the lack of available vehicles. They simply couldn't get their supplies moved. By the time this rumor reached my ears, there was already some noise in the system that Saudi civilians and merchants might have to be "persuaded" to sacrifice their vehicles to our cause, perhaps even while en route from one place to another.

This talk about confiscating vehicles gave me fits. First of all, on principle, the U.S. Army does not confiscate *anything*—all acquisitions are negotiated and compensated. Second, it was I (and not the forward units) who had to stay on good terms with the Saudis. So I decided to nip this problem in the bud. I issued a memo to all personnel, stating in pretty basic terms that they would gain access to vehicles through my command *only,* and if anyone was going to be confiscating vehicles, it would be me. Random commandeering would not be tolerated.

I confess I had an ulterior motive in sending out this memo. It might be productive, I reasoned, for words like "confiscation" and "commandeering" to get out into the merchant community with my name attached.

In any case, the memo went out into our system. Surprisingly, it reached CENTCOM in Riyadh and the Saudi military almost overnight: the grapevine was at work. The Saudis evidently interpreted the memo to mean that I was planning a mass confiscation of Saudi civilian and commercial vehicles in the near future. (A closer reading would have suggested the opposite.) In short order, the phone rang, and on the line came General Schwarzkopf, who told me that he had just read the dumbest memo he'd come across in thirty-five years of military service. Did I know who signed it, he asked pointedly?

Of course, I issued a second memo posthaste, assuring the Saudi Arabian community that we had no intention of confiscating their vehicles, and expressing my regret for any confusion we might have caused. My Saudi friends were gracious, even amused, by my transgressions. I took my licks, and kept my eye out for results. They weren't long in coming. Sure enough, more trucks began to appear, and prices started to come down.

Conducting business with the Saudis and other Middle Eastern nationals was an ongoing educational experience. We had begun on a good footing, given General Schwarzkopf's knowledge of the region and General Yeosock's previous tour of duty in the Kingdom. Within my command, I was fortunate enough to have access to Colonel Roger Scearce's extensive experience. He kept me out of the many pitfalls that yawned in front of us as we did business with our hosts.

Long before entering the theater I had learned that for many Arabs Islam was a way of life, and that any word or deed that

A Desert Storm trio:
John J. Yeosock,
Carl E. Vuono, and
William G. Pagonis

Pagonis and Prince Turki bin Nasser Abdul Aziz, brigadier general in the Saudi air force, at the January 1991 opening of a Dhahran dining hall donated by the Prince for use by American troops.

Members of the 24th ID, B Co. 5th Engineers pose next to the sign that they erected at the Iraqi border along Main Supply Route Yankee.

Photo by Sgt. Guadalupe Hernandez

Members of the 11th Armored Cavalry Regiment are briefed in the parking area at King Khalid Military City.

Photo by Sgt. John Bohmer

The logistical "miracle workers" who planned and executed the initial phases of Desert Shield, in their Dhahran briefing room.

From left to right, first row:
Lt. Col. John Carr
CW4 Wesley Wolf
Lt. Gen. William (Gus) Pagonis
CW1 Mark Otterstatter
Lt. Col. Donald Trautner
Maj. John Barr

Second row:
Lt. Col. Michael Velton
Col. David Mallory
Maj. James Burnett
Col. Steven Koons
Col. Roger Scearce
Maj. Yerry Kenneally
Lt. Col. Thomas Ehlinger
Lt. Col. James Ireland
Lt. Col. James Henrickson

Third row:
Maj. Bruce Laferier
Maj. Dwight Curtis
M. Sgt. John Bohannon
Sfc. Michael Renfroe
Col. Jack Tier
Maj. James Heffelfinger
Lt. Col. Richard Cashon
Capt. David Kolleda
Sgt. Maj. Kenneth Bridges

Gen. Schwarzkopf affixes a third star to Pagonis's collar on February 12, 1991. The promotion symbolized the importance of a single and authoritative logistical point of contact in the Gulf War.

Assisting in the ceremony, at right, is Capt. Gust Pagonis, Pagonis's older son, who commanded a truck company during the Gulf War.

Photo by Ricardo Ferro / Copyright © 1991 *St. Petersburg Times*

Pagonis meets with his friend and ally Prince Mohammed bin Fahd bin Abdula Aziz, who served as an invaluable liaison in his role as governor of the Kingdom's Eastern Province, where much of the logistical planning and preparation took place.

Stand-up meeting in the Bedouin tent, Dhahran headquarters, June 1991.

The stand-up, an old military tradition modified by Pagonis in his earlier commands, was a key managerial device supporting the flow of information across a command which included as many as 40,000 people.

Gus the general
with Gus the
camel at
the Oasis, a
troop rest-and-
relaxation
facility, on
May 27, 1991.

The camel was
a gift to the
command from
a member
of the Saudi
officer corps.

22d SUPCOM staff at work in the Logistics Operations Center (LOC), at the command's headquarters in Dharhan. The LOC handled all day-to-day logistics concerns above the corps level during Desert Shield, Storm, and Farewell.

Photo by S. Sgt. Paul Holman

Portable showers being transported to the troops. Personal hygiene was a priority in the harsh desert environment.

A soldier stops for lunch at a "Wolfmobile" near the port of Ad Dammam, Saudi Arabia. Mobile kitchens such as these brought "home cooking" to troops even in the most remote parts of the theater.

Photo by S. Sgt. Robert L. Reeve

The prime objective of the Coalition effort: the liberation of Kuwait, February 1991.

The ground war lasted only 100 hours, in part because the air and artillery assault which preceded it crippled Iraq's military machine.

Logistics made the celebrated "end run" plan possible. Central to that plan was the criss-crossing of two corps in a remote desert location, and the establishment of mobile log-bases: two highly demanding logistical tasks.

A soldier loading
an M1 tank
onto a flat bed
trailer near
Tapline Road,
Saudi Arabia.
Tanks were trans-
ported hundreds
of miles on heavy
equipment
transporters to
gain time and save
wear and tear.

Photo by Pfc. Gary Oler

A row of host-
country heavy
equipment
transporters lined
up to receive
M109 field artil-
lery, bound for
the port during
the redeployment
phase: Desert
Farewell.

Amenities in the
desert: U.S.
soldiers enjoying
a home-made
swimming pool,
constructed
from materials
at hand.

Up to a thousand 3 x 5 cards were generated each day within the 22d SUPCOM during the Gulf War. The cards played a key role in communications among 40,000 people.

---

8 SEPT 90/ 1910 hours

SUBJECT: Food Service Meeting

- Conducted second theatre food service meeting today
- Great representation
- Still lots of questions on "how do we get rations?"
- 2nd mmc was there and worked out simple pull system.
- Also outlined the theatre food plan so that all are working towards same goal — provide best food possible.

---

are to be retrograded to CONUS for base plate replacement

- 155mm propelling to be destroyed

0 E SEP 1990

---

⑤ 8/9

ACSLOG   Ammo 08 1200 Sep 90
Subject: Ammunition Discharge Operations, DAMMAM Pier
- Barge LB 789 was found leaking
- Bottom row of pallets have wet ammunition.
- Pallets of 155mm ICM rounds and propelling charge that were affected were marked and designated for 100% inspected.
- Defective rounds will be segragated.
- ICM project projectiles with corrosion

SUBJECT: ARAMCO MEETING

NOTIFIED
06 1000SEP90
08

* met with ARAMCO 07 SEP, as a follow on to the MODA letter
* Nothing resolved as far as Abqaiq facilities.
* Hofuf airstrip and hangers released for our use.
* Suffaniyah airstrip and hangers currently under MODA control.
* Numerous abandoned airstrips throughout the eastern province have been released by ARAMCO and we are coordinating with the Airforce for their use.

One solution to housing a half-million guests: a view of the sleeping barge from the dock area.

Photo by Sgt. Winston S. Wilson

Containers loaded with meals ready to eat (MREs) stand ready in Dhahran.

Photo by Sgt. John Bohmer

Soldiers called home using the phone facilities at Camp Kasserine. AT&T, in an example of U.S. support for the war effort, provided direct telephone lines to the United States.

Photo by Sgt. José D. Trefo

Forklift operators move munitions from storage area to break-bulk ships moored at the port of Ad Dammam, Saudi Arabia.

Photo by S. Sgt. Robert L. Reeve

Shrink-wrapped Cobra helicopters are loaded aboard the U.S.S. *Capella*, bound for Germany. Careful cleaning of all outbound equipment was necessary to prevent the introduction of Middle Eastern insects and micro-organisms to the U.S. and Europe.

Photo by S. Sgt. Robert L. Reeve

Vehicles awaiting shipment at the Port of Ad Dammam. The logisticians and their contracted drivers in the Gulf drove over 50 million miles, consuming 1.3 billion gallons of fuel.

Photo by Sgt. John Bohmer

M19 field artillery
bound for the port.
Desert Farewell
was the first com-
prehensive close-
out of a theater of
war by U.S. forces
in this century.

Photo by S. Sgt. Victor Owens

82d Airborne soldiers board "Freedom Bird" bound for home.

U.S. military personnel left Saudi Arabia at a consistent rate of 5,000 people per day, for over 90 days, until most of the individuals called to service were out of the Kingdom.

Christmas at the Pagonis residence, 1991. Joining her husband in Saudi Arabia during the redeployment phase, Cheri helped Gus welcome more than 2,000 troops into their home. At the right of the picture is Pfc. Robert Pagonis on a Christmas visit.

Moving mountains: don't assume anything, advises General Pagonis.

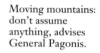

Photo by U.S. Army Specialist Nicholas Minnecci.
Used by courtesy of *Modern Materials Handling*, July 4, 1991.
Cahners Publishing Co., division of Reed Publishing U.S.A.

Logistics in the desert: distances in the Gulf War theater contributed greatly to the logistical complexity of Desert Shield, Desert Storm, and Desert Farewell.

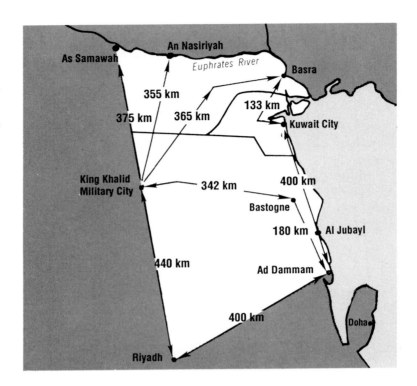

A second complicating factor was the mid-desert crossing of XVIII Corps and VII Corps to accomplish General Schwarzkopf's celebrated "end run." Effective scheduling, and especially traffic control at the "Mother of All Intersections" (indicated with asterisk), were vital contributing factors to Coalition success in the ground war.

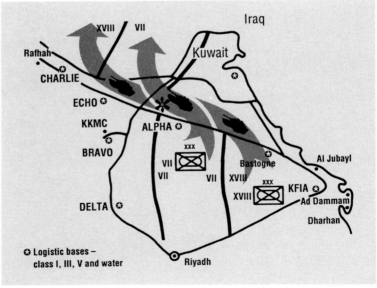

Adapted from *Military Review* (September 1991), pp. 30 and 36.

denigrated or ran counter to the religion would not be tolerated. I had also been advised that debates about social, political, or religious issues were not likely to be productive. I had read that Arabs stand very close to the person with whom they are speaking, and want to make direct eye contact. Failure to do so is a bad portent for business negotiations. Conservative Arabs—who make up most of the population of Saudi Arabia—dress in conservative garments, and are offended by displays of skin. Perhaps most important, Arab women do not interact with men other than their own family members. Except in carefully structured circumstances, they most certainly do not make contact with foreigners.

Other lessons remained to be learned, and these I learned from Roger Scearce. I never knew, for example, that back-slapping is taboo, as is exposing the sole of your shoe while sitting. It is offensive to use one's left hand to offer something—paper, pen, food, and so on—to an Arab. The thumbs-up and "O.K." hand gestures are considered offensive by Arabs—though during the Gulf conflict, our Arab and third-country friends began to adopt the gestures as a symbol of cooperation toward freedom.

In many cases, Western traditions are stood on their heads in the Middle East. For example, if you openly admire the possession of an Arab, whether it be a car, an expensive watch, or jewelry, it is likely to be given to you. You are then expected to reciprocate with a gift of greater value. Before conducting business in the Arab world, you are expected to engage in extensive small talk. You should always inquire about the health of the host's family generally; but it is highly insulting to ask specifically about an Arab's wife or another female family member.

I am a blunt person, and I'm not known as a paragon of patience. But I soon learned that in the Middle East, you have to go slow to go fast. And so we did.

Putting Out a Contract

Our initial contracting negotiations were particularly challenging. Quick analyses of the situation by military leaders, both in the United States and in Saudi Arabia, led to the conclusion that our limited-and-precious transport space should be reserved for combat troops, and for those supplies, such as weapons and ammunition, that could not be procured in the theater. Everything else was our problem, to be found and contracted for.

The sheer magnitude of our needs, projected out over weeks and months, was sometimes staggering. For example, John Carr and the log cell made some initial calculations as to how much water we would need to sustain the XVIII ABN Corps. We were appalled. How do you go to your desert host, just after arriving at his desert home, and announce that you'll need billions of gallons of water over the next few months? Saudi Arabia is not a small country, but its population and its military forces are small. Negotiations are greatly complicated when you must ask the people across the table to think on previously unimagined scales.

We, too, had our learning to do. Doctrine told us to find trucks and procure water from the host nation. This was sensible, especially in the context of a REFORGER, where supply lines were in place and we were moving 10,000 people per month. But when the numbers jumped to 10,000 per day, doctrine began to creak a little bit, and developed some bulges around the edges.

Our accelerated schedule and steep learning curve were complicated by sharp business practices on the part of some Middle Eastern merchants. Especially in the first few weeks of the deployment, supplies of critical items fell far short—in some cases, suspiciously short—of demand. Prices shot up. I didn't see this as defensible behavior, in light of the fact that we were there to protect Saudi Arabia. Some things are universal, including the way people feel when they get gouged. I didn't like it. On the other hand, I knew that I somehow had to reach mutually acceptable arrangements with these people, since contracted support was the key to our survival in the desert.

I decided to meet directly with some of the more important merchants, and talk things through eye to eye. Roger Scearce sat me down before the first of these meetings to spin out a likely scenario. It was common, he told me, for these bargaining sessions to be attended by several people, and to be jointly conducted by two members of the business concern in question. The first was likely to be a young man wearing a Western-style suit and tie, and speaking highly fluent English. The second was almost certain to be an older gentleman in traditional Saudi dress. The younger man would inform us that his superior did not speak much English, and that he himself would translate and conduct the negotiations.

So much for appearances. According to Roger, the elder Saudi would not be as fluent in English as the younger, but would almost certainly know enough English (the universal business language) to follow the negotiations with ease. It would be wise to avoid making asides that might offend the older gentleman. Conversely, if offense was the intent, a comment aimed at the younger representative would most likely strike the elder.

"You'll recognize the head honcho," Scearce told me at our last run-through, "because he'll be the one with the worry beads. He'll either be jiggling them in his pocket, or he will take them out and work them openly."

"Let me see some worry beads," I said.

Roger sent one of his staff out to find some. A lieutenant returned with a small, bracelet-sized loop of smooth stones, strung together loosely and knotted into a tassel on one end. Shortly thereafter, the first scheduled group of negotiators arrived. I dropped the beads into my pocket and we proceeded into the conference room.

Events unfolded almost exactly as Roger had predicted they would. The young man in Western dress offered to translate for his elder, who "didn't speak much English." I don't recall off-hand exactly what it was we were trying to procure from this pair—probably vehicles, at this early stage of the game—but the negotiations crawled along. Well into these unpromising discussions the elder gentleman took out a highly buffed string of worry beads and began to work them over as he listened to the proceedings.

The younger man finished his proposal, which was still overpriced by a factor of two or three. Very deliberately, I took out my string of worry beads and held them contemplatively in my hand. The elder gentleman blinked, looked at them, and then at me, and barely suppressed a smile.

"I like these beads," I said directly to the elder Saudi. "In fact, I really need them. I've got lots to worry about."

The Saudi permitted himself a laugh, and I continued.

"I've got a lot on my mind," I said. "My people need to get settled quickly, so they can perform the task they were sent here to perform. In order for us to protect this country—which of course is your goal as well as ours—we need to concentrate on supporting our soldiers. We can't spend all our time haggling with each other. Now what I need from your company is the following . . ."

I then laid out a framework of what I considered to be an acceptable arrangement. As the discussion became more detailed, I found that I was focusing increasingly on the elder gentleman, until finally the negotiations involved just me and him. The younger Saudi gentleman and my staff members took back seats, and the principals hammered out a deal acceptable to both parties.

In this and all subsequent negotiations I made it clear from the outset that I was not out to break my vendors, but equally that I was not willing to be gouged. I told them that I was not going to insult their intelligence by asking them to make unreasonable concessions, and that I hoped they would extend to the U.S. Army the same courtesy. This was good positioning, but it was also simple common sense. Like my Greek ancestors, Middle Easterners have a keen sense of personal honor. That had to be acknowledged and dealt with. In most cases, we were able to achieve a quick meeting of the minds. And as for the hard-nosed few, I was always able to drop the hint that Princes Mohammed and Turki had told me, personally, that they were sure that the Saudi business community would be eager to cooperate with us. The princes' prophecy turned out to be self-fulfilling.

After our first few contracts were signed, things changed dramatically. Word spread like wildfire that the American military was paying in Saudi *riyals*—a desirable currency—and that payment was made every two weeks. Since the Saudi government was in the habit of paying its vendors only once or twice a year, we were suddenly the favorite clients on the block.

This was a mixed blessing. On the down side, we were swamped with would-be vendors, offering us goods and services not only from Saudi Arabia, but also from Oman, Bahrain, the United Arab Emirates, and even as far away as Turkey. On the plus side, spurred by this unexpected competition, the local merchants loosened up the supply lines and became more cooperative. For example, we were able to cut a new deal with our suppliers of refrigerated vans. On our first days in-country, these vans cost us $1,000 per day. Suddenly, the price dropped to less than $100 per day.

This raises the question of the "blank check." On paper, we never had one. Even in the most chaotic days of August and September, we in the Host Nation Coordinating Cell were guided by the laws and regulations which govern all military spending. In other words, we had a budget that we had to stick to, and we were accountable to the financial officers at the Pentagon for all our expenditures.

In fact, one of the more interesting challenges we faced in the Middle East grew out of the limitations of our own financing and budgeting structure. Military expenditures are broken out into twelve categories. These are referred to as the "colors of money." Each category has its own regulations and restrictions. During our first few weeks in-country, we had access only to Operations and Maintenance funds. Construction money—to take another category—was not approved at the time we were deployed into the theater. And without money designated specifically for construction, it was theoretically impossible for us to put up any new construction—roads or buildings.

But there was a flip side of the "blank check" issue. Over my years of service I had developed strong relationships in every corner of the military. My years on Capitol Hill had also taught me how to get responses from Congress. So when I wanted to get something built, I knew how to tackle the system and secure a waiver of the threshold requirements commonly used in assessing O&M expenditures. An Executive Order issued in November, raising these thresholds, only recognized an existing reality.

Most important, I had been told by Army Chief of Staff General Vuono that if I needed something, I simply had to ask for it. My subordinates and I were expected to observe the rules, fill out the forms, and adhere to doctrine—whenever possible. Beyond that point, we were expected to get the job done.

I should emphasize that the degree of cooperation that we received from our Stateside counterparts, which was nothing less than phenomenal, made an impossible job possible. I could make the request, and usually make it to the right person, but it was they who had to find a way to deliver. And without exception, they did.

In retrospect, the most challenging aspect of conducting business in the Middle East was the Arab's amazingly casual approach to time. For a logistician, particularly one in an emergency situation, scheduling and time management are everything. In the Middle East, these are secondary concerns at best. An iron-clad guarantee that something will arrive today may mean a delivery tomorrow, or perhaps four days from now. My meetings with potential vendors lasted more than an hour—of which thirty minutes were dedicated to greetings and small talk, five minutes to negotiations, and twenty-five minutes to departing wishes of good health. When these meetings were held at a Saudi place of business, they were invariably interrupted by phone calls, visitors, and aides with messages. Scearce assured me that after an initial trust-building period, this pattern of interruptions would subside. Luckily for my sanity, it soon did. When my hosts started stocking the beverage tray with Diet Pepsi beside the traditional Arab coffee and tea, I knew I had arrived.

Again, these problems often arose because the expectations of the two sides were so different. Within their experience and context, Middle Eastern vendors were remarkably responsive to our tight schedules. But the frame of reference was entirely different. When we first issued urgent calls for contracts, large contractors would earnestly ask for 120 days to respond to our solicitation. As politely as possible, we would respond, "Well, you can take 120 hours, since that's all the time that's available." Within a few short weeks, most would-be vendors were submitting proposals for goods and services within our specified time frames. Like so many aspects of logistics in the Gulf, this was another case of good news/bad news. The good news was that multiple bids gave us the leverage to get prices down to reasonable levels; but they also required us to spend many more hours on bid evaluation.

Contracting expert Dan Bartlett, who joined my staff in late September, got us into the habit of diligently checking out all potential vendors. On several occasions, pre-award surveys led us to interesting discoveries. For example, at one point we solicited bids for the rental of fifty trucks. The bids came in, and, starting at the top of the list, we telephoned each vendor and asked to inspect the trucks he was offering to rent.

We got to the first truck farm, at a remote and desolate desert locale, and found that this particular vendor had only thirty-five of the fifty trucks he was promising on the premises. The thirty-five trucks were identified by metallic signs on their cabs: "Ahmed's Trucking." He assured us that he would be able to round up fifteen more trucks without a problem; that in fact the trucks were on their way, and would arrive at the yard in a matter of hours. We thanked him for his time, and told him we'd be back in touch when we reached a decision.

We returned to the base and telephoned the next would-be truck rental agency. The terrain we passed on the way out to his shop looked strikingly familiar. It was soon obvious that we were heading to the same truck farm we had just left. An unfamiliar figure greeted us at the gate and ushered us over to thirty-five trucks, parked in a very familiar pattern but sporting attractive new magnetic panels: "Trabulsi Trucking." Bartlett and I grinned at one another, and I addressed the truck vendor.

"I notice that there are only thirty-five trucks here," I said. "I suppose that the other fifteen are on the road, and will be here in a few hours?"

The merchant looked at me a bit quizzically, and said that indeed, the other trucks were on their way. We shook his hand and headed back to the office.

Later in the afternoon, a third Saudi vendor ushered us out to the same parking lot to inspect the same thirty-five trucks, once again under new ownership. This prompted us to do a little digging, aimed at finding out who actually owned the trucks. Finally, we found him, and suggested that he might want to put in a bid on the contract and cut out the middlemen. He agreed. He submitted a bid which ultimately paid him a higher price, saved us some money, and restored our peace of mind.

Fruitful Negotiations

As noted, once the word got out that the Americans were paying well and regularly, and also that we seemed to have the ear of the royal family, we were absolutely inundated with deals. The magnetic-paneled truck incident, and a dozen similar experiences, raised our skepticism levels to exaggerated heights. As a result, we almost let one of the heroes of the war slip right through our fingers.

A surgeon from the XVIII ABN Corps medical brigade, located about fifteen miles away from our planning center, walked into the LOC one afternoon and caught Roger Scearce during a well-deserved coffee break.

"Listen," he said to Scearce, "there's a Saudi guy running around to different companies in the XVIII with what he claims is a letter from the king. He says he's been chartered to feed all of our soldiers, but nobody knows who he should be talking to."

Scearce replied, "Tell him he should talk to me."

He gave the surgeon the telephone number at the LOC to pass along to the gentleman, and then spread the word around the staff to expect a call regarding food.

The very next morning, a Mr. Zahir Masri telephoned Scearce and told his story. He had, he said, been instructed by the king to feed the American troops. He invited us to send a representative to examine the authenticity of his letter, and—if we were satisfied on that score—to make appropriate arrangements. He was polite but succinct. The implicit message was that if we chose not to avail ourselves of his services, it would be of no concern to him. No doubt he was more than a little put off at having been shuffled around the theater for days on end.

Scearce and Chief Warrant Officer Wesley Wolf then took a trip to the nearby city of Al Khobar, where they had arranged to meet the mysterious Mr. Masri at the luxurious Oberoi Hotel. They were greeted in the lobby by a dapper-looking young man with an excellent command of English. Masri relinquished his letter from the king for scrutiny by our host-nation experts, who soon confirmed that the letter was authentic. We invited Mr. Masri to join us at the LOC the following day to negotiate a contract.

The next morning, Masri arrived at the LOC in Levis and a polo shirt, ready to get down to business. We spent a few moments on introductions, during which Masri explained that he was a Jordanian who had once lived in Tallahassee, Florida; and that his uncle, Mr. Sabi Masri, was a highly successful food producer and distributor in Saudi Arabia. In fact, Masri's company, Astra Foods, operates the largest covered farm in the world, and was already under contract with King Fahd to supply foodstuffs for the Saudi military. When the king approved the deployment of American troops into his country, he evidently concluded that it was his obligation, as a host, to feed his guests. This explained the letter asking Masri to extend his services to our troops.

At that moment, Zahir Masri practically joined the LOC. From that afternoon forward, he and Wes Wolf—my food czar—were virtually inseparable. Together, they developed a food procurement-and-distribution plan that vastly enhanced the quality of meals served in every part of the theater. The use of MREs went down as the use of fresh food went up. Masri and Wolf continued to implement new ideas throughout the conflict, usually with an eye toward improving the availability and variety of fresh foods. There's no doubt in my mind that these developments had a direct impact on the success of the war.

The first weeks of the Masri/Wolf collaboration were full of exciting developments. After a discussion with General Schwarzkopf on the subject, I put out the word that fresh produce would not be distributed to the troops in the logistical "tail" until it had reached the fighting "tooth." Within a week and a half, Masri/Wolf had set up a distribution network which delivered fresh pita bread, fruit, and produce to the troops in even the most forward positions. These provisions supplemented MREs and traypacks (bulk prepared food, often meals like lasagna or chicken, that has been compressed into large cans which are heated, opened, and served). I coined the phrase "a fruit basket in every foxhole," which served as a slogan and watchword throughout the campaign.

Once the Masri family gave us a way to provide fresh foods, we did some quick number-crunching. To our surprise, we discovered that this was a good way to save money. MREs cost about $4.00 each, plus the additional cost of supplements; traypacks were only slightly cheaper. The Masri "A-rations" (that is, fresh and freshly cooked meals) averaged out to about $1.95 each. Wolf and Masri contracted with both Saudi and Filipino cooks, and set up mess halls throughout the theater. They served over 300,000 troops per day with these contract meals, using foodstuffs provided by Astra Foods and paid for by King Fahd. The generosity of the king, as well as the entrepreneurial spirit with which Wolf and Masri approached the vast challenge of food service, greatly improved the quality of life for our soldiers.

Politics and Family

The king pledged the full support from his country when he agreed to the deployment of American forces in the Kingdom, and he more than delivered on that pledge. The Saudi people received us with an openness and generosity that surpassed all of our expectations. As General Schwarzkopf had made clear to me back in the States, it was only fitting that we make an equal effort to abide by their laws and respect their customs.

During the entire time that Americans were in the theater, there was not a single incident of deliberate misconduct on the part of our troops. This is a record that astonished even some within the military. To be sure, there were incidents in which our soldiers unwittingly transgressed against either custom or religious edict—as, for example, when our female soldiers drove trucks, or when our troops drew upon privately owned water wells in the desert. Our approach was to address such issues openly and directly, usually before they developed into conflict. By so doing, we began to discover how to maneuver through the complex web of jurisdictions and responsibilities in the Kingdom.

The Saudis have a civil and political structure much like ours in theory, but which in practice contains more bureaucratic layers. There are mayors and local bureaucrats, called *emirs,* who manage civil affairs; and these town bureaucracies spill outward into the rural regions. Several different police departments address particular areas of the law. Throughout the country, but especially in major population centers, there are military police, religious police, and civil police. Each institution monitors specific aspects of community life. Our challenge was to discern which leader of what institution to address, when we were faced with a question or problem. And there was always one wild card: questions of jurisdiction and responsibility became significantly more complex if the royal family was involved.

One incident early on in the deployment process served as my initiation into the workings of local Saudi politics. A contingent of American soldiers, both male and female, were sent into the city to unload supplies from Army trucks to establish a medical materiel command in downtown Ad Dammam. Unknown to us, the medical center was adjacent to a particularly devout Muslim community. The truck-unloading was sweaty, grueling work, and the presence of perspiring female soldiers in T-shirts with their sleeves rolled up greatly offended local residents. These residents soon complained to the religious police. To compound our difficulties, the female soldiers were subjected to verbal abuse and catcalls from the Saudis who were driving by.

Roger Scearce stepped in to defuse the situation. Scearce described the circumstances to an old friend of his, who happened to be a colonel in the Saudi military. Colonel Kalaf explained that the local residents and religious leaders were taking offense at what they considered an excessive, even obscene, exposure of the body. We quickly arrived at a simple solution: all soldiers working in that area would work in their long-sleeved overshirts. It was a small concession, but one that greatly pleased the religious police, who enforce the *Sharia*, or Islamic law.[1]

The drive-by yelling and catcalling, on the other hand, was a civil issue, which therefore had to be taken up with the local *emir*. We approached this bureaucrat, demonstrated that we had cooperated with Saudi religious arbiters, and asked that he be aware of the distress caused to our soldiers by some members of his local population. The harassment diminished significantly. Eventually, we relocated the entire facility out of this sensitive neighborhood. With Scearce's and Kalaf's help, we learned to sort out our problems and address them to the appropriate authority. This, in turn, allowed us to avoid imposing the responsibility for domestic issues onto the

Saudi Arabian military. However, as a demonstration of the adapt-
ability of the Saudi people, after a few weeks in the Kingdom our
female soldiers were not harassed again while in uniform with parts
of their bodies uncovered. Prince Mohammed led the way in this
matter and ensured that a soldier was treated as a soldier, regardless
of sex.

I did not get a chance to properly meet my Saudi compatriots
until the very end of September, despite the fact that we had been
cooperating on logistical and procedural matters since early August.
I knew from Day One that as soon as circumstances permitted, I
should make the acquaintance of key members of the Saudi military.
The most obvious candidate was Brigadier General Prince Turki,
commander of the Saudi Arabian Air Force located at the Dhahran
airbase. General Turki had already generously offered us the use of
the airfield, and I felt it was important that I thank him personally.

Similarly, I suspected that my command would have to coordinate
movements with the leaders of the Saudi Arabian Army commands
in the Eastern Area and Northern Area—General Salah and General
Alkami, respectively. I sought out each of these gentlemen in an
effort to facilitate military arrangements, and I'm glad to report that
they became my good friends in the process. They were skilled at
both warfare and diplomacy, and by word and deed gave me great
insight into the Saudi mind.

I had realized from my initial dealings with Middle Eastern vendors that hierarchy and rank played a very important role in their
social structure. Nowhere was that more apparent than in my dealings with Prince Turki—not in his actions, but in the actions of those
around him. There was a subtle method of communication employed
with regard to members of the royal family. When Turki's aides
made a request in the name of General Turki, that request was received like that of any other general. But when those same aides
prefaced a request with "the Prince would like . . ." or "Prince
Turki thinks that . . ." you could see people responding in an almost
physical way. Those words carried obvious weight. Being a prince is
an honored position in Saudi society.

I worked fairly often with Prince Turki, negotiating the use of
airfields and similar issues. Both as soldiers and individuals, we hit
it off. He's a very straightforward person, a go-getter. I would approach him with an idea or a plan, he would respond on the spot,
and we would hash out a compromise right there. We moved beyond
the stiffness and formality of "negotiations" very quickly. I owe a

great deal of the success of my logistical plan to him, as well as to the other Saudi officers, who collectively bent their own rules and adjusted their own agendas to help me provide for our troops in the theater.

THE FIVE-PHASE PLAN

When the reservists were called to active duty, General Schwarzkopf announced that there would be no rotation policy. In other words, troops would not serve a 12-month hitch and then head home, as they had in Vietnam. This was a clear signal that we would remain in Saudi Arabia until the Kuwait situation had been resolved to the satisfaction of the Coalition forces. Beyond that, it was also a signal that the Coalition would eventually be prepared to go on the offensive. We logisticians took this as our cue to begin designing a logistical structure that would support a shift to the offense.

Even in the tumultuous early days of Desert Shield, therefore, I began mulling over the logistics of an offensive posture, and considering the implications for our logistical distribution network. My basic rule of thumb was that the depots from which the corps took their supplies had to be located close enough to the front so that once the troops advanced, they could still resupply from those depots. In thinking through this approach, I drew upon my studies of the tactics of both Alexander the Great and the British Army that fought Rommel in North Africa. Both General Schwarzkopf and I, moreover, were determined not to recreate the immobile firebases of Vietnam. Any supply network assembled in Saudi Arabia would have to be flexible, movable, and responsive to the needs of the troops. If and when the troops advanced, the logistics bases (logbases) would have to advance with them.

Planning for a Plan

The simplicity of our initial three-part plan—reception, onward movement, sustainment—was in my estimation a cornerstone of our ultimate success. The plan was easy to understand, and laid out straightforward goals and objectives. As a result, it provided a grid to superimpose on a more or less chaotic situation.

But in late September and on into early October I began to develop a successor plan. I felt that we needed a plan with a similar degree of accessibility and clarity that could guide logistics during the extended conflict.

Perhaps *plan* is not quite the right word to use in this context. Management literature often uses the word *vision* to convey the sense that I mean. One author writes,

> The vision becomes a memory tool, allowing many levels of the organization to make decisions without consulting their superiors. As well, a vision provides a set of decision rules that facilitate speed and ensure less frequent errors by subordinates: Does the solution mesh with the vision's goals or not?[2]

I'm convinced that it's important to build such a vision around non-action-specific goals, because these types of goals incorporate the flexibility necessary to adjust to new challenges. (Reception and sustainment are examples from our survival-phase plan.) For the same reason, I never tell a subordinate how to carry out a specific goal. Dictating terms to a subordinate undermines innovation, decreases the subordinate's willingness to take responsibility for his or her actions, increases the potential for suboptimization of resources, and increases the chances that the command will be dysfunctional if circumstances change dramatically. Our first month in the theater only underscored my sense that our planning process would have to be incredibly elastic.

With this in mind, my colleagues and I devised a "successor vision" to reception, onward movement, and sustainment. The new theater logistic plan had five phases: Alpha, Bravo, Charlie, Delta, and Echo. Right off the bat, anybody who knew the alphabet knew the name of each of the five phases and knew their sequence. The trick now was to differentiate the phases, and get them firmly lodged in people's minds.

The first phase, Phase Alpha, had the guiding principle of "preparation and prepositioning," and developed as a natural outgrowth of our original, three-phase deployment plan. Sustainment of the troops in their defensive positions at the front led inevitably to the development of a network of supply depots from which the COSCOM could draw, and could in turn use to support the divisions and companies through the Division Support Company (DISCOM). (This structure built directly on existing doctrine.) The real challenge here lay in assessing the situation and picking supply depot locations that could serve the current tactical and strategic plans of the mission, and yet didn't limit our fighters' options in the future.

From the moment troops were deployed into the theater, I felt we had to be prepared for the possibility of switching from a defensive to an offensive posture. The supply depots established in Phase Alpha, therefore, might well have to support our troops in a forward movement. This was the goal of Phase Bravo—"movement of the corps" to a forward strategic position, with all the accompanying logistical complications.

Once in such a strategic position, our troops would require every kind of combat supplies and support, including fuel, ammunition, equipment, vehicles, maintenance mechanisms, shelter, food and water, and medical supplies and services. This was the third phase of the plan, Phase Charlie: "the ground offensive." Most likely, the front line would shift rapidly and unpredictably during a ground war, and the supply system would have to be correspondingly flexible.

Our assumption from the start was that the Coalition would win the ground offensive. This meant that we had to identify and prepare for the phases that would follow our victory. The first of these was Phase Delta, which encompassed all logistical needs for "the defense of Kuwait." Intelligence reports suggested that even after the Iraqis had been expelled, Kuwait would make intense demands on our logistical system (and any others that were functioning in the region). It was also clear that during this postwar period, we would have to be implementing the final phase of the plan, Phase Echo, which would orchestrate redeployment of all personnel, equipment, and supplies out of the theater. Field Marshall Montgomery once wrote,

> I hold the view that the leader must know what he himself wants. He must see his objective clearly, and then strive to attain it; he must let everyone else know what he wants and what are the basic fundamentals of his policy. He must, in fact, give firm guidance and a clear lead.[3]

Andrew J. Goodpaster, former Supreme Allied Command, Europe, put it more succinctly: "Be clear about purpose."[4]

Clarity was the watchword of our five-phase plan, which was developed between mid-September and early October 1990. Each phase of the plan grew logically out of the one that preceded it— although as I made clear to my subordinates, the phases might well turn out to be overlapping, or even concurrent. All of the phases were based on existing logistical doctrine. Taken as a whole, they constituted a firm but flexible conceptual framework, available for reworking in response to CENTCOM's changing strategy and tactics.

In Front of the Front

Of course, in the fall of 1990, there were no strategy or tactics for a ground war. One hot and dusty Saturday in late September, while General Schwarzkopf and I were conducting one of our in-transit logistical briefings, I informed the CINC of my intention to develop a plan to sustain an offensive, forward-moving force.

I'll admit that I was a bit hesitant about revealing my ideas to Schwarzkopf. For one thing, I knew full well that an Air Force general had just been relieved of his command for speculating about offensive options with a *Washington Post* reporter. But going public with the media and bouncing ideas off the CINC are two entirely different things. General Schwarzkopf listened carefully to my informal presentation, and then responded with an appropriately empowering statement. "A prudent commander," he said, "should be always looking ahead." Then he flashed me that now-famous smile, which told me to plan away.

I told no one but the members of the log cell of my intention to start planning logistics for offense. To the log cell, I posed the big question: How could we support and supply an offensive maneuver? John Carr and his men went on a two-day retreat, completely isolated from our day-to-day pressures, to think this through. They reached the same conclusions that I was reaching independently. First, we couldn't move the logbases during the offensive. Second, we couldn't position the bases well to the rear of our jumping-off point—the normal place for supply depots—since that would inevitably put our combat troops on too short a tether.

Logically, then, our logbases would have to be positioned right up on the front lines, alongside our current defensive positions, in order to allow our troops to jump out and move forward on short notice. During the first weeks of October, therefore, the log cell began putting together a plan that incorporated forward logbases in the theater in strategic positions.

Meanwhile, the 24th Infantry Division (mechanized) was sitting in port, awaiting deployment into the theater. I wanted to get them out of there as quickly as possible, since they were creating major traffic problems and constituted a relatively easy target for the enemy. General Barry McCaffrey, commander of the 24th, was pushing for deployment for the same reasons. Together, we petitioned our superiors for a forward placement of the 24th's troops and equipment. Truth be told, some of those officers on high-level staffs had grave doubts about the plan. At least one staff officer felt that our troops and equipment weren't up to the job. Another felt that there were good reasons to keep supplies and equipment well to the rear. Fortunately, Generals Schwarzkopf, Yeosock, and Luck came down firmly in our camp. General Luck moved the 24th and several other divisions of XVIII ABN Corps out into the desert, about 200 miles below Tapline Road.

Tapline Road is a paved roadway which wends its way through northern Saudi Arabia, parallel to one of the nation's most important crude oil pipelines. It runs very near to the Kuwaiti and Iraqi borders, and is one of the few paved roads in the country capable of supporting heavy traffic and large trucks. With Schwarzkopf's, Yeosock's, and Luck's support, we sought and gained permission from the Saudi government to use this key road as one of our two "main supply routes" (MSRs). Our second route, known as MSR Dodge, swept in a large arc from Dhahran, southwest through Riyadh, and then back up northwest to King Khalid Military City.

From the outset, I restricted U.S. forces' use of the Tapline Road to tactical support (that is, to the transport of combat personnel, tanks and armored vehicles, weapons, ammunition, and some fuel). All other supplies were transported along the southern MSR Dodge. I knew this arrangement would make the tacticians happy. I also knew that if it came down to a turf battle, the tacticians would beat me in any case. And finally, I suspected that the much longer MSR Dodge would turn out to be a quicker route to the front, since it was four lanes wide on its first leg down to Riyadh, and wouldn't be as congested as the Tapline Road. As it turned out, I was right: the longer road was shorter.

Using rented buses, it was a fairly simple task to relocate the forward divisions in the desert, and to set them up with temporary Bedouin-tent quarters. Getting their equipment and artillery out there, though, was a far more challenging task. With good planning, the MSRs could be made to support a high-volume transfer of supplies across the desert—but only if we could come up with enough transport vehicles. Unfortunately, the U.S. Army had for decades been gearing up to fight a war in Europe, which basically meant staving off an invading Red horde until reinforcements could arrive. Now we found ourselves in a position where we would have to travel up to 1,500 miles just to get into a position to fight. And distances weren't the only problem.

Take tanks, for example. In the Dhahran summertime, the mid-afternoon sun softens up an asphalt surface so much that an average-sized man walking across it finds his heels sinking into the pavement. A convoy of tanks would immediately tear the Tapline Road to pieces. There was also the unsettling possibility that a tank might veer off the torn-up road, blinded by dust kicked up by the tank in front of it, and blunder into the crude pipeline or water lines.

There was only one answer: we needed heavy equipment transporters (HETs)—big, flatbed trucks with huge carrying capacities. We needed HETs in large numbers (say, low four figures), and the Army had a grand total of 112 HETs in-theater. Fortunately, our Coalition allies had additional HETs, and the Saudi private sector was willing to rent us more. This was a lifesaver. We were able to assemble a fleet of nearly 1,300 HETs and tractor trailers, most of which came equipped with experienced third-country national drivers.[5]

The truck fleet provided a host of benefits. First, of course, they protected the roads and pipelines. Second, they minimized wear and tear on tanks, and shifted most maintenance time and costs to truck repair (considerably easier and cheaper than tank repair). Third, they moved their loads quickly—much faster than a tank could have moved itself, for example. Finally, a truck carrying a tank consumed much less fuel than the tank would have needed to drive the same distance.

The HETs did present one drawback. During the hottest times of the year, roughly June to late October, the superheated pavement (which had been baking all day in the sun) sometimes caused HET tires to explode in transit. We decided that this problem could be solved by increasing our stock of tires being requested from the States, and by driving them only at night and in the early morning. We also established a tire-recapping operation in the theater to make our resources go further.

The troops were settled in their defensive positions, fully armed and equipped. Now we had to provide a structure for supplying the troops that had moved out into the desert—by the end of September, some 72,000 of them, mostly members of XVIII ABN Corps. Obviously, we had to sustain our troops; but we also desperately needed to start moving mountains of supplies out of the docks and warehouses, in order to free up space to off-load the constant stream of incoming vessels and planes. Early on, as a temporary measure, we had rented hundreds of thousands of square feet of warehouse space near the port at Ad Dammam and the staging area in Al Jubayl, in order to shelter and keep track of the vast amounts of incoming equipment and supplies. Now those warehouses were bulging, and it was time to get those supplies out into the field.

Since the Tapline Road was already serving as our main tactical supply route, placing supply depots in close proximity to it made good logistical sense. As noted, the road paralleled the Kuwait border, running along almost the entire length of northern Saudi Arabia. My log cell wizards reviewed the then-current state of deployment, and soon pointed to a location about 180km northwest of Dhahran, situated directly ahead of where the 101st Airborne Division was positioned along the Tapline Road. It was here, we decided, that we would place our first forward logistical base—Logbase Bastogne—along with the Screaming Eagles Forward Recon element.

This was not a popular decision among some division and corps staff members. In fact, I had high-ranking visitors from various outfits in the field walk in to my office in Dhahran and tell me in so many words that I was crazy. "That's all the way forward," they observed. "You'll be sitting out ahead of our combat troops, with no one between you and the front."

"Well," I told them, "the Saudis are up there, as well as the Syrians and Egyptians. I think they'll provide adequate protection."

But the real issue, I told them, was protecting our future options. Most of us knew, in our guts, that the proud and tough 101st Airborne was not going to be sitting on its hands forever. If we didn't set up a logbase right up at the front, we might be looking at real problems down the road. The protests continued, but we forged ahead with our plans for Bastogne.

As far as I was concerned, the location was perfect for a large and relatively stable logbase. Logbase Bastogne sat between the XVIII ABN Corps and Kuwait. If the XVIII did move, they'd need supplies, ammunition, and fuel to do so; and Bastogne was positioned to be able to supply them no matter which direction they went. With that end in mind, we placed Tactical Petroleum Terminals (TPTs) at Bastogne. These were 5,000-gallon collapsible fuel-bladders, which provided the means to store and replenish fuel resources forward. Wolf and Masri, my food aces, also placed a distribution center for fresh fruit, vegetables, and bread at the logbase. Now we could finally turn on the tap, and start clearing our mounds of supplies out of the aerial ports of debarkation (APODs) and seaports of debarkation (SPODs).

By the middle of September, it was clear that we had deployed enough combat troops in northern Saudi Arabia to withstand an assault by the Iraqi troops. At that point, the TPFDL—the Time-Phased Force Deployment List, which sequenced incoming units—became much more flexible. I instructed two members of the log cell to evaluate the needs of our command, and then examine the deployment list for companies that could fill in particular gaps. Did we need, for example, a 5-ton truck company, or did we need additional port-operations people? Once we had pinpointed under-manned specialties, I called FORSCOM (General Burba finessed arrangements for me Stateside) and made a request that the TPFDL be shuffled, in order to get the people I needed into the theater more quickly.

In and of itself, the TPFDL is an interesting document. But I see it as symbolic of bigger concerns. Any huge operation needs the equivalent of a TPFDL—and also the means to circumvent it. Situations change constantly, and one must have the capability to adjust accordingly.

And finally, the organization needs in some cases to be able to *stop* circumventions of its TPFDL. After a few rounds of "massaging" the deployment sequence, I found that the people I was requesting on Day One were not necessarily the people I needed most when they arrived on Day Six. I had a pretty good theaterwide vision—but even my relatively broad view didn't encompass all the effects of my requests. After a few forays into tailoring the TPFDL, I decided to back off. I told the log cell to continue monitoring the list, so that we would know whom we could expect in the theater, but not to concern itself with proposed resequencings. Henceforth, we would take our human resources as they came.

We shifted our focus to setting up a second logbase, further to the west from Bastogne on Tapline Road. Dubbed Logbase Alpha, it would be a second large, stable forward location from which combat troops would be able to replenish supplies and equipment, have access to fresh foods, refuel their vehicles, and so on. Together, Bastogne and Alpha provided the foundation for the first phase of a newly developing plan which was then being sketched out by the log cell.

Beefing Up the Ranks

The world watched the situation in the Gulf through the month of October with growing concern. A strict embargo on goods entering and leaving Iraq did not deter Saddam Hussein from increasing the number of his forces in Kuwait. Evidently, Saddam was not going to be moved. Instead, he threatened retaliation against Saudi Arabia, Kuwait, and Israel if attacked. Civilian nationals of Coalition countries were held in thinly disguised captivity in Iraq and Kuwait, obviously for future use as human bargaining chips. By October 4th, twenty-five nations worldwide were contributing forces, supplies, and other support to the Coalition cause.

Embassy after embassy closed its doors in Kuwait. As of October 20th, only the American, British, and French embassies remained open in Kuwait City. A peaceful solution to the conflict seemed less likely with each passing day.

According to the best U.S. intelligence available during this period, Saddam Hussein then had about 430,000 troops in Kuwait. (This number has since been slightly revised downward.) Equipped with 3,500 tanks, 2,500 armored personnel carriers, and 1,700 artillery pieces, Hussein's force outgunned the Coalition forces, and apparently outmanned the American forces by a margin of nearly 2.5 to 1. Since doctrine holds that an attacking force should outnumber a defending force by anywhere between 3 to 1 and 5 to 1, we were defensively secure. On the other hand, even with superior weaponry, we were in no position to drive Saddam from Kuwait.

This was the real significance of President Bush's announcement, on November 8th, 1990, that he was doubling the American military presence in the theater. On the same day, VII Corps began redeploying from its home base in Germany to Saudi Arabia, tipping the balance of forces in our favor. VII Corps includes several mechanized and heavy-armor divisions, comprising more than 6,000 tracked combat vehicles and 59,000 wheeled vehicles. To those in the know, presumably including the Iraqi high command, there could now be no doubt that the Coalition forces were prepared to go on the offensive, if that proved necessary.

Integrating VII Corps into the theater, beginning in mid-November, was a much more organized and orderly operation than receiving the XVIII had been. Although our logistical structure was less than three months old, it performed admirably. We received an additional 220,000 troops over the next two months, along with

769,000 short tons of equipment. Of great importance to us was the fact that VII Corps brought their own logistical support unit, the 2d COSCOM, into the theater right along with them. (XVIII Corps' 1st COSCOM, the reader will recall, was held back in favor of combat units.) According to doctrine, this was the way logistics is supposed to work; and work it did. The VII Corps and its component divisions were able to provide much of their own support from the start.

Once VII Corps began arriving in theater, its soldiers had to be given temporary billets—either in warehouse space near Ad Dammam, or at a staging area in Al Jubayl—until we could move them on to their designated field locations. They were provided with fresh food and water at these temporary billets; and as soon as transportation became available, they were moved forward to a location to the west of XVIII ABN Corps, further out along on the Tapline Road. They were positioned just south of Logbase Alpha, which was already being constructed and supplied as they entered the theater.

500,000 Satisfied Customers

Combat is never a comfortable or enjoyable experience, and can't be made so. But the soldier who is eating well, has adequate supplies and modern equipment, and who feels that he is being supported both by the Army and by the civilian population, will perform far better than one who feels neglected.

Guided by this premise, my organization in the Gulf continued to make quality-of-life innovations long after the bare necessities were in place in the theater. Improving MWR (morale, welfare, and recreation) opportunities for the troops emerged as a key focus of the 22d SUPCOM. We explicitly framed the challenge in business terms: we were a service business, the troops were our customers, and we had to win and retain their loyalty.

This effort took many forms. One of the most important SUP-COM services with MWR implications was our postal delivery system. Beginning in August 1990, we received hundreds of letters and packages each day addressed to soldiers. This torrent increased exponentially as the troop-count rose, and as organized letter-writing campaigns kicked in back home. (Ann Landers encouraged the American public to write to soldiers to show their support. As a result of that column, letters to "any servicemember" jumped to 500 short tons per day—and were eventually assigned a separate APO.) The military postal support staff in the Arabian peninsula expanded from a crew of 13 to 1,300 full-time personnel during the conflict. They processed and distributed over 70 million pounds of mail in the theater. In Stateside terms, this was the largest concentrated postal operation in the history of the United States Postal Service.[6]

In a sense, our extensive MWR activities were just a natural extension of our initial goal of providing the necessities to our troops. We took standard solutions and found ways to extend them and improve upon them. As noted, providing fresh fruits and vegetables entailed only a little extra work for the logistical crew, dramatically improved the quality of life for combat troops, and even saved the king a little money.

The impacts of good MWR are hard to quantify, but I'm convinced that it more than pays for itself. As an example, I'd cite our Combat Convoy Support Centers, better known in the Gulf as "truck stops." Driving for the U.S. Army in Saudi Arabia was no easy task. The Tapline Road was particularly treacherous, given its overcrowded state and almost complete lack of shoulders. (Vehicles drifting off the road were very likely to roll over.) The Saudi civilian drivers—who weren't banned from the Tapline Road until January 1991—also raised the stakes. Each year, some 27,000 Saudis are killed on their highways, out of a total population of 7 million. (In the United States, by comparison, about 50,000 out of 250 million people die each year in traffic accidents.) To this mix, we added 4,500 trucks each day, operated by a truly multinational force of drivers. They commonly drove eighteen hours a day along dangerous and crowded roadways, often transporting many tons of dangerous cargo.

We decided to administer some preventive medicine, in the form of MWR. We had already planned for centers at regular intervals on the supply routes where our truckdrivers could stop, refuel, and have their vehicles serviced as necessary. We went a step further, and integrated "maintenance areas" for the drivers themselves, at distance intervals of 170 miles or less, along the main supply routes. While their trucks were being worked on, the drivers could take a shower and clean up, grab a soda and a Wolfburger (so named in tribute to Wes Wolf), relax, take a quick catnap, or watch a videotape in the lounge.

It's clear that we made the lives of our drivers safer and better. They were more alert, and also more safety conscious in general. This translated directly into a more efficient delivery of goods and equipment, and indisputably saved lives. Our truck-stop strategy also had special benefits for the third-country nationals among our drivers. Many of these drivers were Muslims, with an obligation to stop what they were doing five times a day to pray. The truck stops give them a relatively comfortable and safe place to practice their religion.

I was once asked by a VIP visitor whether it was really necessary to build all these dining facilities out in the desert. My answer was indirect, but it had the desired impact. Among our third-country national drivers, I pointed out, it was customary to stop on the side of the road and cook lunch anywhere where a patch of shade could be found. In the desert, the only shade to be found was most often under your own truck—and we found out that some of our drivers were crawling underneath their trucks, many of which were full of ammunition or fuel, and lighting fires to heat their meals. I suggested to our visitor that the truck stops were a better solution, all around.

The combat support people and our civilian workers obviously loved having conveniently placed facilities where they could pick up a hamburger, a soda, and fries. Our food service experts pondered this success, and came up with their next bright idea. "If the truck drivers love this stuff so much," they told me, "the troops at the front would probably like to get similar fare." I directed Wolf and Masri to put their heads together once again, and design mobile, canteenlike trailer trucks that could take our "fast-food" service to our soldiers in the most forward positions.

Imagine that you've been at some remote and desolate desert site for weeks, or even months, consuming dehydrated or vacuum-packed military rations. One day, unannounced, an odd-looking vehicle with the word "Wolfmobile" painted on it comes driving into your camp. The side panels open up, and a smiling crew inside offers to cook you a hamburger to order. "Side of fries? How about a Coke?" Morale shot up everywhere the Wolfmobiles pulled in—a little bit of home in the desert.

But it was also important to get out of the desert, at least every now and then. The tight constraints of religion and social custom meant that our soldiers in Saudi Arabia could not really unwind. Around Dhahran, the rare day off was usually devoted to laundry. To the manifest relief of the Saudis, we told our soldiers that they were not encouraged to spend much time in Saudi cities except when they were on official business; and when they went, they were expected to go in uniform. As the physical and mental stress of our waiting game with Iraq mounted, we felt it was important to provide some type of escape valve. In Vietnam, people took leaves to Hong

Kong, Hawaii, or Bangkok; in the Persian Gulf, they got the Love Boat. Docked permanently at a port in Bahrain, this contracted cruise ship was a place where the troops could relax for a few days, buy a drink, eat some great food, and enjoy a super floor show.

The waiting game also posed problems for health and fitness. We responded by scheduling regular physical training (PT) for the soldiers, and built basketball courts and baseball diamonds in the desert for them to play on. Later in the game, we even found a way to build temporary swimming pools out in the desert.

For my part, I played basketball with my troops every day. This is my favorite way to work off excess energy, and I'm also convinced that it reinforces important lessons about teamwork. David Packard, co-founder of Hewlett-Packard, had the right idea when he wrote, "I liked basketball and track. You learn a lot of things in athletics, and they're very important in your later career. [For example], you develop a sense of the importance of teamwork."[7]

You also get to exercise judgment, every now and then. There was the time, for example, when Vice President Dan Quayle was visiting the troops at the end of December 1990. We were notified that he had heard about our pick-up basketball games, and wanted to play with us on one of the evenings he was there. Fine with us, we said.

Now, on your average day in Dhahran, we played an anything-goes, no-holds-barred type of game. If it looked like someone might call upon an unfair speed or skill advantage to beat you to the hoop, well, maybe you took him down. And unless someone drew blood, we rarely called fouls. So on the night the VP joined us, I called my team together in a huddle. Quayle and his teammates were already on the court, warming up, throwing foul shots, sinking jumpers. "Look, guys," I told them, pointing at the camera on the sideline. "We're on national TV here. Let's clean up our act a bit on these fouls. We've gotta go out there and play some clean ball."

On the first play, Quayle covers the tip-off, puts a move on one of my guys, and heads in for an easy lay-up. Bam!—one of my teammates blindsides the VP and knocks him on his backside. I could just about see the next day's headlines: "General held in death of Vice President." Fortunately, Quayle bounced up, hung in there, and even got a few shots off. If he had been expecting kid-glove treatment, he adapted his game plan to fit the reality of the 22d SUPCOM.

Planning for Action

Throughout the deployment of VII Corps, we were still operating on the assumption that the 377th Theater Army Area Command (TAACOM), based in New Orleans, would eventually be deployed into the theater to take over the EAC logistical function we had been performing up to that point. In fact, doctrine stipulated that the arrival in-theater of a second Army corps should call forth a TAACOM, and the 377th was fully trained and equipped to carry out that function. The millwheels of bureaucracy started to grind.

Generals Schwarzkopf and Yeosock quickly put a stop to that process. I argued in particular that introducing a new logistical outfit into the theater would be counterproductive, at best. Our outfit had already adjusted itself to the challenges of spontaneous planning, and had forged good local relationships. My superiors ultimately decided that dismantling one headquarters structure and bringing in another one would consume a great deal of time and energy, and might not yield better logistical results. We stayed put, and the 377th headquarters was not deployed to Saudi Arabia.

In fact, we had by this time worked out a pretty tight and effective communications flow. Throughout mid and late November I was in daily contact with Dane Starling, my good friend at Central Command in Riyadh, and Lt. General Ross, the DCSLOG of the Army at the Pentagon. Starling formulated all logistical plans for operations on the theater level, as the CINC's tactical logistics planner. He would then forward the structure of his plan to us in the Support Command, where we would be responsible for logistical arrangements that would make the tactical plan feasible. And Ross—truly one of the unsung heroes of the war—got people Stateside mobilized to do everything possible to support the troops in the field. With information from these valuable sources, and as much guidance as I could give them, my log cell would develop the logistical side of the plan.

This plan would then be presented to General Schwarzkopf during a scheduled briefing session. Very early on, I had gotten in the habit of sneaking John Carr into these briefing sessions with the CINC by having Carr flip my slides in and out of the overhead projector. That way, the head of my log cell stayed as smart and current about the CINC's plans as I did. Carr and I noted the criticisms, and took the logistical plan back to the log cell for refinements that incorporated the CINC's advice. When the plan met with Schwarzkopf's approval, it was then handed over to the LOC for implementation in the field.

Planning was only one of our tasks; monitoring was another. Once a given logistical plan moved out into the field, it proved extremely difficult for the logisticians who were planning operations to monitor it effectively. On the other hand, we couldn't afford to send out our good plans and hope for the best. It seemed to me that a new kind of structure was needed.

This was when I enlisted the help of Ken Guest, my first Deputy Commanding General in Saudi Arabia, in a new assignment. Guest had already proven to be a tough and innovative leader in his own right. Together, we developed a combat command concept called a "Jump Command Post," which was designed to serve as a moving command post far forward in the theater. The Jump-CP would travel to every corner of our farflung logistical "empire," making sure that the troops they encountered along the way understood and were working toward the goals of the command.

As I expected, Guest did a hell of a job. He and his staff, whom I nicknamed the "Ghostbusters," were my eyes, ears, and nose forward in the theater—my constant connection to the troops at the front. They also created a direct link between the log cell and the troops at the most basic level. If the plans of the log cell were not being communicated or implemented correctly, the Ghostbusters would get to those responsible and help them to rectify the problem with their men. In this way, the Jump-CP stayed outside the bureaucracy, but did not undermine the chain of command.

The Jump-CP set up its makeshift headquarters at King Khalid Military City, a Saudi military base located on the northern leg of MSR Dodge. KKMC was a particularly suitable jumping-off point. It was significantly further forward than the headquarters at Dhahran, and it sat along the road that was then being used to take supplies up to Logbase Alpha. Many of our Coalition allies—including the French, British, Syrians, and Egyptians—established their strategic and logistical headquarters along the MSR near KKMC. The Jump-CP, therefore, was able not only to monitor our own troops, but also to maintain constant contact with Coalition forces.

I received two pieces of news in the second week of December which significantly changed the course of my command. I knew from the grapevine that our leaders at CENTCOM felt that the Iraqis were too well dug in along the Kuwaiti border to be easily dislodged by a full frontal attack. The casualties that would result from such an attack were likely to be unacceptably high.

I was not totally surprised, therefore, when General Schwarzkopf contacted me in early December with a new idea. He was now formulating a plan, he told me, that incorporated an end-run sweep up through Iraq, and then eastward into Kuwait. The Iraqis would not expect to be attacked from the desert. In fact, they were pouring all of their energy and resources into defending the southern border of Kuwait, along northern Saudi Arabia, and the Kuwaiti coastline. Schwarzkopf's question was, typically, to the point: "There it is, Gus. Can we support it?"

I told him I thought it was possible. I asked for a week or so to work out the details with my log cell. I knew full well that the CINC was working under several deadlines, but I didn't want to give a half-baked answer to a question of this magnitude. I returned to our Dhahran headquarters, pulled together the log cell personnel, underscored the top-secret nature of our assignment, and put them to work. Our daybooks, phone logs, and other running records from this period make absolutely no mention of this new initiative.

Almost simultaneously, I received word from the Department of the Army of their intention to reactivate the long-defunct 22d Theater Army Area Command, and invest us with that unit's proud colors. This was an honor and a group "promotion" of sorts. We would no longer be a provisional offshoot of the Third Army; we would now be acknowledged as a bona fide organization.

Normally, such an occasion calls for pomp and circumstance. But we were under the gun. The LOC was fully preoccupied with keeping the VII Corps moving forward. The log cell was engaged in its top-secret, pedal-to-the-floor planning for the CINC's proposed end run. There was simply no time for a parade, speeches, or any of the other formalities that usually accompany the designation of a new command.

At the risk of offending my colleagues on the historical protocol side of the shop, I will report that we *did* commemorate the event. On the evening of December 16th—the day we were informed of our new designation as the 22d SUPCOM—we gathered in our main conference room for popcorn, sodas, and the briefest of celebrations. Colonel Mike DiAngelo, who told us that he knew five songs on the accordion, played "Lady of Spain" with great dignity.

The rest of the month of December was dedicated to devising plans for the end run, which were to be reviewed by the CINC in a

meeting on the evening of December 27th. The log cell had concluded that in the aftermath of a successful end run, the new front
line would most likely end up somewhere near the Tigris and Euphrates rivers, far up into Iraq. Accordingly, they formulated a
"two-wheel" plan, which placed small, extremely mobile logbases
far forward in the theater to support the troops as they made their
way across the desert.

At one point, General Schwarzkopf asked on what doctrine we
were basing our structure. I responded, "I got the idea from a fellow
Greek: Alexander the Great."

Schwarzkopf wasn't often at a loss for words, but in this case, he
was. We were betting our offensive on a 2,000-year-old strategy?

In a sense, we were, and with good reason. Alexander the Great
was perhaps the first logistician. "It has long been recognized,"
writes Donald W. Engels in his book, *Alexander the Great and the
Logistics of the Macedonian Army,* "that supply was the basis of
Alexander's strategy and tactics."[8] I read Engels's impressive little
book early in the Gulf campaign, on one of our endless C-12 flights,
and borrowed liberally from Alexander's techniques.

Alexander was a fanatic about mobility, despite the amazing scale
and scope of his enterprise, and he undertook the longest campaigns ever waged up to that point. (At the beginning of one desert
crossing, for example, Alexander ordered all the wagons and excess
baggage in his train burned.[9] The first wagon to be burned, by his
order, was his own.) He was also extremely adept at using the enemy's resources for his own purposes—a trait I carefully mimicked.
Beginning in September 1990, only a few weeks after we got to the
Gulf, I had a small team figuring out where Iraq's depots, railheads,
oil refineries, and other logistics-related resources could be found,
and which of those resources could be put to good use by us. Both
armies, for example, used the same type of fuel. If we could go up
and grab theirs, rather than bringing it all ourselves, a much wider
range of offensive strategies would become feasible.

Of course—as I eventually confessed to Schwarzkopf—we also
drew on more recent antecedents as we planned our logistical support for the proposed end run. One of these historical precedents lay
in the struggle between the Germans and the British in North Africa
during World War II. I carefully reviewed the desert warfare experiences of Field Marshall Rommel. I noted with interest, for example,
that the British successfully played tortoise to Rommel's hare. In part
because of his tactical genius and in part because of his superior

tank armaments, Rommel was generally able to gain ground easily. But the British *held* ground more easily, mainly because they devised effective ways of moving their supply depots westward as Rommel gave ground. In other words, the British—patiently and inexorably—took up the slack that Rommel afforded them. By the time the British were able to introduce a significantly improved tank into the North African theater, they had already crossed and recaptured the desert, and were therefore able to fight the theater's final battles in Mussolini's backyard.

The notion of stripped-down, movable logistical bases was a compelling one—much more compelling, for example, than the firebases of Vietnam. The books by and about Rommel that I read prior to August 1990, along with Engels's book on Alexander, combined forcefully in my mind, and pointed me toward certain kinds of logistical solutions that otherwise might not have occurred to me. We noted, for example, that the British army had successfully used tank-transporting trucks to shuttle its A9 Cruiser tanks across the desert, thereby greatly prolonging the operational life of its tracked vehicles in the harsh desert environment.[10]

Our "two-wheel" plan envisioned that the SUPCOM's logbases would be set up in the desert at a location no farther than one day's round-trip from the COSCOMs which were supporting the corps. These, in turn, would be situated less than one day's round trip from the DISCOMs, which would be providing fuel, ammunition, equipment, and supplies directly to the troops fighting at the front. We added a crucial proviso to the plan: as the troops moved forward, the logbases would have to move with them, carrying only the barest essentials to keep the troops moving and fighting.

In light of my advance warning about the CINC's intention to attack from the west, I decided to establish a substantial 22d SUPCOM presence far forward in the theater. Given the possibility of a SCUD attack on my Dhahran nerve center, I was also interested in creating a redundant logistical headquarters outside of Dhahran. Early in January, we created a mirror command at KKMC. This was the right spot for a number of reasons. First, of course, the Jump-CP had already staked out some space there. Second, it was on one of the main supply routes, near to the troops in the desert. Its proximity to the Coalition forces would facilitate coordination with them. And finally, KKMC was already such a beehive of activity that it seemed possible to squeeze a lot more people in there without the Iraqis catching on.

KKMC is a large complex of military offices, barracks, warehouses, service areas, and commercial shops built in the 1980s for the Saudi military. It rises out of the desert in a spot that, to the untrained eye, looks like Absolute Nowhere. In fact, it straddles the ancient caravan routes of Arabia, and sits in strategic proximity to both Kuwait and Iraq. KKMC was offered to the Coalition forces for the duration.

We didn't have to be offered the space twice. Here we would have the use of modern office space, living accommodations, and recreational facilities. There were also a number of shops ringing the large courtyard in the center of KKMC, some of which continued to be run by their Saudi owners during our stay there. For those of us with recent memories of working out of cars, it was heaven on earth. I dubbed KKMC the "Emerald City"—it seemed appropriate, for such a well-appointed, almost magical forward headquarters—and the name stuck throughout the war, and afterward, when KKMC served as the collection point for all U.S. equipment that was to be redeployed. KKMC was eventually headed up by the energetic and dedicated Brigadier General Tom Jones, a reservist who was activated in December 1990 with his unit of 200 soldiers, and who ably held down the fort through much of the redeployment phase.

By the last week of December, with extensive and valuable input from both corps' LOG experts, the log cell had pulled together a complex plan that outlined how we would move two corps to new forward tactical positions far to the northwest in the Iraqi desert. It was obvious that this was a maneuver which would require very carefully timed and monitored transport.

One fact fairly leaped off the wall: VII Corps would have to move north and a little bit west, and XVIII ABN Corps—then east of VII Corps—would have to jump far to the west, directly across the path of VII Corps. Somewhere out there in the desert, far from the nearest stoplight, we would have to create the Mother of All Intersections.

With the help of the corps transportation planners, we drew up appropriate charts and graphs to illustrate the plan, and went off to Riyadh for the December 27th meeting.

Signing on the Dotted Line

As 1990 drew to a close, there was little question in the minds of American military leaders in the Gulf that active conflict was likely.

Gradually, political leaders worldwide were reaching the same conclusion.

For months, a number of nations had imposed sanctions on Iraq, but these measures seemed to have no effect on Saddam Hussein's policies. By late November, the U.N. Security Council had adopted twelve resolutions censuring Iraqi aggressions against Kuwait and against third-country nationals caught in the conflict. The most recent of these resolutions, adopted on November 29th, authorized "all necessary means" to expel the Iraqis from Kuwait if they had not voluntarily withdrawn by the 15th of January 1991. That date rapidly approached, and there was no indication that Iraq had any intention of relinquishing control of Kuwait.

General Powell, Mr. Cheney, and the commanders of the joint forces met in Riyadh on December 27, 1990,[11] a little more than two weeks before Iraq's U.N.-imposed deadline was set to expire. This was the meeting at which General Schwarzkopf formally unveiled the tactical flanking maneuver he planned to implement, since dubbed the "Hail Mary" strategy. I prefer the term "end run," since, in football, a resort to the "Hail Mary" bomb to the end zone implies that the offense is getting desperate. By the end of December, our forces were by no means desperate.

General Schwarzkopf told the secretary of defense, the head of the joint chiefs, and the assembled military leaders that we would not attack into the teeth of the Iraqi defenses, on Kuwait's southern borders. Instead, he explained, we would outflank the Iraqis, in a vast, clockwise sweep from south to north along the western part of the theater. A strategic air attack preceding the end run would—Schwarzkopf hoped—take out the Iraqi command, control, and intelligence systems, and therefore mask the westward surge of our troops and equipment. The air strikes had to be effective, and our repositioning had to go completely undetected.

After General Schwarzkopf's presentation to the group, the commanders from the two Army corps, the Marines, the Air Force, and the 22d SUPCOM each presented a plan, in broad conceptual terms, of how each intended to carry out its part of the end run. When my turn came, I went through a series of charts and explained the proposed orchestration of the five-phase plan. My presentation laid out the whole logistics operation across the board, and paid particular attention to the crossing of the corps and to forward logbase positioning to the west.

At the conclusion of my presentation, Schwarzkopf turned to me and said, "Gus, we can't move the troops before the 16th of January, after the U.N. deadline expires. We want all of the necessary supplies in place by February 1st to support them out west and up north. Can you deliver on that schedule?"

I looked at the proposed flanking maneuver—it entailed movements of thousands of miles by light and heavy armored divisions, mechanized divisions, and infantry. We would have fourteen days to transport hundreds of thousands of troops, several million tons of supplies, and billions of gallons of fuel, and to set up an effective structure for orderly distribution and resupply.

"Sir," I replied after a moment, "in two weeks we may possibly be able to get the logbases in some semblance of order—using every available soldier and truck in the theater, and working around the clock on all eight cylinders. But, considering the amount of supplies we're moving and the distances we have to travel, I would strongly advise that we start the operation before the 16th."

"That's not possible," he said flatly. "The entire plan hinges on surprise and deception. If you started relocating your logbases tomorrow, we'd run a great risk of being detected. Hussein would shift his defenses westward. Or worse, he'd order his forces to attack before the deadline and preempt our strategy.

"In either case, Gus, we run a grave risk if we move out before the U.N. deadline passes and the air strikes have begun. I'm not willing to take that chance. Are you? How many soldiers' lives is it worth to get a head start on this?"

The atmosphere in the room was charged. Within the Army, General Schwarzkopf was well known for his blunt talk. He was not one to coddle his logisticians.

"It's not worth a single life, sir," I said. "Still, given your proposed deadline of February 1st, I'm convinced that it's impossible to create new logbases adequate to support two Army corps in the field."

"Well, then," General Schwarzkopf said, "what we need to know is exactly how long it will take to get those logbases out there, in position to support a flanking maneuver, assuming you started moving out on January 16th.

"Today is Thursday," the CINC continued, looking at the calendar and then around the room. "We will meet again on Saturday to discuss a revised plan to accommodate these new goals. Thank you for your time, gentlemen."

On the way back to Dhahran, John Carr and I began the reshuffling of our "to do" list. Over the next two frantic days, my team identified every single logistical act we could possibly perform between December 28th and January 16th without tipping our hand to Saddam Hussein. Pushing the limits of our potential and the calendar, the log cell used every precious minute—reshuffling and reshaping, cutting and pasting the plan. By early morning, December 29th, we were tired and punchy, but optimistic: we had come up with a feasible plan that would set up the logistical structure in 21 days, complete with numbers and timetables.

On the morning of December 29th, the group reconvened in Riyadh to discuss the end run strategy. General Schwarzkopf opened the session with an announcement that immediately raised the stakes of the meeting. In the two days that had elapsed since our last meeting, General Powell and Mr. Cheney had briefed the president on the plans that had been presented and discussed, and on that basis the president approved the concept for the ground war. No more practices and scrimmages, we were told; this was the real thing.

This briefing followed a format similar to that of the earlier meeting—after the CINC's introduction, staff representatives presented the details of each command's plan. There was a new strain emerging, though. Here and there during the briefing, stray comments were casually slipping out: "Of course, we'll need 200 more trucks than we've projected. . . ."; "This operation will take four days, or maybe five. . . ."; "This assumes that we'll have 1,000 more people. . . ." With each successive verbal hedge, I could see the CINC's hackles rising. The room became more and more tense.

Finally, it was my turn, and I presented our 21-day plan. General Schwarzkopf stood, turned to the assembled group, and asked, "Does everyone agree that Pagonis's plan can work?" Not one person raised a hand.

Schwarzkopf looked around the room, openly frustrated, and said, "Look. This is not a game. We're getting ready to kick off a major tactical operation for a *war*. Studying time is over. You know your resources—we will not be getting more. I need your assurance that we can successfully work this mission *right now!*"

At that point, still standing at the front of the room with a pointer in my hand, I interjected, "Sir, this logistical plan can happen, and we will make it happen."

Schwarzkopf turned and fixed a meaningful stare on me. "O.K.,

General Pagonis," he responded. "How about signing something to that effect?" The tension in the room was palpable. It seemed to me that Schwarzkopf was using me to make a point to those in the room who had been hedging: fish or cut bait. I took the chart I had been briefing—which included maps and a 21-day timetable of division, corps, and logistics movement—and wrote along the bottom, "Logisticians will not let you or our soldiers down. William G. Pagonis. 29 December 1990."

The CINC took the chart, placed it under the sheet of glass on his desktop, and told me, "I plan to hold you to this." I knew he meant it, and I knew we could get the job done.

Chapter Six

Desert Storm and Desert Farewell

GENERAL SCHWARZKOPF'S second briefing session energized all the U.S. forces, galvanizing them to work together to accomplish our very real mission. The CINC successfully shocked his people out of the planning phase and into action, using me as a catalyst. I found out later that several of my colleagues thought I had jeopardized my career by signing that piece of paper. In fact, it helped me get my own people motivated to achieve our common goal.

The logisticians had agreed to refrain from carrying out any preparations that might make the Iraqis suspicious about General Schwarzkopf's end run plans. But the two weeks between the adoption of the plan and the scheduled commencement of the bombing campaign could still be put to many good uses.

As noted, we established a forward logistical command at KKMC, bringing us much closer to the center of the planned action. We also set up a third logbase, tucked right up below KKMC, which we code-named Logbase Bravo. Sited directly on the northernmost leg of the MSR that went north from Riyadh to Iraq, Bravo served as a perfect forward location for the loading of trucks on a massive scale. These trucks were to be sent northward as soon as the Air Force dropped the first bomb on January 16th. Their contents would constitute the guts of two new logbases, Charlie and Echo, which were to be located up to the northwest of KKMC, almost on the Saudi/ Iraqi border.

It was a strange interlude—a deceptive calm before the storm—as the hours ticked down to the U.N.'s January 15th deadline. While we loaded every truck we could find and pointed them north, the world waited anxiously. In the first week of January, Saddam Hussein declared that "the results of this battle will be great, and all the world and future generations will talk about it." On January 8th, President Bush asked Congress for authorization to use "all necessary means" to expel Iraq from Kuwait. Congress gave him that authority four days later. In the interim, Saudi officials informed Secretary of State Baker that they were now prepared to go to war. Egypt told the U.S. military that Egyptian troops would be part of the Coalition attack force. The trap was about to spring on Saddam Hussein.

COMMAND IN TWO PLACES AT ONCE

Creating a second, "shadow" command at KKMC fully tested the 22d SUPCOM's methods and structures, and especially its methods of generating and disseminating information. We were now functioning in two distinct headquarters on almost opposite sides of the theater. From this point forward, at least until the ground war was over, we had to depend on our tried-and-true organizational devices.

The SITREP (situation report), for example, would still be the only official document going out of the command, and it would originate at the Dhahran headquarters. Stand-ups and sit-downs occurred at both locations; "Please See Me" time was scheduled to reflect where I was on a given day. Thanks to modern fax technology, 3 x 5 cards generated at either location could be read and turned around almost immediately.

It was a bit like a master-clock/slave-clock relationship—except that at any moment KKMC could have become the master clock. The creation of this command engendered an increased ownership of responsibilities. Inevitably, soldiers traveling back and forth from one headquarters (HQ) to the other missed scheduled meetings, and their subordinates had to jump in and cover for them. Similarly, subordinates often had to make decisions on their own initiative. The combination of clear objectives and tight, redundant information systems prevented foul-ups and disconnects.

At KKMC, our supply experts in various specialties and those from the COSCOMs stocked trucks with all the necessities that would be needed to establish supply logbases in forward positions. In Dhahran, we focused on APOD and SPOD operations, and made sure that the resupply network from the center outward was smooth and efficient. The log cell, meanwhile, concentrated on fine-tuning the road traffic schedule, on which the successful crisscross movement of the VII and XVIII corps would depend.

This major challenge deserves some elaboration. General Schwarzkopf's end run scheme placed the VII Corps—which was the "heavier" of the two Army corps in the theater, with more tank and heavy-armor battalions—in a long line, starting up north nearly to the Euphrates River and running down through the breach zone between Iraq and Saudi Arabia. The corps would proceed from its deployment in Saudi Arabia directly northward along the Wadi al Batin, a large natural depression in the desert. Meanwhile, XVIII ABN Corps—a lighter, more mobile force—was to set up behind the VII and proceed behind them toward western Iraq. This meant that the XVIII, which would begin from a defensive position east of the VII, somehow had to get to an offensive position west of the VII. The two corps would have to cross paths in order to get to their respective destinations. This was a daring maneuver, to which delays and logistical bottlenecks could have dealt a serious blow.

A plan for building an overpass at the Mother of All Intersections was briefly considered, but it was abandoned when it was decided that this wasn't the best use of our limited engineering resources. Nor did we have the time to pull off this type of construction. Instead, the log cell located a logical intersection in the travel routes of the two corps, and then pieced together a schedule incorporating movement of the two corps, movement of the Coalition forces, and transport of fuel, equipment, and supplies to support the troops once they reached their destinations. With heroic efforts, they boiled down this very complex movement into a simple plan, which we presented to the two corps commanders and all of the division commanders. Once it had been understood and accepted by all parties, we drew up a timetable charting the movements of the individual divisions. Responsibility for adhering to the schedule was assigned at the division level.

Once this plan had been disseminated, we awaited the final countdown. Midnight, January 15th, 1991, came and went with no signs of withdrawal. We had laid our best plans, and packed all our trucks. We hunkered down and waited for the air war to begin.

A NEW STAR IN THE DESERT

Of course, planning the movement of the Army corps did not go off without a hitch. As I have said before, it is hard for one division or command to effectively see the whole picture clearly in a military campaign. And despite all the changes in the Army over the last several decades, some things never change. For example: all colonels are equal, except that a colonel who belongs to a two-star general is a little more equal than one who belongs to a one-star. As January started, it became increasingly apparent among the higher ranks that the SUPCOM was suffering for having a two-star commander. In some cases, two stars don't speak loudly enough.

General Schwarzkopf called me down to ARCENT in Riyadh shortly after New Year's. Never one for preliminaries, he jumped right in: "Gus, I've talked to Secretary Cheney. I've talked to General Powell. We're going to make you a three-star."

"I don't think that's necessary, sir," I replied. I wasn't being modest; I honestly didn't think it was necessary. In addition, I knew that gaining a third star would disqualify me for a whole range of interesting two-star positions back home, after the war.

The CG didn't miss a beat. "Hey, I didn't ask *you*," he said flatly.

The promotion, he explained, was not so much a reward for work done so far as it was a maneuver to facilitate the much more difficult work to come. Schwarzkopf wanted me to be a co-equal with the two corps commanders. He knew full well that Generals Luck and Franks always went out of their way to cooperate with me. But intrarank collaboration was not as consistent a few rungs down the organizational ladder. An extra star on my collar would go far in ensuring that their subordinates and mine would cooperate fully, in the coming weeks, as they carried out the complex logistical arrangements involved in moving the troops to their forward positions. Dividing material assets on the battlefield would prove difficult enough, without petty political arguments getting in the way as well.

So in mid-January, concurrent with the first successful strikes of the air campaign, General Colin Powell was walking the halls of Congress. In selected Senate offices, he made a personal plea for my immediate promotion. Powell's case was evidently persuasive, since I was nominated and confirmed as a three-star in about two weeks—a process that normally takes at least three to five months.

As it turned out, my promotion made the work of my subordinates immeasurably easier. I could afford to squint a bit at difficulties caused by my two-star rank, in part because I spent so much time dealing directly with corps commanders, as well as the commanders at ARCENT and CENTCOM. In those contexts, rank wasn't an issue. My subordinates didn't have that luxury. That third star magically opened doors and cut red tape for them, and paved the way for more successful logistical arrangements as we approached the ground offensive. We could now divide critical resources on the battlefield to best support the overall action, without the added worry of internal politics. Also, the CINC was already thinking about redeployment of our forces and had decided I would remain behind to be his CINC-forward and the single point of contract to get the Air Force, Marines, Navy, and Army personnel out of the theater with their equipment. This position, he reasoned, would have to be a three-star one.

DRIVE OUT BY FORCE

The deadline had passed, and Saddam had not withdrawn his troops. On January 17th, just after midnight Saudi Arabian time, Coalition air forces launched an assault on strategic and military targets in Iraq and Kuwait. They targeted supply lines running between the northern and southern parts of Iraq; they demolished enemy radar and intelligence capabilities; and they systematically destroyed enemy tanks, SCUD missile launchers, airplanes, and other weapons and military vehicles. These strikes were conducted on a truly frightening scale: 2,500 tons of ordnance in the first twenty-four hours alone. They effectively blinded the Iraqi armed forces.

U.S. Navy ships, meanwhile, stepped up their level of activity out in the Gulf, kicking off the long charade that was designed to suggest that the Coalition intended to attack from the sea. Any remaining Iraqi command-and-control capabilities were forced to focus on the distracting menace just over the horizon in the Gulf.

Setting Up the Ground War

Two days into this massive assault, Phase Bravo—the "movement of the corps"—commenced.

Trucks carrying personnel, tanks and armored vehicles, weapons, ammunition, fuel, and supplies started their engines and moved out onto their travel routes in the early dawn of January 20th. During the next month, those roads saw a constant flow of movement—twenty-four hours a day, seven days a week. By the time the pipeline was flowing at full speed, an average of eighteen trucks per minute was crossing through a single point on the northern route. This rate was sustained for an entire month. At one point, I had my helicopter land on the west side of the highway to check out a transportation movement-control point. The traffic was so dense that I couldn't get across to the east side of the road. We were finally forced to crank up the helicopter and fly to the other side.

By February 3d, both corps had closed in their attack positions. VII Corps had traveled more than 330 miles, and XVIII ABN Corps had jumped some 500 miles, with no significant glitches. This is a tribute to everyone involved—corps, division, COSCOM and SUP-COM personnel, and our Coalition partners who moved in and out of our lines with precision. It's worth noting that all of this was accomplished under the constant threat of chemical and biological warfare, random SCUD attacks, and so on. We owe special thanks to those contracted civilians from Saudi Arabia, South Korea, Pakistan, Egypt, the Philippines, India, Bangladesh, and a dozen other countries who drove up and down our MSRs, in many cases entering enemy territory to supply Logbases Charlie and Echo. In the early hours of the ground war, many of these drivers were working without gas masks, fully aware of the dangers they were confronting.

On February 20th the corps were in place, fully equipped with all classes of supply, and ready to go on the offensive. The 1st and 2d COSCOMs, under the extremely competent leadership of Generals Zeidt and McFarlane, respectively, and supervised by Generals Guest and Whaley, shifted into high gear and really made things happen. Logbases Charlie and Echo, established to resupply the XVIII and VII corps, respectively, were stocked with large but movable quantities of Class I supplies (food and water), Class III (fuel), and Class V (ammunition). Meanwhile, we were developing plans and identifying locations for four additional logbases deep inside Iraq. These projected logbases were positioned using our "90-mile rule": the distance from one supply location to the next had to be less than ninety miles, so that a supply truck could make the round-trip between two logbases in twenty-four hours or less. If the conflict dragged on for an extended period of time, supplies would leapfrog to XVIII ABN Corps from Logbases Oscar and Romeo and would resupply the XVIII ABN Corps; and they would jump north to VII Corps via Logbases Hotel and November.

The corps waited in their ready positions for three days, while we continued to pump supplies and provisions into the logbases. By the time the ground war kicked off on February 24th, we had brought forward enough food and water to sustain the troops for 29 days; there was adequate fuel to keep everyone moving for 5.2 days; and our ammunition would hold up for at least 45 days. Four days later, when the ceasefire took effect, we still stocked 29 days of supply (DOS) of food, about 5.6 DOS of fuel, and more than 65 DOS of ammunition.

In other words, during the course of the 100-hour war, our logistical picture got better and better. Our resupply lines were nearly flawless. Food stocks stayed constant, fuel supplies increased slightly, and ammunition stocks increased significantly. This is astounding, given that fuel consumption by the two corps approached 4.5 million gallons per day, or 880 truckloads. One day's worth of ammunition for the VII Corps weighed 9,000 tons, and constituted 450 truckloads. The XVIII ABN Corps required slightly less ammunition resupply: about 5,000 tons per day.

This was only accomplished through precision planning and hard work. While the armored and combat units moved forward on the attack, a constant stream of trucks continued to traverse the main supply routes, moving fuel, ammunition, and other basics forward from the ports and airfields to Logbases Echo and Charlie, and then forward again from those resupply posts into the field. The twenty-one DOS increase in ammunition comprised 294,000 tons of material. In practical terms, this was 17,850 round-trip truckloads.

This, of course, is the logistician's perspective. Out on the battlefield, the Army and Marine divisions were blasting forward with great courage through minefields, barbed wire, and fire trenches, taking the outflanked Iraqis completely by surprise. Coalition forces simply swept aside the ineffective barriers that had been erected by the enemy. Within hours, there were more than 5,500 enemy prisoners of war (EPWs). Over the next two days, Coalition attacks met with similar spectacular success—so much so that a lot of our planning turned out to have been unnecessary. Forward Logbases Oscar and November, for example, ended up being used solely as trailer-transfer points for relatively small lots of fuel and ammunition. The assault advanced so rapidly and ended so quickly that establishing full logbases within Iraq never became necessary. One of the criticisms I have heard of our logistical efforts is that several units of the VII Corps almost ran out of fuel. However, this criticism seems off the mark. Brigadier General Guest was only twenty-five miles away with 300 5,000-gallon fuel tanks, simply awaiting instructions from the Logistics Operation Center to move to any critical position on the battlefield.

Back at KKMC and the 22d SUPCOM headquarters, we spent the ground war fine-tuning our resupply mechanisms, in the event that the conflict began to get extended. Meanwhile, we decided to accelerate plans to redeploy troops and equipment out of the theater.

The War Hits Home

I meet with skepticism, even disbelief, when I tell people that I didn't issue a single order during the ground war. This is only a slight stretch of the truth. Yes, people sought and got guidance. But the people in my command knew exactly what they were supposed to do in almost every conceivable circumstance. They had been trained and encouraged to think on their feet. I felt they could even deal with the inconceivable.

The inconceivable happened on the evening of February 25th. I was in my quarters at KKMC reviewing paperwork and jotting responses to 3 x 5 cards. At about 11 o'clock, a call came into the LOC from the Dhahran headquarters. A SCUD missile had eluded the American Patriot missile system and hit one of the barracks at Al Khobar—a building temporarily housing about 125 soldiers from the newly arrived 99th Army Reserve Command and the 14th Quartermaster Detachment. The SUPCOM hadn't pulled together all the details of the accident, but it was clear already to those in Dhahran that there had been some casualties.

I packed my things and headed down to Dhahran immediately to see what I could do to help out. By the time I got there, the death toll stood at twenty-eight, and another ninety-six wounded soldiers had been evacuated to medical facilities. I went to the hospital immediately. On the way, I learned that our soldiers, although new to the theater, had taken all the prescribed precautions. They were just in the wrong place at the wrong time.

It was a freak accident, a grim illustration of the fog of war. SCUDs were essentially unguided missiles, which crashed and exploded wherever they happened to be aimed. The hit on the barracks was a shot in the dark. If the missile had fallen ten meters shorter or farther, or to either side, there would have been no casualties.

A final, terrible irony in the situation was that this group of soldiers, who had arrived in the theater less than two weeks earlier, were all from small towns in Pennsylvania, very near to my and my wife's hometowns. I spent the next day, the 26th, in my quarters, writing letters home to the parents and families of the deceased. It was one of the most difficult things I had to do in my entire tour of duty in the Gulf.

Death is a tragedy for those who are touched personally by it. But in the context of war, death is also a continuing threat to the living. Losing twenty-eight young soldiers—or one old soldier—kills a piece of the commanding officer's heart. But that officer can't give in to tragedy, or more tragedy may follow. I could not allow the surviving soldiers of the 99th, or any others in my command, to lose their focus. Focus keeps soldiers alive.

THE END OF THE BEGINNING

I emerged from my quarters and returned to headquarters in Dhahran on the morning of February 28th, just in time to hear the 8:00 a.m. announcement that a ceasefire was in effect. We took just about one minute to celebrate; then we began taking up every single inch of slack in the logistical reins. For weeks, the 22d SUPCOM had been a high-pressure hose, spewing supplies northward and westward at full pressure. Now we had to make absolutely sure that as we began to back off we didn't drop the hose and let things fly off in a million directions.

In retrospect, there were several aspects of our logistical structure that were never tested, as a result of the brevity of the war. For example: we had brought such a huge amount of supplies forward that the commanders in the field never had to ration their consumption. In an extended conflict, that would not have been the case. People would have had to cope with getting only 50 percent of what they asked for, rather than 110 percent.

Similarly, we never had to test our maintenance capabilities or our medical facilities in any serious way. We had developed a plan for on-the-spot cannibalization of damaged equipment; we never implemented it. The elegant "two-wheel" resupply structure (port-to-logbase, logbase-to-forward) got tested in the build-up phase, but was not called upon for heavy resupply.

But the men and women in the 22d SUPCOM, as well as their counterparts in the corps and Stateside, worked wonders. It was they who moved mountains. During the entire conflict, not a single mission was cancelled, postponed, curtailed, or even delayed for lack of logistical support. I'm very proud of our soldiers.

THE TOUGHEST PHASE

From a logistician's perspective, the most difficult phase of the Gulf War was the final one: redeployment. This retrograde action, code-named Desert Farewell, began almost at the instant the ceasefire accords were signed in Safwan. After exhausting, flat-out exertions to support the war effort, we logisticians now had to throw our enormous machine into reverse. Our fire hose now had to be a vacuum cleaner. Without missing a beat, we had to begin moving personnel, supplies, and equipment back out of the desert to the airports and seaports, for shipment out of Saudi Arabia.

As already noted, domestic concerns in the Kingdom were one consideration. We had been invited in to do a job; now the job was finished, and the president directed a prompt departure, to keep our promise to the Saudis. Our personnel were more than eager to carry out this welcome order.

There were also broader security issues to consider. The Warsaw Pact had just disbanded. The Soviet Union was then in the initial stages of disintegration, and our political and military leaders (like their counterparts in Europe) were suddenly playing without a rule book. In U.S. Army circles there was some concern about the readiness of our combat divisions in Europe, whose strength and numbers had been depleted through diversions to the Gulf.

A speedy redeployment, both to the continental United States and Europe, was therefore of the highest priority. Fortunately, our planning for this activity was already far along, in part because my new log cell head—Colonel Randy Geyer, a gifted reservist logistician from Indiana—had come to me with an urgent request during the short-lived ground war. Geyer told me that in his opinion, Phase Echo, the preliminary plan for redeployment, was relatively weak, and needed a great deal of refinement.

I took Geyer's advice, and put the log cell to work on the job, which gained urgency as the war approached its unexpectedly rapid conclusion. They came back to me shortly with a sophisticated plan in two stages. Stage I described a personnel redeployment, which would take place as fast as was humanly possible. Included in this stage would be redeployment of the two corps' combat power—the tanks, artillery, and ammunition needed to ensure their rapid reconstitution in Europe and the United States. This would involve the movement of some 365,000 troops, along with their equipment, in less than ninety days.

Stage II, as described by Geyer's log cell, was even more ambitious. Although the time frame would be longer—perhaps up to a year or more—this stage would involve work that had never before been done on the scale that was now anticipated. It had certainly never been done in the desert. We would have to account for, segregate, clean, and load onto vessels and planes all of the equipment and supplies that were left behind by the departing forces. It was a staggering prospect.

Stage I: Round-Ups and Flights Home

Before we could take steps toward achieving these monumental goals, we had to deal with the conclusion and the immediate aftermath of the war. "The battle is fought and decided by the quartermasters," wrote Field Marshall Rommel, "before the shooting begins."[1] By Rommel's measure, Saddam Hussein's "Mother of All Battles" was over long before it began. Coalition forces had achieved such a ferocious, devastating level of air and artillery firepower, and then applied such a well-disguised left hook (in the form of the end run), that the majority of the soldiers in the Iraqi forward lines were trying to surrender well before the ceasefire started. Many of these troops were conscripts, held in service by coercion at the hands of Hussein's Republican Guard. Iraqi soldiers had seen their fellows and their superior officers tortured, or even killed, for alleged treason. Few had eaten more than survival rations in the previous month. As soon as our combat troops had subdued the Republican Guard—which in fact did fight with skill and courage—most of the remaining Iraqi conscripts wanted nothing more than to be done with the fighting.

Luckily, we had gotten the jump on this situation. A few weeks before the start of the ground war, Brigadier General Joseph "Big Joe" Conlin came stalking through my command, talking to anybody who would listen about enemy prisoners of war. A big, gruff, former football player from New York, Conlin was a rough-and-ready version of the Flying Dutchman, looking for someone to hear his message. "We've got to start building prison camps," he said to various leaders around the theater. "Mark my words. We're going to have 100,000 prisoners."

A 3 x 5 card brought Conlin to my attention, and I soon had him tracked down and brought into my office. "You're right, Joe," I told him. "We are going to need those prison camps badly. I think you ought to come and work for me, since I've got everything you need to build 'em with. Let's work together."

After a bit of high-speed political maneuvering, and with strong support from General Yeosock, Conlin and some 9,000 troops from his 800th MP brigade were attached to the 22d SUPCOM, and immediately started constructing EPW camps, drawing upon our stocks of barbed wire, lumber, tents, and so on. This crash effort began in the third week of February. A mere five days later, the camps were far enough along to start receiving and processing the first wave of prisoners. This was close timing, since the 101st Division brought in 450 captured Iraqis on the 20th of February, before the ground war had even begun.

As the ground war progressed, U.S. troops rounded up staggering numbers of EPWs—but no more than Conlin had warned us were coming. For the most part, the process went smoothly, but there was one small hitch. We had been planning to transport EPWs southward to the new camps in empty ammunition trucks: trucks would come north full of ammo, and would head south full of EPWs. But as demand for ammunition plummeted with the collapse of the enemy, empty ammo trucks were harder and harder to find at the front. We fell back on our old standby, the rented bus, and moved the prisoners south.

The Saudi Arabians were unprepared to handle large numbers of EPWs immediately. (They agreed to start accepting and processing prisoners after March 2d.) As a result, we received all of the 70,000 EPWs who were taken during the first few weeks. Once the Red Cross geared up enough to take responsibility for the EPWs, we gladly transferred authority to that organization, which in turn released the EPWs to the Saudis.

The EPW camps remain an untold story, in large part because the Geneva Convention prohibits exploitation of prisoners of war, including publication or broadcast of their pictures. (In this media age, if it isn't on TV, it doesn't exist.) From my point of view, the camps were not only a triumph of planning and execution, but also a remarkable demonstration of the humanity of our American troops.

Many of these prisoners came to us in a pathetic condition. They were immediately offered whatever medical attention they needed. They were fed, cleaned, and clothed. When they awoke on the morning after their first night of internment, they were stunned to discover that our troops had shot an azimuth to locate Mecca, enabling them to face in the direction of that holy shrine for their morning prayers.

All I can offer is anecdotal evidence—but I gathered that evidence firsthand. The American soldiers extended themselves, personally, to the surrendering Iraqi troops. Our soldiers were handing over their field jackets and their rations to the shivering, starving Iraqis as they crawled out of their foxholes. The enemy—who had been told that we were heartless butchers—were absolutely at a loss to deal with this kindness. It speaks volumes that there was not one escape attempt at any of our camps. In fact, many of the prisoners asked if they could stay on with us rather than be sent back to Iraq.

I recall one visit I made to an EPW camp to make sure everything was running smoothly. It happened to be the camp in which most of the high-ranking Iraqi officials were being held. A half-mile or so out of camp, I began to hear an indistinct chanting, that sounded like "uh UH, uh UH." My first thought was, "Look out—prison riot!" But when I got within eyeshot of the prisoners, the chant became distinguishable: "George *Bush*, George *Bush*." Apparently, one of our soldiers had told them that a big American general (meaning me) was coming to the camp. The enemy soldiers were so grateful for their humane treatment that they were cheering their own leader's chief tormentor.

The overwhelming characteristic of the war, in both the military and civilian ranks, was professionalism. I hope I'm not betraying a confidence by relating the following story, but I think it speaks well for an institution that is often criticized: the media. On the afternoon of February 27th, I took a helicopter tour of the theater. By coincidence, the distinguished journalist John Chancellor had arrived at KKMC that morning, looking for an interview with me. I always try to take care of the media, but this was something special. Chancellor had walked with the legends—Eisenhower, Bradley, and the rest—and here he was out in the middle of the desert looking for me. Bending the rules a bit, I invited him to join me on a helicopter tour.

We headed out over the desert to get the bird's-eye view of the 22d SUPCOM's logistical empire. First I showed him the stockpiles of ammunition at Logbase Bravo; then we flew toward Logbases

Charlie and Echo for an overview. We saw a few surrendering Iraqi prisoners, which prompted me to recount an incident of a few days before.

While flying over the desert, I had noticed a lone individual urgently waving a white flag. It was obviously a surrendering Iraqi. I asked the pilot to circle so we could get a better view of what was happening. When we approached the area again, there were at least two dozen would-be prisoners on the spot. We circled once more to land, and by the time we made our third approach, some fifty prisoners had gathered to be taken into our custody. There was a serious language barrier, but I hopped out of the helicopter and motioned southward, in the direction of the nearest EPW processing area.

Upon hearing this story, Chancellor suggested that the incident would make great copy: "Three-star general singlehandedly takes 50 prisoners."

I earnestly asked him not to do it. For one thing, I felt I couldn't make light of the true desperation of those pathetic prisoners-to-be, who were only pawns in a much bigger game. More important, I didn't want to demean our fighters up north, who even then were engaged in deadly tank battles with the tenacious Republican Guard. Chancellor honored my request—and that night, filed a brief story on the men and women who were working a logistical miracle in the desert. Sensational journalism was not his method; and to me, this was the mark of a true professional.

The 22d SUPCOM did not participate extensively in the immediate postwar defense of Kuwait, which as I defined it included the reconstruction of a civil authority in the wake of Saddam Hussein's depredations. "Task Force Freedom," as the Coalition occupying force was dubbed, pulled together a number of very talented soldiers—including Brigadier General Ken Guest, former commander of my Jump-CP—to provide food, fuel, water, and medical supplies to the Kuwaitis at the very end of the war and at the beginning of the peace. It is worth noting that the Civil Affairs Brigade which General Yeosock arranged to have attached to the 22d SUPCOM once again ensured that there was a single point of contact in the theater, in a turbulent transitional period.

In addition, through Operation Provide Comfort, we moved surplus supplies up across the Turkish border to Kurdish refugees fleeing Iraq. We sent them tents, cots and blankets, clothing, water, excess MREs, and traypacks. This was first and foremost a humanitarian gesture, but it was also a practical plan from the logistics standpoint.

The Kurds needed these supplies desperately, and whatever they could use, we were happy to give up, knowing that we would otherwise have to pack it up and ship it home, or destroy those MREs that had exceeded their usage dates. In subsequent weeks and months, surplus food and clothing was sent to needy populations elsewhere around the world.

Leaders of the Iraqi and Coalition forces met in Safwan, Iraq, on March 3d to work out terms for a ceasefire. (I distinguished myself by dozing off at the conference and falling off my chair—the result of having worked all night to help prepare the site.) Simultaneously, commanders of the various combat units were hard at work putting together reverse TPFDLs, which scheduled the redeployment of their personnel. When President Bush made his announcement to the people of the United States on March 6th that the war had ended, planes were already on their way to Dhahran to transport soldiers back home. On March 8th, the first wave of 5,000 soldiers left Dhahran headed for the United States.

The redeployment of troops continued at a consistent and remarkable pace of 5,000 soldiers per day. Maybe by the standards of, for example, Chicago's O'Hare Airport, 5,000 people a day doesn't sound like a lot. But remember that we were effectively running both a military outprocessing unit and a customs operation, helping the Saudis keep control of their borders while also making sure that no contraband goods went home to the States. We were basically working off of several runways, and they were busy round the clock. The combat troops had accomplished their mission with valor, and they deserved to go home. By April 1st, more than 165,000 U.S. troops had been sent home; and by the time ninety days had gone by, we had moved more than 365,000 soldiers.

Stage II: Removing Mountains

For the support personnel, on the other hand, the ceasefire only marked the beginning of a new mission. Out there in the desert, we had staggering quantities of stuff—food, ammunition, fuel, and a thousand other items—that now had to be brought back in and dealt with. We didn't want to just leave it there, and we had told the Saudis that we wouldn't.

Most of the people working in the 22d SUPCOM had already been in the theater nine or ten months when the ceasefire took effect. It was easy to see that they were exhausted, and on the verge of burning out. Nevertheless—and believe it or not—most of them still wanted very badly to stay in Saudi Arabia and help clean up. They wanted to stick it out for the duration.

I am paid to be realistic. I knew that this particular clean-up would take at least a year, and maybe longer. I simply couldn't ask these committed soldiers, who had already given so much of themselves, to stay on in the theater; nor could I ask their families and friends to make additional sacrifices. In early April, my problem was solved for me: the Army decided that all reserve units had to leave the theater. It was then that my long-time crew went home, and the first of 6,000 new troops—all volunteers from the reserve and the National Guard, along with new active-duty personnel— arrived in-theater to staff and run Operation Desert Farewell.

The switch of personnel was nothing new for me. In less than a year in the theater, my command had turned over the equivalent of five times. This latest ebb-and-flood cycle would simply bring our grand total to six. Once again, we implemented aggressive training programs, and put our new people to work, using the plan that had been worked out by Geyer's log cell. I was greatly aided in this process by the arrival of reservist Major General Marvin Back, an accomplished business executive, who despite being a newcomer himself made this latest transition go smoothly.

Desert Farewell was the first close-out of a theater of war by United States forces in this century. We left huge amounts of equipment to rust and rot in Germany after World War II, and it took months, even years, to get all the troops home. In the wake of Korea, some materials were shipped to Japan, but the process was apparently a haphazard one. Our departure from Vietnam was so abrupt that we left billions of dollars' worth of equipment behind. But we were obligated to do better in this case. President Bush's agreement with King Fahd specified that there would be no American military presence in Saudi Arabia after the conflict. In addition, we felt a moral obligation to clean up the huge mess we had made in his country. Accordingly, this would be the first war in modern military history in which everything was accounted for, cleaned, sorted, labeled, and shipped off in an orderly and comprehensive fashion.

We approached the task of repacking with a long-term vision. Some of the material, of course, was repacked onto prepo ships which would return to their ready positions in the Indian Ocean. (We could not forget how those ships had bailed us out, only a year earlier.) Other supplies and equipment were designated for shipment to American military bases throughout Europe, Asia, and Central and South America, in part to replenish stocks that had been depleted to supply the Gulf. Kuwait was making requests for limited amounts of military supplies. Beyond that, everything else had to be shipped back to the States.

We did everything in reverse, and then some. For example, we set to work, along with our VII Corps colleagues, repainting our tan tanks green, to make them suitable for redeployment to Germany. Throughout this long and unglamorous phase, we benefited greatly from Army Vice Chief of Staff General Dennis Reimer's "guardian angel" activities. General Reimer understood why what we were doing was difficult and sometimes dangerous, and he ensured that we got the support we needed.

As mentioned in previous chapters, we set up four "washrack" units to clean and sanitize vehicles so that they could meet stringent U.S. Department of Agriculture standards for goods arriving from the Middle East. More than 2,000 vehicles were washed each day: not just a quick rinse, this was instead a complete scrub-down to assure there was no loose sand or dirt anywhere on any piece of equipment. On many of the tracked vehicles, including the M1 tank, the soldiers actually pulled the engines out to clean them and then reassembled the vehicle. In addition to ground and air vehicles, all the stores of ammunition—more than 350,000 short tons—were cleaned for shipping. During redeployment, the washracks constituted the largest operation in the theater.

We had to bring adequate supplies of water to each of the four sites (in some cases by truck; in other cases by temporary pipeline). Down by KKMC, a group of ingenious young soldiers situated the washrack so that the water would run off into a gully and drain into a reverse osmosis unit, which purified it again and put it into a large tank to be recycled. In several cases, asphalt had to be laid down to support vehicles on the washracks. At one of the sites, a jury-rigged assembly line for shrink-wrapping large equipment had to be set up. And finally, sterile staging areas had to be completed at the port, to hold materials and equipment until ships became available.

Out in the desert, troops swept the terrain for lost or abandoned ammunition, weapons, vehicles, supplies, and construction materials. Once everything had been gathered up, it was sorted, and then shipped or scrapped.

We worked as quickly as safety permitted. In the first 120 days of Desert Farewell, we cleaned and shipped more than 117,000 wheeled and 12,000 tracked vehicles, 2,000 helicopters, and 41,000 containers of supplies. As the end of 1991 approached, only 30,000 short tons of ammunition remained on the ground in Saudi Arabia, and with the help of civilian contractors, that too would soon be gone. I departed the theater in January 1992, and was succeeded by Brigadier General Ed Brown, a superb logistician with a broad range of experience in the Gulf, which more than equipped him to finish the job. Six months ahead of schedule, the bulk of the redeployment was completed; and for this logistician, at least, the toughest phase of the war was finally over.

CONCLUSION

The three phases of the Gulf War should really be seen as part of a whole. Together, they comprised a war that was fought less on the battlefield and more in the LOC, more along the MSRs and less in Washington and Riyadh. It was months of logistical preparation that allowed our forces to wrap up the air and ground wars in 1,012 hours. It was months of planning—before and during the war—that enabled us to redeploy successfully out of the theater.

It was, once again, the goodwill and patience of our Saudi hosts that enabled us to prepare the field of war, and then repair it.

And I'm convinced that it was the talents of our soldiers—especially, in my experience, the talents of the logisticians—that allowed us to put it all together. I'll have more to say about these remarkable CSS soldiers, and their 500,000 colleagues-in-arms, at the end of this book.

Chapter Seven

Building Blocks
of Leadership

TAKEN AS A WHOLE, Desert Shield, Desert Storm, and Desert Farewell comprised an extremely complex challenge in leadership and logistics. The environment was harsh and, to most of us, alien. The host-nation culture was similarly unfamiliar. Over my seventeen months in the theater, our circumstances changed constantly. Strategic and tactical plans changed on short notice, and our logistical planning had to follow suit. A steady stream of new personnel entered the theater—at first to supplement our ranks, and later to replace those who had completed their mission.

So why did things run as smoothly as they did? It was a result of both external and internal factors.

I've already laid out some of the external factors that contributed to the success of my command and the overall logistical effort. There was, for example, the fact that the Army had spent the prior two decades retooling and reinventing itself, in terms of both personnel (through recruitment and education) and equipment. On another front, we had strong civilian leadership provided by President Bush, Secretary Cheney, and Secretaries of the Army Marsh and Stone, who defined the military's goals and then gave us the resources and the latitude to accomplish those goals. There was a similar clarity of purpose and supportiveness at the highest ranks of the military, including Generals Powell, Schwarzkopf, Yeosock, Luck, and

Franks. Not to be overlooked, of course, was the generosity of the
Saudis, the timely support of other members of the Coalition, and
the strong moral and physical support of the American people. All
of these factors contributed to our context, and nothing would have
been possible without them.

We also had strengths that were internal to the organization that
became the 22d SUPCOM. One of those strengths was my particular
approach to leadership, especially as amplified and improved upon
by those around me. That leadership style became the property of
hundreds of people. This style was important not because it was Gus
Pagonis's approach, but rather because it allowed other people to
lead. And in the end, it was leadership that made it possible to solve
our formidable logistical challenges.

LOOSE AND TIGHT LABORATORIES

From a logistician's standpoint, the military is a structure that de-
pends both on flexibility and on rigidity. It is both loose and tight,
to use contemporary management jargon. This dualism is captured
in military doctrine, which provides a sort of operational "template."
Like most templates, doctrine is rigid—but only up to a point. Past
that point, it becomes extremely flexible. It first lays out guidelines,
but it then demands innovation and adjustment on the part of the
leader in those cases where the guidelines come up short.

The hierarchical and bureaucratic structure of the military also
captures this special dualism. When I began my first day as a newly
commissioned officer, I suppose I could have charted out how my
military career could be expected to progress: first this level and type
of responsibility, then that, then that, and so on, year by year. Perhaps some of my colleagues actually thought like that. I didn't, and
I'm glad I didn't, since that would have been missing the point. The
Army, despite its long-standing reputation for enforced homogene-
ity, is not an ant colony. Within the Army's vast hierarchy—which
determines everything from career patterns to day-to-day chains of
command—there is a great diversity of experience. Orders are issued
and obeyed, and yet highly individualistic people grow and flourish.

It took me many years to appreciate the subtle benefits that grow
out of these paradoxical, sometimes contradictory elements. When
the Army is functioning at its best, it can be stable without being
stultifying. It can take risks without posing undue risk to people's

lives. It can create individual "laboratories," within which officers and noncommissioned officers can experiment with the tools and techniques of leadership.

Well before I knew it, I was running such a laboratory. Throughout my years in the military, I have tested and tinkered with approaches to management and leadership. I have rummaged among the techniques of effective leaders, both in the military and in business, and have incorporated them into an increasingly coherent vision, which is implemented by means of an increasingly comprehensive set of tools. These tools supplement, rather than substitute for, conventional doctrine and bureaucracy. They enrich our contexts, and sharpen our edge.

Most important, they improve the flow of information. This, in turn, helps formulate and disseminate the short- and long-term objectives of the organization. It motivates and empowers my staff, maximizes the use of their talents, and therefore encourages innovation.

Like most researchers, I've benefited from the occasional accident and lucky discovery. This reflects the realities of leadership, which guarantee that while you're trying mightily to design your perfect organization, nothing is standing still, and everything is demanding your attention in the here and now. Sooner or later, you are practically forced to stumble onto something important.

I'm a soldier, so I'll present the following techniques as orders: do this, do that. But I'll also state in advance that the last such order in this chapter will be for the reader to ignore any advice that doesn't make sense for a specific context, or for them personally.

Finally, if everything seems to be rational and sequential in the following pages—all ready to be captured in a critical-path diagram or a flow chart—it would be wise to be skeptical. In summaries like these, a lot of false starts, dead ends, and stubbed toes don't show up.

KNOW YOURSELF

Let's begin this exploration with a quote from that ancient Chinese warrior and poet, Sun Tzu, who wrote, many centuries ago:

> Know the enemy and know yourself; in a hundred battles you will never be in peril. When you are ignorant of the enemy but know yourself, your chances of winning or losing are equal. If ignorant of

both your enemy and of yourself, you are certain in every battle to be in peril.[1]

In my opinion, the fundamental key to being an effective leader—and the key to all successful human interaction—is to know yourself. You've got to be in tune with what makes you happy. You have to understand what you're good at. And every once in a while, you've got to sit down and take a brutally honest look at your shortcomings. And since people are a moving target, this process of self-analysis should go on constantly throughout one's career, formally and informally.

Take myself, for example: I know from years of self-analysis that I am a creature of habit. I love order. If someone moves a pencil in the holder on my desk, I can tell. (My Alpha Chi Rho fraternity mates in college used to rearrange the items on my dresser to get my goat.) This is either a useful trait or a not-so-useful trait, depending on the circumstances.

I also have a voracious appetite for knowledge. But I'm the first to admit that my intellectual fare has to be cooked certain ways. Charts, graphs, and tables do it for me; textbooks and long information papers don't. I also know I have a particular capacity for processing information, especially data that are presented visually.

I've always been impatient with any sort of hierarchical structure that impedes, rather than empowers, those in lower echelons. This first surfaced during my days as a newspaper boy in Charleroi, Pennsylvania. The instinct is right; the impatience is not always helpful.

I'm a great believer in the economical use of time. Early in my career, this was simply a personal preference. Over time, however, it became an absolute necessity. I think any leader with significant responsibilities can identify this same pattern in his or her past.

I'm a real meritocrat: I believe that people should be rewarded for doing what they do best. By extension, they should also be encouraged to focus on what they do best.

And finally, I'm a great verbal communicator. I love to get up and work a crowd. On the other hand, writing a position paper (or a book) is not the first thing I want to do when I get out of bed in the morning.

Augment Yourself

There are two reasons why these kinds of hard-won self-perceptions are important. First, they let the leader play to his or her strengths.

Second, they let the leader augment strengths, and compensate for perceived weaknesses.

The heavy responsibilities of leadership, and the time those burdens consume, tend to crowd out introspection. As a result, the people who ought to worry the most about self-knowledge sometimes wind up ignoring it. My advice is: find the time. (We'll get to time management later.) If you can't find the time on the job, take a sabbatical to a Greek island—I recommend my father's island, Chios—with its good food, beautiful scenery, and gracious people.

PRESENT YOURSELF

Once you have a handle on who and what you are, and what you do and don't do well, you have to go to market—to present yourself as a leader. "For a leader to secure commitment from subordinates in business and political organizations," writes Abraham Zaleznik, "he or she has to demonstrate extraordinary competence or other qualities that subordinates admire. If the leader fails to demonstrate these personal qualities and is not maintained in his or her role by tradition, the leadership compact begins to disintegrate."[2]

Zaleznik asserts that tradition underwrites leadership in the military. I don't agree; I think I have to earn my stars every day. Fortunately, the opportunities for earning your stars, both in the military and in business, are almost unlimited.

Learn to Listen

Presenting yourself begins with figuring out to whom you're presenting. In that sense, listening skills are absolutely critical. They are also very rare. I'm reminded of the party game "telephone," where the same message is passed down two lines of people, and at the far end comes out completely different. Why? In part because people don't speak carefully, in part because people don't listen carefully, and in part because people embellish and change what they hear for all kinds of reasons.

I've run informal experiments at work in which I may say to several dozen people, "Walk out those doors, turn left, and go down the steps." Invariably, half of them go through the doors and turn right, and subsequently *insist* that that's what I told them to do. Over the years, as will be explained in subsequent pages, I've learned to listen harder and better. There's no magic to it. Taking notes can prevent your mind from wandering. Taking a course in listening skills may be a great investment. And, as a wise commanding officer used to say to me, "Never pass up the opportunity to remain silent."

Knowing what you're listening *for* is extremely important. What are the ground rules? What will you be expected to take away from a given session? I'm reminded of the time, a couple of years back, when my wife scheduled a public appearance for me. "You're just going to give an informal talk to a relatively small group," she said, somewhat mysteriously. "Don't give it a second thought."

On the appointed day, we drove off together, and eventually pulled into a school parking lot in the Virginia suburbs. My audience was a graduating kindergarten class. I was apprehensive, but as it turned out, the kids were very quiet and attentive. They were seated in rows, construction paper mortarboards perched on their heads. I set the stage with some ground rules. "O.K.," I said, pointing at my plastic name badge, "my name is General Pagonis. You and I both have jobs to do here today. But they're different jobs. My job is to tell you about what I do all day, and your job is to listen very carefully to what I have to say."

A little hand shot up from the back row. It was attached to a girl with a serious look on her face. "Mr. General sir," she said thoughtfully, "if we finish our job before you finish yours, can we go home early?" I'd bet on that girl as a future great listener.

Learn to Communicate

Good verbal skills are the starting point of good listening, of course. The leader at every level in the organization must be able to present himself or herself effectively, and articulate the message within the time that's available. From my perspective, nothing replaces rehearsal. Rehearse the presentation several ways—for example, what will you do if the allotted time is cut from thirty minutes to five minutes?

Most people think they're terrible public speakers, and most of them are wrong. Moreover, almost everyone can get better at this task, by means of videotapes, coaches, and so on. As for that small subset of people who honestly can't improve in this area, they can train and use a proxy. If the CEO is uncomfortable on his feet, he can delegate the speechifying to a trusted vice president. Obviously, the ground rules need to be worked out—who introduces whom, how the VP's role in the event is explained, and so on. But these details are relatively easy to deal with.

Learn to Read Body Language

Good interrogators watch the eyes of their subjects to see which part of the brain is being consulted. I maintain that you can learn as much from a colleague's delivery as from his or her substance. Are you able to make eye contact? What is your colleague doing with his or her hands? Are there lots of crossed arms and crossed legs in the room, indicating tension or anger? In small-group sessions with newcomers, I usually ask people to introduce themselves—a good opportunity to pick up on body-language cues. At the same time, of course, others are watching you. It makes great sense to monitor your own body language, and to disclose only what you want to disclose.

In the same general way, you can read (and be read by) audiences, big or small. You can see if your message is getting across, and, if necessary, fine-tune your presentation on the spot to connect better.

Use the Orientation

Orientation of new employees, for example, provides multiple opportunities. One of these is the chance to establish yourself from Day One as a leader in the eyes of your new arrivals. If they are ever going to be open to persuasion, it is probably in the first week. Use that opportunity. Point to what's good about the organization, and how you intend to support them. Set some initial expectations, which gives them another means to evaluate their leader. (What's important to the Old Man, anyway? What's he all about?)

In the Gulf War, I personally welcomed as many of the 50,000 troops who came under my direct command as my schedule allowed. Upon their arrival, the soldiers were generally tired, disoriented, and a bit scared. In my impromptu remarks and in the Q&A period that followed, I tried hard to offer both concrete direction—do this, don't do that—and a more general reassurance. (Early in my tenure, I had one of these orientation sessions videotaped so the message would still be available even if I wasn't.) From past experience, I knew what their expectations were, and I either confirmed those expectations or let them down gently. Finally, I encouraged them to ask people already in the command what they thought of me. "Ask them if I'll take good care of you," I suggested.

Humor is an important element of the orientation experience. Humor underscores a leader's accessibility and humanity, and when newcomers are trying to get a handle on what makes this individual and this organization tick, it can play a crucial role. I used to tell my troops that when a movie was made out of Desert Storm, my role was going to be played by Dustin Hoffman. "Of course," I continued, "my wife is convinced it's going to be Danny DeVito." I also wound up my Gulf War orientation sessions by donning a wide-brim camouflage hat adorned with a huge red feather, and telling the troops with mock seriousness that this particular "look" was reserved for three-star generals.

MBWA

I am a devout believer in management by walking around—although given the distances involved in Saudi Arabia, it was most often driving around or flying around. Almost every afternoon, I got out in the field, talked to my troops and civilian contractors, and tried hard to get a firsthand feel for what was really going on. I visited warehouses, walked the docks, surveyed the airfields, and went out into the desert to touch base with the folks running the truck stops and filling the TPTs. Simultaneously, I got a chance to talk to our "customers"—the soldiers, airmen, and marines whom we were there to support—and find out whether or not they thought all their needs were being met.

This is in part an outgrowth of military tradition, which holds that a leader ought to be present in person to share the risk that he is imposing on his troops.[3] But equally important, it reflects my determination to be seen as a leader—the one who's in charge here—and to make personal contact with as many people as possible in my command. People contribute most willingly when they are shown that their contribution has value. Having the leader show up makes that point forcefully.

Management by walking around represents one of the best ways for a leader to get the straight story. The Duke of Wellington had this impulse. He would spend all morning with his top aides, who would give him their side of the story; then he would spend the afternoon riding his horse into every nook and cranny of his command.[4] General Eisenhower, too, was out poking around incessantly.

For the private or the mail room clerk, seeing is believing. If they see you, they're likely to believe in you.

The Personal Touch

This is a grab bag of small gestures, which are necessarily different for every leader depending on his or her own inclinations (know yourself). But it comes down to finding opportunities to make unusual, informal, and rewarding contacts with one's subordinates.

For example, I play basketball with my troops almost every day at lunchtime. I may not get much credit for my three-point shot, but I'm sure my young teammates respect my willingness to get out on the court and mix it up with them. In the same spirit, whenever I came across a particularly desolate or isolated outpost of our logistical empire—such as the equipment dump in Ad Dammam—I always arranged to talk up their achievements, send cold sodas after the fact, and schedule a second visit after an appropriate interval.

While we were in Saudi Arabia, my wife, Cheri, ran two different weekly dinners for the troops. We met and got to know hundreds, even thousands, of young people this way. They got to know me as well, and took their impressions of me back to their colleagues. I have no doubt that for every one soldier we made contact with in this way, another half-dozen were exposed to me indirectly, through story telling after the fact. And of course, Cheri's charm and openness always won them over to the fact that the general and his wife were everyday people.

Manage Your Time

The better you are at what you do, the more valuable your time is. This is good, since it means you are likely to be well compensated in one currency or another. But unless you're an artist or a craftsman, this is likely to mean that you are getting spread thinner and thinner. More and more people need your help, and as a leader, you're expected to give it to them.

This calls for effective time management. Effective leaders dole out minutes like hen's teeth. They develop efficient habits and stick to them. One of my favorite time management stories concerns Ulysses S. Grant, who was often untidy but rarely sloppy with his time. "He sat with his head bent low over the table," writes John Keegan of Grant's after-dinner despatch writing ritual, "and when he had occasion to step to another . . . to get a paper he wanted, he would glide rapidly across the room without straightening himself, and return to his seat with his body still bent over at about the same angle at which he had been sitting when he left his chair."[5]

We don't all have to walk across the room bent over double. But the effective leader has to eliminate wasted motion in his daily routines. He has to set a schedule, and stick to it. A key ingredient in this discipline is understanding the times of day when you are most likely to be productive at certain tasks, and protecting those times of day from interruptions and distractions. For example, right after a run or a swim, I can conquer almost any pile of paperwork. At another time of day, that same pile could conquer me.

Certain things can only be done at specific times of day—for example, phoning the Pentagon from Saudi Arabia. There are a surprising number of these more or less inflexible responsibilities, around which the rest of the day's schedule must be built. This adds urgency to the challenge of time management.

Once habits are established, the leader has to protect them, and look for signs that things are going awry. In the Gulf, I watched the flow of paperwork like a hawk. Why? Because I had learned that if I got a lighter-than-normal load one day, it simply meant that the system had broken down. The paperwork load would be doubled the following day, demanding time I couldn't easily give it. I constantly drummed this priority into my staff: set a rhythm, and *stick* to it.

Leverage Yourself

This obligation extends to subordinates as well. To the extent that daily procedures are routinized, time is saved, and decision making is reserved for the important questions. While I was in Saudi Arabia I did a lot of my paperwork in transit. My staff knew where I was going to be and when, and how much time I'd have between Point A and Point B. Invariably, when I left Point A, my driver had a pile of fresh paperwork in hand.

But even the most efficient leader runs out of hours in the day. This is when alter egos become critical. When it came time to leverage myself over more people and more distances, I invented a group that came to be known as the "Ghostbusters."

The Ghostbusters, who numbered about a dozen people at the height of my command, were my stand-ins. They were not in the formal chain of command; instead, they went out into the field as my ambassadors. Quite frequently, they were outranked by the people they dropped in on. I took the time to train them personally, and to constantly update them—they knew the details of the five-phase plan just as well as I did. They were not spies, but rather mobile advisers. Most often, they went out to discover whether a given plan was being implemented as expected. But they also made my presence felt.

For example, during the Gulf redeployment phase, I got a request that our MPs be allowed to load live ammunition in their weapons, rather than leaving ammo magazines in their ammo pouches. I was not inclined to grant the request, fearing that it might lead to accidental deaths, or to international incidents. My Ghostbusters did a quick survey of the situation which brought additional disincentives to light: for example, it turned out that many of our incoming MPs were National Guard volunteers who had only been designated MPs at their mobilization station. They knew little or nothing about the circumstances under which they were required or permitted to fire their weapons. All in all, live ammo seemed like a bad idea. Training was more to the point.

In a sense, the Ghostbusters were my third base coaches—in and out of the dugout, talking to the manager to nail down the strategy; and then back out onto the field with signals for the runner on second. Maybe for the runner this isn't as compelling as a signal directly from the manager himself, but at least the runner is assured that the manager has weighed in.

KNOW THE MISSION

Knowing oneself is one kind of hard work. Knowing the mission is a different kind of hard work. I think it's an easier task, though, in part because there are more kinds of data, and they're usually easier to get at.

I mentioned before the necessity for an "extraordinary competence." Simply put, every strong leader has one or more of these skills. Alexander the Great understood people, and had an amazing grasp of logistics. Ulysses S. Grant understood topography—perhaps one reason why he was a remarkable horseman. Most successful business start-ups have a single figure, pushing them from behind, who simply knows more about something—how to make it, how to put it to use, how to sell it—than anyone else.

Work Hard

This is the motherhood-and-apple-pie entry in this chapter, but it needs saying. Nothing beats hard work and experience. Every one of my twenty experts, the men who were the first to join me in Saudi Arabia, was thoroughly versed in his particular trade. They had no trouble setting up their operations single-handedly, because they knew exactly what it took. They had little trouble earning the respect of their subordinates, who arrived in subsequent weeks and months, because our incoming troops—like most talented subordinates—were more than eager to learn from an expert.

Working hard is an ongoing responsibility, and it has good effects both up and down the ladder. As chief logistician in the Gulf, I felt that I had to be able to give Generals Yeosock and Schwarzkopf good answers to whatever questions they asked, at any time. This meant that, at least within the limits of the human brain and memory, I had to stay constantly abreast of where everything stood at all times. When I had a block of time open up unexpectedly, I used to take out our Red Book, which included up-to-the-minute status reports on all of our operations, and study it intensively.

Oftentimes, this focus on the nitty-gritty minutiae of my command led me into unexpected areas of thinking, and helped me anticipate the next major challenge. One of our major challenges in the Gulf was to stay a step ahead of the needs of our Saudi counterparts, some of whom tended to ask for things late in the game and then want them yesterday. One day several months after the ground war ended, as I was poring over my Red Book, I realized that our now-inactive firing ranges would soon be traversed by Bedouins again, and that those ranges were probably full of unexploded "duds." We made the removal of that unexploded ordnance a top priority, well before the Saudis thought to ask us to.

This was not easy work, but it paid off many times. By sticking to this kind of discipline, I got the reputation for anticipation, accuracy, mental toughness, and holding the reins tightly. When you have that sort of reputation you find that you begin to get better questions asked.

There is another aspect to working hard, and that is taking care of yourself physically. The Army makes physical demands that aren't normally made in the private sector, but good health is universally important. Endurance has to be built up; stress has to be reduced. I am convinced that corporations will devote much more attention to this problem in the future—not only because of the increasing costs of health care, but also because leaders are such a rare and valuable commodity. On a related point, I've discovered that unless the leader legitimizes physical fitness, it tends to be seen as unimportant. I exercise in part to avoid burnout, and I tell my people they're responsible for doing the same thing. A burned-out manager is of no use to the organization.

Hard work, including physical fitness, isn't a prescription with universal appeal. But it's inescapable. Peter Drucker says that leadership is "mundane, unromantic, and boring. Its essence is performance."[6]

An old Chinese proverb emphasizes the converse: "Lots of noise at the top of the stairs, but no one coming down."[7]

Build a Vision

"Where there is no vision," the Bible tells us in Proverbs 29:18, "the people perish."

Every successful venture grows out of a vision. Max De Pree writes that "the first responsibility of a leader is to define reality."[8] It's the vision of the enterprise that motivates, embraces, and sets limits, all at once. Such a vision may begin to hint at strategy, but it is almost certain to express values.

In the 22d SUPCOM, we created the first of our two visions based on my own experience, and also on the concise guidance provided by General Schwarzkopf before I left the States: take care of the combat troops. Early in the chaotic period of Desert Shield, we began broadcasting a five-word phrase: "Good Logistics Is Combat Power." The emphasis was on the positive; the five words were carefully chosen for their toughness, immediacy, and memorability; the ideas behind the words were complex. The sentence was easy to scan and to decode, and yet its implications were fairly complex. It had staying power.

Once the fighting ended, "combat power" became a secondary concern, and a new vision was needed. We settled upon General Yeosock's phrase, "Not One More Life," which not only emphasized the need for safety and security in a still-dangerous theater, but also linked Desert Farewell to the two dramatically successful operations that had preceded it.

Act on the Vision

Once the vision is articulated, it needs to be disseminated out into the world. This we did with a vengeance. We printed our mottos everywhere—on correspondence, at the bottom of all presentation charts and slides, on napkins, in our SUPCOM newsletter, on wall displays, on medals and citations, and in a hundred other places. You couldn't read very much or travel very far in my command without being reminded of our overriding mission in the Gulf.

The forceful vision helps your subordinates understand what they should strive to accomplish, but it doesn't give much guidance as to how to *get* there. This is the point of my next two topics: goals and objectives.

Set Goals

Amassing 80,000 people and saying, "Good Logistics Is Combat Power" won't get you where you want to go. It would be about as effective as assembling a brand-new team for a football game and saying, "Win."

Instead, the vision needs to be brought down one level of abstraction, and translated into a series of goals. My sense is that these goals should be top-down—that is, generated wholly or in large part by the leader(s)—and that they should be nonquantifiable. I suggest the former because it's important to strike a middle ground between concreteness and abstraction that still has enough emphasis on vision. I suggest the latter for the same reason. The bean-counters and quantjocks will get at your plans soon enough; meanwhile, let your vision have as much time in the sun as possible.

In the Gulf War, our goals took the form of phased plans. Our first, under-the-gun statement of goals consisted of three phases in four words: reception, onward movement, sustainment. Later, as the role of Coalition forces evolved, we elaborated on this early version, but tried hard to hold on to its simplicity.

To revive the football metaphor, when the vision is "win," the objectives might be along the lines of "shut down the offense," or "more productivity from the special teams," or "protect the quarterback." These are clear targets. They don't change much, except over long periods of time. They tell the team how to begin acting on the vision: emphasize this, worry less about that. They stop well short of dictating terms to talented players.

Set Objectives

This is the level at which visions, people, and resources come together in specific action plans. I generally insist that objectives be set by the people who will be responsible for carrying them out—and ideally, by those responsible for monitoring their implementation as well.

This is an absolutely essential underpinning for my notion of centralized planning coupled with decentralized execution. Although this is not exactly a new idea in management circles, I still find that many people are confused by it. How can you have something both ways? The answer lies in dividing responsibility along the lines I've just described. Visions and goals come from the top; objectives come out of the management trenches.

Objectives tend to be concrete, quantifiable and quantified, and tied closely to schedules. They change rapidly. A typical objective in the Gulf might have been to "reduce ship off-loading time from two days to one day without impacting safety." In football, an objective might be to "average 3.5 yards per carry on runs off tackle."

There are countless examples in military history that illustrate the perils of holding the reins too tight. Hitler located his headquarters far from the front—not a mistake, in and of itself, for civilian leadership—but from those relatively remote locations he then attempted to supervise the actions of his troops down to the minutest details. Unfortunately for his staff, he had an excellent memory for technical details and numbers, which he enhanced by an almost obsessive study of technical manuals. Hitler's memory was "the terror of his entourage," and he used it to enforce a near-total centralization.[9]

Thoughtful guidance, provided at the right moment, is crucial. During the redeployment phase, I one day found myself sitting through a briefing that was based on the premise that the Saudis would ask us to leave—lock, stock, and barrel—within twenty days. We were then at least several months away from being able to leave the theater. I couldn't fault my young logisticians, who after all were simply trying to anticipate all scenarios; but I had to amend their objectives to coincide with what I knew to be reality.

Watch Your Language

This is not an argument to ban swearwords or offensive jokes from the workplace—although as the work force expands and changes its composition in coming decades, that might well be a smart course of action. (George Washington attempted to prohibit cursing in the Continental Army, mainly because he thought it crude and unnecessary.) Instead, I want to make a pitch for semantic clarity. A shared understanding of the meaning of words is absolutely necessary as people set out on a complex undertaking.

"The military," writes van Creveld, "is forever seeking ways to make communications as terse and unambiguous as humanly possible."[10] At the same time, of course, the military is addicted to jargon and acronyms. Sometimes this verbal shorthand is helpful. It can lend vitality, intimacy, and accessibility to language that would otherwise be dreary. But if you're going to use words like "Ghostbuster" or "skull session" to describe important functions, you also have to make sure that people know what they mean. I use my bulletins, described below, to define terms; and this is one reason why I insist that people familiarize themselves with the bulletins.

Under the heading "watch your language" should also come another point: think of the impact of what you say. The casual aside or pleasantry from the head office can have huge rippling impacts out there in the organization. I once volunteered the opinion that a sergeant had perhaps been put in the wrong job; several hours later, he had a new job. This undercut the chain of command, and also led to an outcome that wasn't measurably better than the original posting.

Build Momentum

Max De Pree has argued that a leader is obligated to provide what he calls "momentum," which comes from "a clear vision of what the corporation ought to be, from a well thought out strategy to achieve that vision, and from carefully conceived and communicated directions and plans which enable everyone to participate and be publicly accountable in achieving those aims."[11] I agree. On a toboggan ride, momentum gets you through the flat spots; it gives the cyclist a chance to rest his or her leg muscles. The leader is in a unique position to push from behind, to add urgency, and to keep edges sharp throughout the organization.

Plow the Field

Change is uncomfortable. In most cases, it creates winners and losers. The leader has to help people prepare for change and live through it. This is especially true if the leader is ahead of the game—if he or she perceives before the rank and file that the old formula won't work much longer. Good communication helps, but some sort of compensation is better. As one student of human organizations has suggested, "In introducing change, protect incumbents by compensating them for their losses."[12]

In general, I avoid reorganizations. I think the efficiencies they make possible are far outweighed by the disruption and anxiety they create. When I do make a structural shift—usually as small a shift as I can get away with—I plow the field ahead of time. For example, I know where my key people are going to wind up, and I'm prepared to tell them why the change will be good for them, over the long run. During the Gulf War, I did form provisional units to fill voids to accomplish the mission, but once established, they only had minor changes made in them.

Behave Yourself

When a leader asks an organization to act on a vision, he or she must accept responsibility for embodying that vision—in other words, for behaving in ways that consistently reinforce the vision. It's not simply a question of being a good role model. Appropriate behavior involves examining objectives, and making sure that your implicit and explicit messages are in synch.

For example, in Desert Farewell, we promulgated the message of "Not one more life." This was intended to focus our people on safety and security. One day, it struck me that many of the people at our headquarters looked like the walking dead. They obviously weren't getting enough sleep, and they were poor advertisements for safety. But on further reflection, I realized that it was *my* behavior that was to blame. My staffers were trying to keep up with my 18-hour days, and then add an hour at the beginning and end of each day. I was putting them in a bind, and I had to change my schedule (in part by taking work home out of the office) so they would go home at a decent hour.

The point is to set standards, across the length and breadth of the organization. These are ethical standards, quality standards, and behavioral standards—levels of performance that people understand and can work toward. If they are not embodied and advocated by the organization's leader, they cannot prosper.

DEVELOP YOUR SUBORDINATES

I've never met or read about a successful leader of a complex organization who didn't focus on cultivating his or her subordinates. It's good for the leader, good for the subordinates, and good for the organization. "As the War Department moves you on up," General Eisenhower once wrote to a younger general, "you will find greater and greater need for people upon whom you can depend to take the load off your shoulders. The more you can develop and test these people now, the greater will be your confidence in them when you are compelled to thrust bigger and bigger jobs upon them." [13] Robert Kirby, the former head of Westinghouse, once said that the first thing he did upon taking a new job in that organization was to identify his potential successor in that job. This was the only way, he explained, that he would ever be able to move on himself.

Peter Drucker puts it this way:

> Because an effective leader knows that he, and no one else, is ultimately responsible, he is not afraid of strength in associates and subordinates. Misleaders are; they always go in for purges. But an effective leader wants strong associates; he encourages them, pushes them, indeed glories in them. Because he holds himself ultimately responsible for the mistakes of his associates and subordinates, he also sees the triumphs of his associates and subordinates as his triumphs, rather than as threats. [14]

Development is not only a function of training. It's also an outgrowth of constructive evaluations and goal setting, and an effective structure of compensation and other motivational devices.

Know Them

This may sound painfully obvious, but a good leader knows where the levers are. Since good subordinates are the best levers, you've got to know who's there to be called upon, and for what. This is a combination of personal traits and organizational position.

In the Army, it's the sergeant majors—the highest-ranking noncommissioned officers—who really implement policies in the trenches. I therefore made a special point of welcoming new sergeant majors into my command, telling them that I would count on them to instruct and motivate their own subordinates, setting standards and instilling discipline. Every organization has its functional equivalent of the sergeant major. The trick is to find them and use them effectively, without undermining the chain of command. My effort was always to make contact with these subordinates, several steps removed from me, and to encourage them to work their problems through the hierarchy. I was there as a last resort—but I was there.

Train Them

Whenever I enter a new command—and after I've gotten my feet on the ground, several times a year after that—I arrange to take a day or two away from headquarters with a group of key people from the command. We use this brief respite from our everyday activities to take a long look at what our organization is doing. These organizational effectiveness (OE) sessions give us a chance to work as a group, in a focused way, on identifying our short- and long-term institutional goals.

I find that these OE sessions are a great opportunity to get things out on the table, deal with differences, and eliminate confusion. To the extent that my management style and leadership techniques are unfamiliar to my subordinates, I have to be prepared to lay out all of the pieces at once, and give people a chance to understand how each part contributes to the whole. By so doing, of course, I also present myself. I convey my personal style and my visions for the future. It is essential for a leader to completely understand his leadership style and get it on paper. This is easier said than done, but it is critical if your subordinates are to understand why you do things and what you expect from them. Anyone who comes into an organization I have led is always given a document about what I consider my leadership style. Feedback I have received over the years from subordinates is that this one document has been invaluable to them, and has allowed them to be more comfortable immediately. This was critical with the rapid turnover of personnel in the 22d SUPCOM.

Follow-up OE sessions conducted within the same command are less focused on orientation and more focused on revitalization. We regroup, and—in relatively broad-brush strokes—reach renewed agreement on our shared goals and on the responsibilities of each individual to achieve those goals. Generally speaking, two kinds of problems emerge for resolution. In some cases, individuals have reached an impasse with each other, and need help breaking that impasse. In others, an individual or group has drifted into a position of opposition: to a policy, trend, and so on. People are at odds with each other or with the institution, and need help.

As noted, OE sessions are held at a site away from the command locale. This gets us out from under our distractions, and it also puts us on neutral ground. (Given the Army's tight budgets, we head for an underutilized military installation, rather than a corporate conference center.) To enhance the "neutrality" of our sessions, an outside facilitator is retained. Since he or she must have a clear understanding of my goals and techniques, I try and develop a long-term relationship with a few individuals skilled in this type of facilitation.

At the beginning of every OE session, I arrange to have plain white 3 x 5 cards placed at each person's seat around a table. As the session gets underway, participants are encouraged to write their questions and observations on these cards, which they are asked not to sign. The cards, participants are told, will be collected throughout the session, and will be read aloud at a designated time late in the session. At that time, questions will be answered and observations responded to. Almost invariably, this system of anonymous communication, in the context of a clear and simple process, helps surface some of the more volatile and difficult issues facing the command, bringing them out into the open where they can be dealt with and defused. I even plant a few cards surreptitiously—that way, I'm assured that the more important points of my organizational style will be surfaced and discussed.

Another technique I use is a version of what I call "three-up, three-down." Individuals are asked to assess in writing the performance of their peers, subordinates, or superiors in terms of three strengths and three weaknesses. (Obviously, this exercise presupposes that a certain amount of trust has already been built up.) As soon as I adopted this technique, I started reading that I wasn't a very good listener. Well, the first dozen times you encounter a specific criticism, you may choose to ignore it; after that, you're just being foolish. I took my critics' comments to heart, made adjustments, and was very pleased when "good listening skills" began turning up as one of my *strengths*.

Over the day or two of the OE session, the group participates in role-playing sessions that concentrate on team building. Individuals assess the one-, two-, and three-month objectives of their area of the command, as well as projecting a 24-month goal toward which they would like to work. I always set aside at least an hour and a half at lunchtime for people to take a break, get some exercise, and relax. And I end the sessions on an informal note, usually a barbecue or potluck supper for participants and their families.

These sessions have proved to be so valuable that my wife, Cheri, has run sessions specifically for spouses. Spouse OE sessions allow soldiers' husbands and wives to discuss the military and their relation to it in a structured way. Information from these sessions is channeled to improve the organization, in the same way suggestions from regular OE sessions are processed. For example, Cheri may tell me after such a session that my officers' spouses feel that those officers are working too late, or too many days a week; this is a perspective that I have to factor into my approach to management.

Our OE sessions help reinforce the values and the goals of the Army, mainly by stressing the fact that what matters is not weapons, vehicles, or buildings, but people. The sessions combine formal education and informal support, and help develop a "critical mass" of individuals who are both sensitive to the vision of the institution and adept at the interpersonal skills necessary to the completion of a mission. I'm sure that every complex business could identify similar needs, and devise good ways to meet those needs.

Training can't be restricted to these formal opportunities for learning, of course. Training is the constant and continuing responsibility of the leader. In my commands, I try to anticipate when a new or newly heightened challenge is coming upon us, and get my managers committed to training their people intensively before that time. "Be a teacher," I tell them constantly. In such a situation, every minute spent on training saves hours of time, further down the road.

The best example from the Gulf came during redeployment, when in a short span of time almost every individual in my entire command changed. We had to educate the newcomers in every minute detail of the command—for example, in the fact that our Muslim drivers would not work on their holy days (Thursday and Friday). In less than a month, we trained more than 6,000 new volunteers to do a wide variety of complicated tasks, with almost no loss of efficiency or decline in safety standards.

Finally, I am convinced that training is a great way to avoid institutional stagnation. The machine that is functioning at 100 percent efficiency may be the hardest to change—and may therefore get left behind by changing circumstances. I push my subordinates to push *their* subordinates to stretch themselves. What kind of specialized training could they pick up that might push us in a new and productive direction?

Review Them

Interpersonal skills, along with technical skills, smarts, and experience, are building blocks of performance. But it's not enough to put someone into a position of responsibility and then let them go. People demand and deserve feedback.

The Army has a formal institutional review mechanism, known as the Evaluation Report (ER), by means of which each individual is rated annually by a superior officer or NCO of his or her command, and also senior-rated by a second officer or NCO. The ER examines technical skills; assesses interactions with subordinates, peers, and superiors; and projects potential for advancement and present and future value to the organization as a whole.

Unfortunately, at least in my experience, the ER is not always used to its full potential. It can and should be a learning tool for the ratee. But when things go wrong—such as in the case of a personality conflict between the rater and the ratee—it can degenerate into a club in the hands of the rater. One sufficiently negative rating can effectively end an individual's Army career, short-circuiting any possibility of advancement.

In the worst case, the individual gets blindsided. He or she doesn't even know that the performance rating is unsatisfactory until it's a done deal and in the file. I have a simple solution: make sure that a bad ER also reflects badly on the rater. Why? Because that rater is the one with the responsibility to train his or her subordinates. Direct and focused feedback on performance, on a schedule that allows response and improvement, is a vital element of development. If that doesn't happen, the leader should be judged at least as harshly as the led. I realize this concept is almost impossible to achieve, but I still think there is some merit to it.

For many years now, I have implemented officer evaluations by

means of a two- or three-step process, and I have encouraged my
subordinates to adopt the same method. Normally, an ER occurs
after someone has been in a position for about a year. I make a point
of setting up two meetings for pre-ER evaluation sessions, scheduled
to take place at regular intervals during that first year of the individual's tenure. At these first two meetings, I candidly talk about how
I see the individual's strengths, and I highlight what he or she has
done well. I also identify those areas in which I want to see improvement. Because these sessions are understood to be dry runs, the subordinate usually feels free to point out things that I may have missed,
or things that might be getting in the way of good performance. In
other words, I can learn things about myself and my command that
I might otherwise have missed.

This three-step process doesn't always result in perfect ERs, but
it does give people (rater and ratee) a chance to deal with minor
character flaws or idiosyncracies before they become career-threaten-
ing issues. It helps them figure out what the ratee enjoys and is good
at, so that action, rather than reaction, is the focus.

Earlier I made the case that in order to lead you have to know
yourself. By the same logic, your subordinates have to know themselves before they can assert leadership. When you help people develop a better understanding of their abilities, and help them test
those abilities in new ways, the entire organization benefits.

Motivate Them

"A prince should show that he is an admirer of talent," wrote Machiavelli, "by giving recognition to talented men, and honoring those
who excel in a particular art."[15]

The private sector has a great deal more flexibility and experience
than the military in the realm of monetary compensation, so I won't
belabor that obvious point: people need to get paid well for what
they do well.

Perhaps because I have never had the luxury of being able to hand
out large bonuses, raises, or even titles, I have had to concentrate on
other types of recognition. The Army is sometimes criticized for
being overly preoccupied with medals and citations, but this is one
wellspring of that preoccupation. You have to use the tools that are
available to you.

I take care to send handwritten thank-you notes to subordinates
who have turned in an exceptional performance. I single out people

by name at meetings, applauding their good work. When medals and other awards come down the pipe—as they do quite regularly—I try to make an appropriately big event out of it. I'm not one for high-flying and exaggerated language, but I do make sure that the photographer is there to record the moment for Mom and the local newspaper.

Going out of your way underscores the significance of an award. Wal-Mart's president, the late Sam Walton, used to show up at 2:00 a.m. on the night before the opening of a new store, with coffee and donuts for the crew who were frantically putting on the finishing touches.[16] Walton's motivational technique is interesting for its novelty and flexibility: he didn't simply settle for a "cashier of the month" award; instead, he thought up a new and institution-specific type of reward.

The other component of motivation, of course, is staying out of people's hair. One of the leader's continuing goals is to build trust; and one way to do that is to demonstrate that you are willing to place your trust in someone else. Recognizing and placing value on the intellect of subordinates, granting them autonomy in defining objectives and meeting them, is a key motivational device—and it doesn't cost anything. Give them enough guidance so that they don't flounder and waste time, and then get out of their way.

"Mistakes will be made," comments William McKnight, former CEO of 3M Company, "but if a person is essentially right, the mistakes he or she makes are not as serious in the long run as the mistakes management will make if it is dictatorial and undertakes to tell those under its authority exactly how they must do their job."[17]

NASA learned this lesson the hard way in November 1973, when a team of astronauts in the Skylab space station turned off the radio and refused to deal with Mission Control, which had offended the team's professional pride by being too intrusive.[18] Applaud your people when they're good, and also make sure you leave them alone long enough to be good.

Break Molds

Although I hate institutional reorganizations, for reasons outlined above, I'm a strong advocate of reshuffling the deck in creative ways. I'm usually the captain of my basketball team. (This is a general's perk that I invented.) In that capacity, I don't hesitate to experiment with my lineup, moving people around on the court to find out which position suits them best.

When people get in a rut, they tend to get complacent: "I know how to do this, no problem." Once they start thinking like that, they are at great risk of getting sloppy, or falling off the cutting edge—or even of forgetting how they got there in the first place. Some American League baseball teams have started requiring their pitchers to take batting practice again, despite the fact that the designated-hitter rule almost guarantees that they won't have to go up to the plate. Why? Because it helps the pitchers understand the psychology of their opponents, and how their own skills can best be put to use.

The commanding officer or NCO does not have the firing power of his civilian counterpart. The Army makes it difficult to get rid of somebody, unless they violate their oath, break the law, or transgress against moral standards—and even then, the decision is left to an impartial board. I try to make a virtue out of the necessity of assignments. Everyone has skills and abilities; the trick is to match the individual with the challenge. The leader who fires someone too quickly, or shunts someone off into another department, risks hurting both the individual and the larger institution. Breaking the mold shouldn't translate into breaking the individual in the mold.

In the Gulf, as in my previous commands, I made a point of personal growth beyond the limits of the job. I trained the members of my personal staff to be multifunctional. My driver/bodyguards had to be aware of far more than their vehicle-maintenance and protection responsibilities. For example, they were the maintainers of the 3 x 5 card system mentioned earlier, and which I describe more fully below. The best of them could get on the telephone with their counterparts at other commands and move things along, according to my instructions. Obviously, managers have to be sure that subordinates don't start getting selective in the information they channel. Within that overall caveat, though, I try hard to break molds, and push responsibilities down into the system.

DEVELOP YOUR TOOLS

The leader creates visions; leaders and good subordinates together develop goals and objectives. A third major ingredient in the leadership mix is tools, which individuals use to carry out objectives, and which organizations use to reinforce the vision and assess progress toward objectives.

I have developed a collection of tools that seem to reinforce each other very effectively. Some are old techniques only slightly modified to accomplish new ends; others are bigger departures from tradition.

The Bulletin and the SITREP

I first started using Command Bulletins back in 1977, as a commander of a transportation battalion at Fort Eustis. By that point in my career I had put together what seemed to be a pretty distinctive management style. As I have said, I decided that the most efficient and effective way to make sure that everyone in my command understood my expectations was to commit them to paper, and make them required reading for everyone.

By design, my bulletins aren't numerous or lengthy. But they do cover all of the issues that are major and consistent concerns to the command. Some are durable and travel with me from job to job, such as assignment of responsibilities during VIP visits, the expected level of cleanliness in quarters, how to prepare for an internal audit, and budgeting and reporting procedures, and, of course, my leadership style and techniques. Others are more command-specific, such as the one I wrote to help troops understand and be respectful of the Saudi Arabian culture.

Since the bulletins are supposed to be practical guides, the topics they cover are presented in very specific detail. On the other hand, they are liberally salted with explanations of the philosophy and techniques of my leadership style. Once a soldier reads my bulletins—which every person entering my command is required to do—he or she not only knows what behavior is expected, but also has a pretty clear sense of what I'm about as a person.

I hammered away on the theme of the bulletins at every possible opportunity. For example, at briefings with relatively new officers I simply asked for a show of hands: How many had read the bulletins? If I heard a question I had already answered in a bulletin, I steered the questioner toward that bulletin in no uncertain terms. My expectation was—and is—that my subordinates will refer to the bulletins for guidance as they confront new situations. Again, I aim for centralized planning with decentralized execution. The bulletins sometimes give the whole answer; more often, they help subordinates shape better questions.

During the Gulf War, we also complemented the bulletins with a daily situation report. The SITREP was a statistical summary, distributed first thing in the morning to all members of the command. It was also sent to General Schwarzkopf's Central Command, General Yeosock's Army Central Command, and the Pentagon, representing as it did the single official status report and update on the activities of the 22d SUPCOM. Before the first meetings began each day, therefore, everyone had an opportunity to be briefed on the status of the command. Like the bulletins, the SITREP served as a common platform of information upon which people built during the course of the day. I often said that I was providing my people with a house—walls, stairs, floors, and so on—but that I wasn't furnishing the house. That was their job.

The Stand-Up

The "stand-up" is one of two types of meetings in my leadership tool kit. It's almost like it sounds: during this meeting all of the participants stand up except me.

The stand-up is a morning meeting and is as old as armies and businesses. It probably started simply as a means of counting noses. General Eisenhower made a point of getting his top officers together every morning for a combined status report and pep talk. I've tried to respect these objectives, but I've also amended the morning meeting in two fundamental ways. First, anyone in the command, regardless of rank, was welcome to attend. Second, the entire assembly would stand during the session.

The first of these two modifications was a deliberate effort to reinforce the free-and-open exchange of information within the command. To ensure that there was a reasonable mix of people present, I required that one representative of each specialized function attend the meeting—most often, but not always, the commanding officer.

The second modification worked toward other purposes. At the stand-up, only I sit (along with a note-taker). Everyone else stands. From the outset, I wanted to place a strict time limit on the stand-up. I was determined that it should start precisely on time (at 8:00 a.m.), and end at or before 8:30. Early on, I discovered that making people stand up keeps the ball moving at a quicker pace. People speak their piece, and then quickly yield the floor to the next person. On the rare occasion that someone starts to get long winded or wax philosophic, an unmistakable kind of body language begins to sweep through the crowd. People shift from foot to foot, fidget, look at their watches—and pretty quickly, the conversation comes back into focus. It's an interesting phenomenon. I can't recall the last time I had to crack the whip. The peer group has great power.

I once read about a corrupt sort of stand-up that Hitler engaged in. Apparently, he would sit himself down at a map table while his generals stood around him discussing the campaign in minute detail. It must have been a bit like being sent to the principal's office. Hitler evidently used the technique as a power play and an intimidation tool. He also allowed his stand-up generals to drone on into the small hours of the morning, which presumably didn't help them stay sharp.

Earlier in my career, the stand-up commonly consisted of a mere half-dozen people. Not so in Saudi Arabia. In early August 1990, word got around that this strange 8 a.m. meeting was the best place to get the straight skinny on what was happening in-theater. Soon, so many people were attending that we had to move to a larger location. On any given day, about three out of four of those in attendance didn't need to be there. They simply wanted to keep up with what was happening.

During the Gulf War, the stand-up was a chance for people to make quick status reports and then throw out questions for clarification. Topics tended to bubble up as dictated by outside circumstances. Sometimes we heard first from people who were attending to a continuing problem; other times we listened to a new challenge or opportunity. From week to week and month to month different groups dominated the front ranks of the standees. Early in the war, when construction was a key concern, the engineers seemed to be front and center. Later, the MPs and ammo experts came to the fore.

The stand-up, as it evolved in the Middle East, was a mix of loose and tight. There was no agenda, and no one was excluded. On the other hand, all functional areas had to be represented. If a designated attendee couldn't make it, he or she had to take responsibility for sending a subordinate instead. That subordinate had to be prepared to make appropriate contributions, and to brief the absent superior officer at the earliest possible moment.

Communications flowed in every direction, including some unexpected ones. For example, once it became apparent that certain people could always be found at the stand-up, other people began attending the meeting to catch up with those individuals.

The burgeoning size of the stand-up was invaluable for communications across functional areas, but bigger wasn't necessarily better for all purposes. For example, trial balloons didn't float well at the stand-up. Certain kinds of confidential issues, such as personnel problems, were inappropriate for that context. At the suggestion of Ken Guest, therefore, we established a daily meeting of the "Top 6" generals. This meeting also started exactly on time at 8:30 a.m., and never went more than thirty minutes. Most mornings, we managed to conduct our business in a half hour or less.

The Sit-Down

I run a second meeting in the early evening, known formally as the "1700 command and staff meeting," and informally as the "sit-down" or "1700" (5 p.m. on the 24-hour military clock). As the name implies, this is a meeting at which we sit down, enabling us to engage in a more concentrated kind of analysis.

My staff in a predetermined set of specialized areas present the guts of their business in a series of charts and graphs, and collectively we brief each other on the status of the entire command, topic by topic. As at the stand-up, the sequence of the presentations shifts and they get more or less emphasis according to what's happening in the theater at a given moment. But unlike the stand-up, the presenters and the other members of the staff are expected to take time to dissect and delve into issues.

Whenever possible, I like to have the "action officer"—that is, the individual who is responsible for a particular event, battalion, movement, and so forth—give the briefing, rather than their superior in that functional area. In my experience, this is the best way to get good answers fast. The action officer knows off the top of his head whether he has enough trucks for a specific task, or if his people are adequately trained to perform a given maneuver. In addition, it is an opportunity for me to size up my action officers, and to recognize their contributions publicly.

The presentations observe a specific format, although individuals are free to elaborate on the basics as necessary. The prescribed format is another kind of "three-up, three-down" analysis. Each officer presents three areas in which significant progress is being made, and also identifies three areas that are currently posing real challenges.

This format elicits very good information. First of all, people like a chance to toot their own horns. And, having done so, they're surprisingly willing to point out their area's shortcomings. The fact that this exercise is performed every day also softens the blow, since today's "down" can and eventually should be one of tomorrow's "ups." Also, the action officer will list what corrective action was taken to fix the down. This is a great way to correct problems rapidly at the lowest level. An example of this during the Gulf War had to do with unloading ships. The standard was twenty-four hours for a roll-on-roll-off vessel. This particular ship was off-loaded in twenty-six hours. Next to the down the action officer commented that two hours were lost because the bus didn't show up to take the stevedores from their quarters to the pier. The corrective action was to preposition the bus thirty minutes before departure to allow for reaction time if there was a problem with the bus. Prepositioning a bus thirty minutes before pick up was more cost-effective than losing two hours in off-loading a ship with critical cargo for the war.

One important task in the sit-down is to establish a fast and efficient pace of business. Once you lose the back several rows at a briefing it's very hard to get their attention again. I don't hesitate to move things along, sometimes by interrupting with a question, or by offering a summary statement.

A friendly and informal tone is an important element in the sit-down. (For one thing, it's the only way to get people to challenge the boss, and the boss—in this case me—absolutely has to be open to challenge.) In the Gulf War, we obtained a few popcorn makers, one of which was permanently installed in a small room next to our conference room. Throughout the sit-down, big bowls of popcorn circulated up and down the tiered rows of seats. (Once a week we showed a Three Stooges movie to accompany the popcorn, and to stress informality.) So although the pace was fast, the atmosphere was friendly, and consistently focused on problem solving. It was highly unusual for anyone to try to pin blame on anyone else. Instead, people listened hard, made good contributions, and helped information flow.

Two final points on stand-ups and sit-downs: variety is the spice of life. Have your subordinates run these meetings occasionally. This underscores that other people are valuable, and that you are not indispensable; it also prompts subordinates to work on communications skills. A good note-taker can provide the information of the meeting as if you were there, plus allow others who missed the session to be updated.

Speaking more generally, work environments change constantly, and regular meetings should reflect and encourage that change. If some aspect of your meeting schedule stops working, adjust it, and say why you're doing so.

The 3 x 5 Card

If someone in the Army has heard anything at all about Gus Pagonis, what they've probably heard about is 3 x 5 cards. I've seized upon these humble little cards as a way to goose the hierarchy, and push news—of both problems and opportunities—all over the command.

The system, which I talked about somewhat earlier in the book, is as simple as the technology on which it's based. When someone wants to draw attention to a potential problem, get an answer to a question, or just pass along some information, they fill out a 3 x 5 card and send it to some appropriate destination: either across a functional line, or up the chain of command. That card keeps moving through the hierarchy, or across functions, until it reaches someone who can respond with good authority. The card is annotated with some kind of response, and then goes back down the organizational ladder to the person who wrote it.

Most often, a 3 x 5 card is sent merely to report on or update a decision made by someone out in the field. The information gets disseminated to all the appropriate parties, and may prompt discussion at either the stand-up or the sit-down. Other times, a tough question gets asked, and makes it all the way to my desk. In Saudi Arabia, about 1,000 cards were generated every day. Of these, between 60 and 100 got to me, arriving by messenger in a steady stream, all day long. I would scan them, scribble a comment, and turn them back over to the courier. Green ink was reserved for me. When the system saw a card with green ink, the system knew that the problem had gotten to my desk.

The 3 x 5 system is a rough equivalent of a good E-mail system in the private sector, and I have used my 3 x 5 card system in staff jobs when my staff all had computer terminals at their desks. Actually, I used E-mail and 3 x 5 cards simultaneously. I think, however, that the lowly 3 x 5 has several advantages over its high-tech relatives. First of all, they are the ultimate in portability: you carry them in your pocket. Second, you're not depending on power sources, batteries, modems, or other variables. (We did use a fax for the period when we had two headquarters.) All you need is a card, a pencil, and some means of moving the cards from one location to another. I believe messages that are transmitted verbally, or from screen to screen, are too ephemeral to be effective. The 3 x 5, by contrast, doesn't go away. As it moves around, it physically nudges people into action. It's less of a solo manifesto and more of a group solution.

Like the stand-up and sit-down meetings, the 3 x 5 card system reinforces the idea of communality and teamwork, and underscores the value that the system places on open communication. But unlike the meetings, the 3 x 5 lives outside of schedules. Once a card is written, it gets sent to headquarters on the next available vehicle. Cards travel up and down the command within hours or minutes of being written, and are guaranteed a 24-hour turnaround. Most make the circuit much more quickly. Why such a speedy turnaround? If an action officer gets an answer within hours rather than days, then he or she has that much more time to act on the problem at hand.

During the war I received cards from soldiers of all ranks, at locations as close as within the LOC or as far afield as inside Iraq and Kuwait. By the same token, my aides and I had a pretty good sense of those areas that we hadn't heard from in weeks, sometimes months. During Desert Farewell, for example, material dumps were critical. It was in these facilities, located in and around ports, that decisions were made about what would be salvaged and what would be scrapped. I made a point of visiting these facilities and soliciting 3 x 5 cards on specific topics, such as retrieval of certain goods on a monthly basis.

One of the best aspects of the 3 x 5 system is the elimination of lengthy papers. It is amazing how all the information needed by a decision maker can be placed on a 3 x 5 card. I normally tell my people that if it won't fit on a 3 x 5 card, then they are telling me too much. Also, fitting information on a 3 x 5 card teaches subordinates to write precisely and to the point. It cuts down on everyone rewriting the paper as it moves to the top. Furthermore, it accelerates the movement of the information to the right decision maker in a timely manner. Three by five cards have reached me in hours or less when a paper could have taken days. Remember: bad news doesn't get better with time. The card sysem also allows the sender to provide his or her version of an incident. Finally, the bottom line is that a 3 x 5 card can have a tremendous effect on a decision maker, especially if it is sent from the lower levels of an organization to the top. Actually, by the time 3 x 5's get to me, action has normally been taken and a problem eliminated by the chain of command. I always have a special holder on my desk for 3 x 5 cards so that I can get to them ASAP and see to it that they don't get lost in the normal paperwork.

Please-See-Me Time

I make a point of setting aside up to an hour and a half each day for 15-minute blocks of what I call "Please-See-Me" time (PSM, for short). These blocks of time get allocated in a number of ways.

Sometimes a 3 x 5 gets a green-ink scribble: "PSM." The recipient then gets in touch with my staff and takes the next available slot. In other cases, issues arise about which I want to know more, but which don't (yet) warrant taking up valuable time at a stand-up or sit-down.

PSM time blocks not scheduled by me can be reserved by anyone in the command who has a problem or a question. Scheduling is based on first come, first served, and no pulling of rank is allowed. I have turned away generals to keep appointments with privates—and surprisingly, the generals seem to approve of this policy.

I get uncomfortable when I start seeing that my PSM time blocks are filled for the foreseeable future. The Boston Celtics have sold out every one of their home games for over a decade; nevertheless they hold back a certain number of seats for sale on the day of each game. I take that to mean that they're worried about seeming remote and inaccessible to the man on the street. Since my PSM time is supposed to help make me accessible, I keep after my staff to hold aside a block or two, here or there, for the occasional walk-in.

APPLY YOUR TOOLS

Tools are made to be used. I have stumbled upon a number of techniques and circumstances that make good tools work better. Because I'm a logistician, most are designed for use before the fact, rather than after the fact.

Find Leverage Points

Trying to get things done in a huge organization has been compared to pushing around a 200-pound sponge: you lean on it, and it swallows you.[19]

The solution is to find what I call leverage points, where you can apply your tools to greater effect. Is the 200-pound sponge sitting on a platform? Could you get a forklift under the platform?

One such leverage point is the in-house newsletter, as well as other types of internal communications. I made a point of getting in touch with our editor regularly, giving him guidance without yanking his chain unnecessarily. In a similar vein, I was pleased to discover one day that among our reservists in the Gulf were several network TV producers and cameramen. I gave them an opportunity to make a short video about Desert Storm, and they soon produced an extremely high quality show which we put to all sorts of good uses.

One very successful consulting firm got its start in a Midwestern city by identifying and commanding what it called the "strategic narrows" of that city—the four or five top-tier companies whose actions were usually imitated by the second- and third-tier companies. Leverage points accomplish the same thing within an organization.

Make It Visual

This is another motherhood-and-apple-pie statement, but since so many people seem to ignore it, I'll go ahead and say it: a good leader uses visual tools.

This first became clear to me in the context of the sit-down, where certain presentations that should have been barn-burners came off as dry as dust. Worse than being boring, they didn't *tell* me anything.

From that point on, I insisted that my officers take care in making sure that their slides and charts were graphically compelling, and that they conveyed useful information. It's easier said than done, but it's absolutely worth doing right.

One reason is because if it's done right in one application, it's usually right for another application as well. For example, many of the charts generated for use in the sit-down also wound up in the Red Book, referred to earlier. This red three-ring binder captured all pertinent information about logistics in the theater, including the

progress of specific actions and movements, the deployment of soldiers and materials, the status of contracting, host-nation relations,
and so on.

I requested from the start that all charts presented during the
sit-down (and therefore eligible for inclusion in the Red Book) have
three characteristics. First, they had to be substantive. Second, they
had to be useful—that is, they had to not only report on a given
situation, but also suggest directions for future planning and serve
as a tool for decision making. And third, they had to be visually
informative and appealing, or else they would waste people's time.

For example, I required substance, usefulness, and visual appeal
in follow-up presentations as Desert Farewell drew to a close. A set
of charts prepared by the log cell describes the entire operation of
reception, onward movement, and sustainment.

One of the charts summarizes the movement of cargo ships during
the operation in a very interesting way. It would have been simple,
but not particularly compelling or easily decodable, to put up a list
of numbers stating how many ships entered the theater, how many
were off-loaded, and so on. Instead, the message of the chart was
communicated in large part through graphics: a boat is placed in the
Atlantic, with text indicating that every day 100 ships were en route
to Saudi Arabia; a ship is placed at the dock in Ad Dammam, with
the legend "15 ships discharged daily"; and an aircraft is shown
filled with soldiers, heading toward Southwest Asia, and marked
"5,000 troops entering the theater per day." A list of compounded
totals, written simply at the bottom, completed the chart.

Charts are indispensable for daily interaction, and they present
information of statistical and historical significance. Every element
on those slides had to add something—and once a chart ceased to
inform decision making, it was immediately removed from the
lineup. A chart can develop a life of its own, and, before you know
it, several people will be maintaining these unneeded charts when
they could be working on other productive efforts. In the Gulf, I
used to tell my subordinates that we were making history, and that
these charts were the written record of that history. They had to be
done right. But I had a rule: if we were using forty charts for our
1700 sit-down update and added two new charts, the staff were
required to present two charts for elimination. Sometimes we would
exceed the forty-chart standard, but not for long. If you want to
keep your meeting to a specific time frame, watch the number of
charts used and how long each person talks.

Skull-Session It

Another innovation which I have found absolutely invaluable is what I call the skull session. The best way to describe this tool is by means of the tried-and-true football analogy. The skull session, I tell my troops, is a way to do our Monday morning quarterbacking on Saturday night. In other words, rather than sit around for hours or days after a disaster berating ourselves, we try to anticipate and head off the disaster. It works, too.

Before implementing a particular plan, I usually try to bring together all of the involved parties for a collective dry run. The group includes representatives from all appropriate areas of the command, and the goal of the skull sessions is to identify and talk through all of the unknown elements of the situation. We explore all possible problems that could emerge, and then try to come up with concrete solutions to those problems. Skull sessions reduce uncertainty, reinforce the interconnection of the different areas of specialization, encourage collaborative problem solving, and raise the level of awareness as to possible disconnects in the theater. They also teach soldiers to think differently—more expansively—in the long run. They are both near-term scenario-building exercises, and longer-term vision-expanding exercises.

One of the most common questions asked of me by journalists, both during and in the wake of Desert Storm, was, "What was your biggest surprise?" I took that question to mean, "What weren't you prepared for? I always frustrated the journalists on that score, since I could honestly say that there was *nothing* that surprised us, and nothing that we weren't prepared for. This is not to say that nothing went wrong. Lots of things went wrong. But the fact is, we never had a problem for which we had not already discussed potential solutions. This happened, among other reasons, because of the skull sessions. We were able to stay on top of events because very few were unanticipated.

REEDUCATE YOURSELF

It's almost redundant to say this at this point, but here goes: learning is never over, no problem is solved forever, and good answers may be found in unlikely places.

Measure and Quantify

Some leaders would put this first. Even though I'm a logistician, I'll risk putting it toward the end. I don't think it's worth generating a lot of numbers if you don't know what they mean, or how to use them. Most of the advice in the preceding pages is designed to set the stage for meaningful number crunching.

Objectives, as described above, are quantifiable. So are other kinds of longer-term trends that cut across functional areas. Most corporations have solid expertise in this area, so I'll defer to that expertise. Once you're sure the stage is set adequately, crunch away. Check all those numbers against some kind of reality, as described below. And finally, make sure that the information is available in a format and on a schedule to be put to some kind of sensible use. I used to tell my deputies in the Gulf that information was only useful if it could be acted upon—and information could only be acted upon if it was made available to action officers with sufficient lead time.

Find Your Critics

According to organizational theorists Kaplan, Drath, and Kofodimos, leaders are all too often cut off from their critics: "The exercise of power keeps executives from getting personal criticism that could lead to the awareness of deficits."[20]

I've already advocated management by walking around. Keep your ear to the ground. Read between the lines of the 3 x 5 card, and look at facial expressions during meetings. It's amazing how much people tell you without saying anything—and how easy it is to follow up in person when you get one of these cues. My father was right: you've gotta get your hands dirty.

Find Evidence to the Contrary

And finally, look for evidence to the contrary. By this, I don't mean contradictory evidence. I mean that evidence that pops up just after you've settled on a course of action, and is just a little bit irritating and unsettling. It may be only a slight variation on something you've already come to grips with, but all the same, it's just different enough. Most often, it's the people down in the ranks who know where the *real* bugs are in your proprietary software, or the real limits in your new manufacturing process. As you set out to bet the company, it's worth taking a deep breath, and listening to that evidence to the contrary with a fresh ear.

You have to be prepared to reverse yourself. During the Gulf War, I received a request to move the Bedouin tent that housed our LOC a few feet in a given direction. The reasons seemed compelling enough, and I wanted to give my people some free rein. A few hours later, though, I got the bottom line for this seemingly inconsequential hopscotch: $50,000. I made a point of telling people at the next sit-down that I had made a dumb decision, by acting on partial information.

Sometimes the evidence to the contrary is first felt in your gut. I recall, for example, that hectic interlude when General Schwarzkopf assigned to one of the Army units the responsibility for setting up facilities for the peace talks in Safwan, Iraq. Except for providing tents and building materials, my command had no direct responsibility for these preparations. But the night before the talks were scheduled to begin, I found myself with a gut feeling that all was not well in Safwan, and I flew up there in a Blackhawk helicopter to take a look. Nothing had been done; all of the necessary materials were stuck in a monumental traffic jam on the road from Kuwait. To make a long story short, we flew back, pushed the materials up the highway, and worked all night setting up the facilities, finishing a half-hour before General Schwarzkopf and the other participants in the negotiations arrived.

A leader has to be prepared to act on these kinds of hunches. Until we figure out exactly how the brain is wired, we'll have to assume that "evidence to the contrary" is being sorted and sifted in ways that sometimes show up in your gut.

TAILOR THE SYSTEM

In this chapter I've tried to present my ideas and tools in a way that may help in the picking-and-choosing process. The main headings, such as "Develop Your Tools," are ends. The entries under those headings, such as "The Sit-Down," are means toward those ends. I'm pretty confident that the ends that I've outlined are important to leaders in almost any context. The means to those ends may be less universally applicable. They have worked for me, and I think they've worked as a package, reinforcing each other. But they won't work for everyone in all places, or at all times. People change; circumstances change; technologies change. Leading 50,000 people is very different from leading 50 people. Don't shed light where there isn't any darkness, as a wise old officer used to caution me.

My final prescription, therefore, is to tailor your system. This grows naturally out of the previous step: reeducating yourself. You've developed ways to measure and quantify progress; now apply the lessons of those statistics to retool. You've turned up the critics and listened to them; now act on their criticisms in a positive way. You've found plenty of evidence to the contrary; now get tough, and use it.

Chapter Eight

Lessons in Leadership and Logistics

AT THE OUTSET of this chapter, which examines some of the lessons I've learned and observations I've made as a result of my three decades in the service, it might make sense to pose a logistical challenge to the reader. As we think through the many aspects of this puzzle, we will inevitably invoke questions of leadership as well. With these two issues fresh in our minds, we can proceed to assess some enduring lessons in leadership and logistics.

So, let's imagine that you decide you want to take 1,000 of your closest friends to a Penn State football game. (Perhaps you're interested in observing the grand master of teamwork, Joe Paterno, at work.) This plan, for better or worse, is your strategy. We'll assume, first, that you have at least 1,000 close friends, most of whom would be pretty likely to accept your invitation. We'll also assume that once they've accepted, you can be confident that they'll show up at the appointed time and place. What's your first step? It's when you ask this question that you begin to think logistically: Given the stadium strategy, how are you going to implement it?

First, you might want to think about ticket supply. If the season schedule is already sold out, of course, you're out of luck: time for a new strategy. On the other hand, if Penn State isn't drawing, you have nothing to worry about—you hold off buying tickets until after all your RSVPs are in. You count your acceptances on the day before the game you've selected, go downtown, buy just enough tickets a few minutes before the box office closes (retaining the use of your money for as long as possible), and pat yourself on the back for a job well done.

What about the gray area, though? What if your team sells enough seats, regularly enough, so that you can't count on a last-minute purchase? What happens if, at the end of next week, 1,000 friends have accepted and you can only scare up 900 tickets? If there are 2,000 tickets available right now, should you buy your 1,000 now and forget about it? Or should you hang on to your money for a few more days? Should you buy a few extra? Would you be comfortable throwing away 100 tickets on the day of the game?

Then there's the issue of transportation. You've decided that you really need to bus your 1,000 friends from the train station at Lewistown to the stadium. (They've never been to the Happy Valley before.) Through a quick calculation of friends-per-bus, you figure that you need ten buses. Unless you own a bus company, you'll have to hire the buses. You find a bus-rental outfit in the phone book, call them up, strike a deal, and sign a contract: "ten buses to and from the stadium on such-and-such a day for such-and-such a price."

Now you've cracked the transportation nut, right? Maybe. Or maybe you start to hear troubling stories about fly-by-night bus companies in the area who are overselling their vehicles and depending on equally fly-by-night subcontractors to bail them out. Can your contracted bus company deliver what they say they can deliver? How much time are they allowing between the end of the previous job and their scheduled arrival at the train station? Is that allowance realistic? If they own only four buses, where are the other six supposed to be coming from? Will they all be equally well maintained? What if one breaks down en route—is there any kind of backup? Do the buses have radios?

And wait a minute: you've told your friends to meet the buses at the train station. It's a big train station. Maybe you should have said, "Meet me at Track 1, at the train station." Now what? A second round of invitations, with better instructions?

The tickets arrive in the mail, and you notice on the back that the university takes no responsibility if you or your friends get hit by a thrown or kicked object. You start to wonder: Are *you* liable if your friends get injured? Under what circumstances? And speaking of injuries, what kind of medical care is available, if worse comes to worst?

Maybe the stadium only sells hot dogs. You begin to wonder if any of your friends hate hot dogs, are allergic to hot dogs, or have religious objections to eating hot dogs. If so, what will they eat? If there's a two-beer-per-customer limit, how will you treat 1,000 friends to a beer?

What if it rains?

Most important of all: in my premise, I asked you to assume that you had at least 1,000 close friends, and that once they had accepted, they would show up at the appointed time and place. But the first thing I tell my junior officers about logistics is, *Never assume anything!* The logistician who assumes things quickly goes down the chute.

I've played out this example at some length because—at least for a football fan—it frames some key logistical questions in accessible terms. For example: What are the supply and transport issues inherent in a particular strategy? Where are the potential bottlenecks? Is there a sequence according to which these issues have to be addressed? Can they, or should they, or must they all be addressed simultaneously? At what point (if any) does the strategy get modified to accommodate logistical realities? What kinds of experts need to get involved, and when? What can you assume about this situation? *(Answer: nothing! Attack assumptions!)*

The stadium parable also suggests some questions that are less obvious. To take just one example: Should the strategist and the logistician be the same person? On the scale of the stadium example, of course the answer is yes. But on a larger scale, or over greater distances, the answer at some point becomes no. (How big a party do you throw before you hire a caterer?) If a half-million people need to be moved to the other side of the world to accomplish some complex and dangerous goals, it's surely time for a division of labor. But a division of labor, too, holds inherent risks. If you divide the strategic and logistical tasks among two or more people, how do you ensure that all of these people understand and buy into the strategy? How do you keep them all pulling in the same direction?

This is where leadership comes in. Logistics is people, at its heart; and that means that it's never an exact science. "Logistics is a word that sounds scientific," as one trio of private-sector logistics scholars has pointed out. "It implies that we know the answers and have the techniques. It may hint at a field of activity relatively devoid of human content until we remember that, even in this golden age of technology, there are still more people in this world and in this country lifting and transporting things than are engaged in any other principal job assignment."[1]

Murphy's Law says, "If it can go wrong, it *will* go wrong." The logistician acknowledges the real-world wisdom in that law, and responds in two ways. First, he or she tries to keep as many options open as long as possible, even after identifying and pursuing a particular alternative. Second, within the constraints of time and budget, he or she tries to build (just enough) redundancy into the chosen alternative so that a minor oversight, shortfall, human frailty, or mishap won't doom an entire strategy. The logistician doesn't deny Murphy's Law, but instead tries to quarantine its potential impacts.

In the wake of operations as big and complex as Desert Shield, Desert Storm, and Desert Farewell, there are literally millions of observations that could be made. I'm sure that generations of students at the various senior service colleges will be looking at our experiences carefully, and will be teasing out observations and lessons topic by topic for decades. My own recommendations are necessarily going to be a bit selective. My contracting ace, Dan Bartlett, has recently written a 24-page monograph comprising his observations and recommendations on contracting, based on his Gulf War experience. I'm sure that every one of my several dozen functional experts could write a similar paper; and pulled together, these very useful commentaries would run hundreds (or thousands) of pages.

I'll stay at a higher level of generalization. First I'll make some observations about what needs to be fixed, from my perspective; and then I'll summarize what *doesn't* need to be fixed. As I make these observations, the reader should remember (as I do) that we all need to think in terms of trade-offs. Every additional dollar that we allocate to logistics will have to come out of the dollars that are needed for more and better combat equipment. These will be tough decisions, in which a lot of people will participate. The reader should also understand that there were certain things that we were unable to do during the Gulf War, because we didn't have certain kinds of equipment. Tight budgets and tough choices have been the order of the day for many years.

My point in all of this is not that the American taxpayer should be asked to buy everything that the Army can think of, in order to respond to every conceivable type of crisis. But it's clear that if we can collectively agree upon a number of plausible scenarios (which would obviously include a rapid deployment to the desert), we can then procure at least a bare minimum of the kinds of equipment that will support that deployment.

WHAT NEEDS TO BE FIXED: TRANSPORTATION

The first point to be made is that in the Gulf we had serious shortages of certain kinds of transportation-related equipment. Although sealift was not in my domain, it's clear to all of us who were involved in the Gulf War that the United States needs to augment its fast-sealift capability. Given the increasing need for our Armed Forces to project themselves rapidly into a theater—perhaps without any military logistical infrastructure—we must ensure that we can move our troops and equipment across the oceans. The eight fast-sealift ships that were available to us in the Gulf did a remarkable job. In fact, based on that performance, Congress has already taken the necessary steps to purchase more such ships.

In the same vein, the C-17 aircraft, which can carry a tank far forward into battle, will be a tremendous asset and improvement. The current C-141 transport can't carry a tank (although the C-5A can). The C-17 also has the capability to land on dirt runways, which may be necessary in cases where the infrastructure is not as good as Saudi Arabia's. In this case, too, Congress has approved more funding for this valuable force-projection tool.

Different needs arise once the equipment is on the ground. For example, our divisions had an average of only six Heavy Equipment Transporters (HETs) apiece. In total, the Army had only 112 HETs available, and the Marines 34.[2] (By contrast, the Iraqi army had more than 3,000.) This was in part the result of our Eastern Europe scenarios, in which it was assumed that we could use railroads to move our tanks eastward, at least up to the point where the rail gauges became incompatible.

The tight fiscal constraints of recent years have created a zero-sum game for the Army: if you buy more of this, you'll have to buy less of that. Up until the Gulf War, it was assumed that we'd be better off using our limited resources to buy relatively more tanks and relatively fewer trucks. But in Saudi Arabia, we soon learned that HETs saved us from two major kinds of problems, already discussed in previous chapters. One was wear and tear on our tanks; the second was wear and tear on the roads. If we had driven our tanks on road surfaces that were heated to 120 degrees, for example, the resulting damage to the roads would have made it impossible to move our logbases out of Dhahran and up to the front. The incoming supplies would then have buried us in Dhahran.

Logisticians are paid to look at reality. The only realistic alternative to full-fledged HET companies is to count on either in-theater availability, worldwide cooperation, or both. This doesn't seem like a safe bet. We might not have made it in the Gulf without the HETs that Saudi Arabia, Germany, Egypt, and the Eastern bloc so generously provided. In how many contexts can we count on our allies, let alone our former Warsaw Pact adversaries, to equip our armed forces? I think that we're now moving toward solving this problem, since funds are being made available to form HET companies within our Army corps. In an ideal world, we'd have something like a 1 : 3 truck-to-tank ratio; we'll have to see what the real world permits.

The performance of our third-country national drivers was nothing short of heroic. But a truck is no good without a driver, and as we address the issue of HETs, drivers must also be considered. Full-fledged HET companies will solve part of the problem. But to the extent that we decide to rely on local and/or contracted drivers, we need to understand fully what we're getting in to. We have to recognize that practicing Muslims won't drive on Thursdays and Fridays. We need to anticipate difficulties if large numbers of drivers are driving into a country that is apprehensive about concentrations of foreigners. We have to take responsibility for treating our drivers as well as we treat our soldiers. (At first, many of our drivers were being asked to drive north without gas masks, even though all of the U.S. soldiers directing their efforts were required to carry their masks with them at all times! We did eventually procure enough masks for the host-nation drivers as well.)

HETs ensure mobility, but so do sufficient numbers of highly mobile equipment, called HEMTTs (heavy expanded mobility tactical trucks). This includes tankers, cargo trucks, and wreckers capable of traversing the rough terrain where tanks are expected to go. Lacking enough of these in our system, we put them all forward in the DISCOMs; but a clear case can be made for having them in the COSCOMs and the SUPCOM as well. Why? Because the SUPCOM had to go into terrain that was very rough and difficult. We were fortunate that the weather held up, and that the rains didn't cause a total disintegration of the limited road networks that our engineers were able to build behind our attacking units. The 5,000 rented tankers with commercial chasses had a very difficult time as it was; they would have been immobilized if the roads had washed out.

WHAT NEEDS TO BE FIXED: MATERIALS HANDLING

Another critical shortage was in the area of materials handling equipment (MHE), which includes forklifts, mobile cranes, and so forth. As was the case with the HETs, we managed to rent, lease, and otherwise contract for our MHE in Saudi Arabia. But those 500 ships, thousands of airplanes, and millions of tons of equipment that they carried would have been utterly useless to us without the means to unpack them and prepare their contents for transshipment. We need improvement in two general areas: first, in the category of rear-area equipment, which can be solved with buying or renting commercial equipment; and second, in the category of rough-terrain, forward equipment, which is more specialized, isn't normally available in the host-nation civilian economy, and must therefore be brought into the theater by the armed forces.

Equipment alone will not solve our problems in the MHE area. I, for one, am convinced that the Army has to create and maintain formal MHE companies. I've noticed that every healthy soldier in the world thinks that he's an ace forklift operator. Most of them are wrong. We need to identify specific people, and then train them in these demanding jobs.

A third key equipment shortage was in refrigeration vans, needed to keep water cool and food edible. Every single one of these had to be rented in-theater; and fortunately, the Saudis happened to have more than 2,000 of these available for lease. Clearly, we would have been in a very difficult situation if the host nation had been either 1) poor, 2) hostile, or 3) both. Refrigeration vans are, of course, only indispensable in the desert. But as we engage in new and deeper rounds of defense budget cuts, we should keep this precedent in mind. Is there critical equipment needed for, say, arctic combat that we don't have access to?

Equipment shortages weren't our only problems. In-theater processing of containers also presented a major headache, for a number of reasons. One big contributing factor was multiple consignees for a single container. (These containers are the 40-foot variety that travel down U.S. highways on tractor trailers.) This resulted from the eagerness of our Stateside, European, and Korean shippers to fill every container to the brim, which would ensure that every ship was filled to capacity. Given our limited shipping capacity, this made good sense—at least until those ships disgorged their cargoes in Saudi Arabia. Then it turned into a classic example of suboptimization. We had numerous mixed loads, and even a large number of unidentified containers. The documentation on the ship's manifest didn't always jibe with what was in the containers. We had to open some 28,000 of the 41,000 arriving containers right there on the docks just to find out what was in them. We hauled a lot of containers 2,000 miles out into the desert only to find that 10 percent of their contents were intended for the front-line troops, whereas 90 percent belonged to units back near the port.

Early in September 1990, I issued an edict: 90 percent of incoming containers had to be single-consignee. The remaining 10 percent, if absolutely necessary, could be mixed. This held up for a few months, until VII Corps arrived in the theater and the supply flow intensified again.

In the wake of the war, there has been some criticism of the Army's bar-coding system.[3] In my experience, the system worked well enough, as long as the information encoded was correct. Bar-coding is no different from any other data-storage/data-retrieval system: garbage in, garbage out. Industry is certainly ahead of us on this count, but I don't think the Army has any apologies to make. We drew from an inventory of some 5 million different items, which is 10 to 100 times the level of complexity of inventory management in the private sector.[4] I'm told that the Army is now working to develop a sophisticated bar-coding system that won't penalize either the shipper or the receiver, and will allow the computer control to extend past the port to entry to the field units.

Meanwhile, it seems to me that we will have to swallow hard and live with some 20-foot containers, in addition to the standard 40-foot model. Use of a smaller container will ensure that a single consignee can fill that container up. Failing that, we will have to live with the fact that some 40-footers won't be full, and that therefore some ships won't be full. This, again, is a case where a logistician can make a good case for suboptimizing the shipping function in defense of the overall mission.

WHAT NEEDS TO BE FIXED: DOCTRINE

In the broad sense, the Army's logistical doctrine doesn't need to be fixed, and this is good news. I think most observers would agree that there were some hidden biases in our doctrine, mostly because our past experiences and post–World War II expectations steered us toward war in Europe. All in all, doctrine guided us well, and allowed us to improvise as necessary. Contrary to some fanciful media reports—such as the one that compared me to the lightfingered Milo Minderbinder in *Catch-22*[5]—the 22d SUPCOM was not a band of logistical outlaws. Our innovations and provisional structures fit well under the umbrella of doctrine.

Doctrine, moreover, is not revised on the basis of one data point, but on the basis of multiple data points. In Panama, during Operation Just Cause, we had unlimited supplies of potable water, since the Panama Canal Commission was willing and able to make water available to us. But the Army couldn't decide, based on the Panama experience, that well-digging units could be eliminated from doctrine. In a less affluent or receptive desert environment than Saudi Arabia, those water units would have been indispensable.

Nevertheless, I think we can anticipate some adjustments to doctrine. One of the most important concerns the single point of contact. Had we followed doctrine to the letter and not created the Support Command, we would eventually have had several logisticians simultaneously attempting to control critical and limited logistical resources. I think our experience demonstrated the clear advantages inherent in having a single point of contact for all resource management and contracting, especially in a host nation where certain resources are limited.

My expectation is that henceforth a TAACOM (like the 377th, based in New Orleans) will consist of at least 100 active-duty soldiers, commanded by a brigadier general. If there's a war or serious threat of war, that general and those 100 soldiers will be sent in to set up the theater. They will be at the top of the TPFDL, in part because they'll travel light: duffelbags and checkbooks.

I make this projection with some confidence, because Army Chief of Staff General Sullivan has made a strong case that the future Army will be a projection force—projecting power into a region on a rapid basis—rather than a forward fielding force. This means that in most future conflicts, the first job of the logistician will be to "capture" the host-nation infrastructure. That, in fact, was the role I performed for Yeosock in Saudi Arabia. I used his transportation group, his POL (petroleum, oils, and lubricants) specialists, and MPs to "capture" and channel the civilian infrastructure, and it worked well.

I suspect that a key element of the 100-person active-duty TAA-COM will be the Materiel Management Center (MMC) with exclusive responsibility for putting in requisitions for materials from the States. Again, the single point of contact has multiple advantages. Only an organization with that kind of theaterwide vision can determine whether the requested item can be obtained locally, or is sitting on a prepo ship, or is already in a nearby warehouse. In the 22d SUPCOM, we were able to do some of this, sometimes—in fact, by November 1990, we were screening up to 90 percent of all requisitions this way—but before and after that point in time, our percentages were much lower. The result was that a lot of material wound up in-theater that eventually had to be shipped back again.

I should underscore the key role of the prepo ships one more time. While we were "capturing" the Saudi infrastructure, we were living off the equipment and supplies brought to us on those ships. I've already made the point that the prepos enabled us to survive during those first few weeks in Saudi Arabia, and any future doctrine will have to take this obvious fact into account.

It seems clear that the logbase concept proved itself, at least in this particular desert context. Our willingness to place these bases alongside (and in some cases, in front of) the combat-arms troops was surprising to some, but I would argue that it didn't contradict established doctrine. Instead, we tailored doctrine to the needs of the theater. We restricted the logbases to the smallest number of absolutely indispensable items—food, fuel, water, and ammo—mainly to ensure that they'd be movable as the front line advanced.

The log cell, and the division of labor between the log cell and the Logistics Operations Center (LOC), drifted a bit further away from logistical doctrine. I'm not prepared to argue that all logistics units, everywhere, henceforth have to set up a log cell. Nevertheless, it makes eminent sense to separate out the long-range planning function from the logistical operations that support combat on a day-to-day basis—and also to make sure that the former stays closely tuned in to the latter's activities.

As I've made clear, the mix between reserve and active-duty units has turned out to be a great boon to the logisticians. Our reserve units, which as noted above made up almost three-quarters of my command, were highly talented and motivated. I must emphasize a personal conviction at this point: that we cannot afford to move any more spaces from the active CSS force to the reserve structure. In fact, I'd argue, we must contemplate moving some spaces in the Materiel Management and Materiel Control areas back from the reserve side to the active CSS structure.

WHAT DOESN'T NEED TO BE FIXED: EQUIPMENT

Observations like these should include comments in the "if it ain't broke, don't fix it" category. The most obvious point to make here is that by and large, our equipment worked—either well, very well, or spectacularly well. This was a remarkable performance in and of itself; it was all the more remarkable because the public's expectations regarding that performance were so low. These expectations were based, in part, on the failed 1979 mission to rescue the Iranian hostages, which came to an unhappy end on a very similar-looking desert. Those gloomy forecasts simply didn't take into account all the improvements of the intervening decade. The M1A1 (Abrams tank) and the M2 (Bradley Armored Personnel Carrier) performed superbly and demonstrated on the field of battle that they are the best tank and carrier in the world. Both in the daylight and at night the Apache helicopter achieved the same result—total devastation of the enemy.

Some of the good equipment-related news could only emerge in a true combat situation. For example, we logisticians learned that we had overestimated the fuel-consumption rates of the M1 tank, mainly because the tanks had never been driven more than about 100 miles in our desert training centers. When greater distances began to be covered in combat situations, the tanks got better mileage, and the logisticians got a better feel for what we can expect in the future.

There was early concern about the blades on our Apache helicopters being abraded by sand thrown up in updrafts; this concern was greatly exaggerated and the problem was easily remedied. The concerns about our weaponry being too "high tech," and therefore too easily fouled and choked by fine desert sand, were also unfounded. We discovered early on that changing filters on a regular basis avoided most of these kinds of problems.

Finally, there is the category of "wish it could be like that next time, too." There are two main entries in this category. First, the

Saudi infrastructure, particularly its northeastern airports and sea-ports, was absolutely first-rate. Several dozen ports around the world poured hundreds of fully loaded ships into two Saudi ports—Ad Dammam and Al Jubayl—and except for some brief shortages of warehouse space, those two ports were up to the task, and then some.

Second, and even more important, Saddam Hussein made the mistake of letting the Coalition say when the war would start and how it would be fought. For reasons I've never seen adequately explained, he didn't seize the initiative when he had it. He then failed to back down even after it was obvious that he couldn't prevail militarily, and that we were resolved to eject his forces from Kuwait. He was, in effect, only an intermittent aggressor, and I don't think we can count on being so lucky in the future. Most aggressors are more determined.

MILITARY LOGISTICS AND BUSINESS LOGISTICS

As many a soldier and businessperson has discovered, analogies between the Army and the private sector don't always hold up. Some of the dissimilarities between the two sectors are fundamental, and important; others turn out to be not so important. Before we can decide who can learn what from whom, we have to make sure we're comparing apples to apples.

What's the biggest difference between logistics in the military and in the private sector? Without a doubt, it's our respective bottom lines, and how we think about them. The military focuses on life and death, whereas business measures profit. Both my youthful entrepreneurial experiences and my MBA training convinced me that profit is an important and meaningful measure—in the long run, it determines whether a given company lives or dies. But *real* life, and *real* death, tend to change all the calculations. We in the military must sacrifice some measure of efficiency to maintain a higher margin of safety. We stockpile a little (or a lot) extra, just in case. We build a redundant system, such as my shadow command at KKMC, just in case.

"If the logistic system in question is not to be hopelessly fragile and liable to catastrophic breakdown," writes one observer of military affairs, "if it is to function under changing circumstances and be capable of switching from one objective to the next; if, in short, it is to be capable of coping with the uncertainty that is the result of enemy action and, as such, inherent in war—in that case a certain amount of redundancy, slack, and waste must not only be tolerated but deliberately built in."[6] There are few for-profit concerns that live comfortably with redundancy, slack, and waste.

Another difference, which I think is an important one, lies in the management of career paths, and specifically, when it is that individuals are normally asked to assume major responsibilities. The military places a great deal of responsibility on very young people. A captain in his twenties may have personal responsibility for hundreds of lives. A technician barely out of high school may control machinery worth millions of dollars. The young Air Force pilot brings these two awesome responsibilities together, holding both lives and a hugely expensive piece of technology in his hands. There is no comparable experience to be had in the private sector, at least so early in one's professional life.

Believe it or not, that's just about my whole list of real differences between management in the military and in the private sector. To strengthen my case, let me run through some of the differences that may appear to be important on first glance, but which I think tend to fade away under closer scrutiny.

Different, and Not So Different

For example, it is often said that it is patriotism, pure and simple, that accounts for most heroic accomplishments by individuals or groups in the military; and that there is no equivalent motivating force in the private sector. There's certainly some truth to this. If the United States were faced with invasion from, say, Manitoba, I'm absolutely sure that the patriots of North Dakota and Minnesota would perform magnificently. And it's also true that there's probably nothing else that would motivate those people to perform in just that way. Rational human beings wouldn't make the ultimate sacrifice for Amalgamated Widget Co., Inc.

But we can certainly point to successful military interventions (perhaps even the Gulf War) that weren't dependent upon excesses of patriotism. And it seems to me that the motivation systems in the private sector are often different from the military's in degree and focus, rather than in kind. The truth is, great companies can inspire great performances on the part of their workers. For the right company—one that is in desperate trouble, and can make a compelling case for its survival—workers will make extraordinary sacrifices. In some cases, they will even *buy* the company.

It is frequently suggested that the officer's ability to give orders, and to expect that they will be obeyed, is a major difference between management in the military and in the private sector. When the general tells the private to hop, as legend has it, the private hops. That's true enough, as far as it goes; but all of my experience suggests that someone in my position has to win the loyalty and respect of his or her subordinates—their hearts and minds—before they can hope to get anything done well. Yes, the military is an authoritarian and hierarchical structure, designed to elicit obedience. But this is no guarantee that orders will be obeyed blindly. I alluded earlier to the "radio difficulties" that an officer encounters just after issuing a dumb order. Suddenly the radios don't work, and the order is ignored. The private sector certainly has its own version of this phenomenon.

The turnover rate is certainly much higher in the Army than in industry. I welcomed over 6,000 new people into my command in August 1991 alone—a near-100 percent turnover of my command at that time. This huge influx represented a considerable challenge in terms of vision building and education. On the other hand, many of these people arrived with both a common base of procedural experience (they were all soldiers) and a specialized base of knowledge in common (they were all logisticians of one sort or another). It seems to me that whereas industry hires its workers in much smaller batches, it doesn't have the benefit of these shared experience and knowledge bases. The advantages and disadvantages are offsetting, more or less.

I have also heard it said that a big difference between management in the Army and in the private sector is that the private sector is much better at getting rid of people—and, when necessary, of whole functional areas. Not so in the Army, or so the old military adage would have it: "Staff grows, paper flows, no one knows." This distorts reality. It's true that a low-status assistant vice president in business could probably fire a staffer more easily than a general could kick a subordinate out of the Army. But the general is not helpless. For one thing, he can arrange to have the offending individual shifted out of his command. (I have never done this, because it only means that you're passing the buck to the next guy.) He can also write up the offending soldier's next ER in such a way as to guarantee that the officer will want to leave the service, or will be asked to depart for reason of failure to be promoted.

There is another kind of evidence that suggests that our experience in the Gulf has relevance to business. As noted in earlier chapters, approximately 70 percent of my command consisted of reservists, most of whom came to me directly out of the private sector. Several of my one-star generals—including Tom Jones and Joe Conlin—were CEOs on loan to the Army through the reserves. Of course, the 22d SUPCOM was first and foremost a military organization. But it was heavily influenced by businesspeople. The good ideas in leadership and logistics that came out of the Gulf were tested and approved on the spot by people whom I consider to be some of the private sector's finest representatives.

Finally, there are a number of experts from the private sector who have already analyzed the logistical effort in the Gulf War and have concluded that our experience holds useful lessons for business. "Many of today's global or globalizing companies face critical logistics challenges of their own," writes Graham Sharman, a director in McKinsey & Co.'s Benelux office and a specialist in logistics. "The Gulf experience provides some useful lessons for such companies." [7]

LOGISTICS: OBSERVATIONS FOR THE MILITARY

I'm tempted to use the word *lessons* rather than *observations* to introduce this section. The reader should understand that the military learns lessons on many different levels. On one level, it learns as we did in the Gulf: every single day, in almost every aspect of its operations, with constant recalibration and fine-tuning. But lessons on this level aren't necessarily durable; they may need revisions within hours or days, and what's certain on Monday may be uncertain on Thursday. It will be years before we know with certainty which lessons of the Gulf War are durable. For that reason, I'll stick with "observations."

LOGISTICS: OBSERVATIONS FOR THE PRIVATE SECTOR

In a celebrated 1962 *Fortune* article, business expert Peter Drucker referred to physical distribution as "the last frontier of cost reduction. We know little more about distribution today than Napoleon's contemporaries knew about the interior of Africa. We know it's there, and we know it's big, and that's about all."[8]

Things have improved somewhat over the last three decades. Logistics, both in the military and in the private sector, has emerged from the Dark Ages. A recent colloquium sponsored by the Shell Oil Company identified two basic kinds of reasons for this increasing and overdue emphasis on logistics.

In the category of *contextual* changes, the authors of the study cite oil-price shocks, with the resulting emphasis on fuel efficiency; environmental concerns; faster market dynamics; increased volatility in exchange rates; and a tension between decentralization and integration. The key words describing contemporary logistics are, according to the authors, "dynamic, uncertain, consumer-driven, information-driven, operational decisions, integration, decentralization, flexibility, effectiveness, complexity."[9]

In the category of *technological* developments, the authors cite flexible manufacturing tools, new model-building tools, new computing tools, new industry-specific knowledge, better practical applications of existing theoretical models, and better data acquisition and processing.

Others cite these same forces, and point to the 1980s in particular as the period during which "the previously quiet logistics evolution became a revolution . . . [and changes] stimulated progressive North American enterprises to implement far-reaching changes in the culture and basic philosophy of logistics."[10]

This progress is very good news, since by most reckonings, the amount of money invested annually in logistics-related activities is roughly 11 percent of a country's GNP, and accounts for about 15 percent of the sales price of a product.[11] In recent years, producers and distributors in the United States have spent more than a half-*trillion* dollars annually on logistics—a figure about ten times greater than the average annual expenditures on advertising during the same period.[12]

For many years, logisticians in the Army have looked to the private sector for innovation. In some areas, such as bar-coding and satellite-based tracking, that is still the case. But our logistical successes in the Gulf War suggest to me that our colleagues in the private sector may now get some good guidance from us.

I have defined logistics as the integration of transportation, supply, warehousing, maintenance, procurement, contracting, and automation into a single function that ensures no suboptimization in any of those areas, to allow the overall accomplishment of a particular strategy, objective, or mission. Until the 1960s, these subfunctions were considered separate. There was an attempt made in the 1960s, under the broad rubric of "physical distribution," to integrate warehousing and transportation. This was a step in the right direction, but—as my definition suggests—it did not go far enough. There were, and are, many more functional areas that need to be integrated into the logistical realm.

Why, in an era of decentralization, is integration the way to go? Because, as I see it, logistics is a field that is particularly prone to suboptimization. Our logistical mission in the Gulf was to protect and provide for our troops, and thereby aid in the liberation of Kuwait. In support of this mission, our Stateside shippers made heroic efforts to stuff every Gulf-bound ship absolutely full, in part by topping off each vessel with mixed-consignee containers. Meanwhile, on the receiving end, our port operators were swamped, and—in support of the same overall mission—pleaded with me to ban mixed-consignee containers.

Create a Kingpin

What was needed to resolve that conflict and avoid suboptimization was a logistical "kingpin"—someone who could assess the imperatives of each functional area and decide upon a solution that best supported the mission. In the Gulf, I was lucky enough to be selected to serve as that person. I would argue that every complex organization that is involved in materials management, handling, and distribution needs my equivalent.

Some might argue that this integrating role belongs to the CEO. I disagree. The CEO has plenty of other things to worry about—monitoring the overall business environment, long-range strategy and planning, financial strategies, integration of the board of directors' guidance, and so on. The CEO, in other words, has to come up with the plan that logistics supports.

I am convinced that all companies above a certain size and complexity need a senior vice president of logistics, with explicit authority to cross functional boundaries. The Gulf War was a remarkable distillation of the factors that argue for a single point of contact in logistics—in fact, it was an extreme case—but I think that most companies experience attenuated versions of the same challenges we faced. Could we afford to have two corps competing for the same limited resources? No. Can a corporation afford to have its operating divisions working at cross-purposes? Of course not. A single point of contact in the logistics area is a good way to avoid suboptimization.

In fact, according to one study, many companies with acknowledged expertise in logistics already have some version of this person in place. In this select group, about three-quarters of the wholesalers, retailers, and "hybrid" wholesale-retail companies report having senior logistics officers at the vice president level or higher. But among the general manufacturing base, where one might expect an emphasis on logistics, only a third of companies report having a high-level logistician.[13]

Go for Credibility and Versatility

Where should such a logistical kingpin come from? Currently, many companies promote their most accomplished functional-area head into the position, but I think this is risky. It's very difficult for a person with a one-dimensional background in logistics to rise above that background. The integrator risks emphasizing what he or she knows best—and therefore risks not integrating. To cite a simplistic example, our senior vice president of logistics recently promoted out of the transportation area may always lean toward the solution that includes the lowest shipping rates. But most products with short life cycles can't go by barge.

Obviously, the top logistician has to have some relevant functional background to have credibility within the organization. (Within the Army, I was known as a port operator, an authority on LOTS, and an architect of REFORGERs, among other things.) But this kingpin has to have other qualities and experiences that are even more important. He has to be a motivator, an empowerer, and a politician, at least to the extent that people in all functional areas will be confident of his backing when their ideas further the objectives of the firm.

Equally important, the senior logistician has to have "skills sideway" and "skills upward." If he really is going to have authority to cross boundaries, he has to be able to deal with powerful colleagues on the vice presidential level. And he has to be someone the CEO *wants* to deal with—someone with whom the CEO wants to drink a cup of coffee, float a trial balloon, or blow off steam.

Sometimes I think the best person for this difficult position might be the founder of a small, successful business, most likely one with a heavy logistical component. This person has already done it all. He hasn't had the resources to hire specialists, so he's done it himself. He's had to get along with all kinds of people. He's had to train himself to keep his eye on the ball, even when day-to-day distractions were at their loudest. He's a proven orchestra-master.

There's at least one potential problem with this suggestion. The small-business ace is used to getting his way—whereas the senior VP of logistics *always* has to be prepared to be overruled, and come up smiling. For example, he may come up with a plan to shut down a half-dozen satellite warehouses in favor of a centrally located facility; and he may be able to demonstrate conclusively that through layoffs and other economies, this will save $1 million a year. The CEO may listen to this scheme, accept all of its elegant calculations, and still shoot it down. Why? Because only he knows the human resource implications, companywide, of firing a hundred people. Only he knows the ins and outs of the company's long-range expansion plans, and how warehouses (and local goodwill) fit into that picture. And if the company has a long-standing policy against layoffs, only the CEO can quantify the costs of abandoning that policy.

I have mentioned the notion of trial balloons, and I think it's important to acknowledge that in many or most cases, it's the CEO who comes up with the bright ideas. After all, CEOs get where they are because they've got higher than average amounts of vision and drive. Early on, General Schwarzkopf needed a sense of whether the end run scheme was supportable. Logisticians were able to give him an early reading, including some suggestions for revisions, that enabled him to "go public" with a stronger plan.

Grow Log Cells and Ghostbusters

I am firmly convinced that my corporate counterparts need a log cell, or its equivalent with a different name. Why? Because in my experience, it's all too easy to get a hundred high-priced people to spend a thousand hours talking about a disaster that has just happened. It's much, much harder to get ten people to spend a hundred hours trying to anticipate and head off a disaster. In fact, if a company doesn't make an explicit commitment to this kind of preventive medicine, it won't happen.

The organization needs to gather together a group of very talented people and take good care of them—which involves not only good compensation and career paths, but also an emphasis at the highest levels on good tasking and effective follow-up. The goal of this select group could be simply stated: "Help us identify our unknowns. Tell us what could go wrong with this proposed plan, and how we might avoid those bad outcomes."

I used my log cell only for logistical issues, which was as far as my theater responsibilities extended. But there's no reason why a corporate log cell, broadly defined, couldn't tackle other kinds of issues with complex inputs. Do we have a companywide succession planning function? How can our organization best investigate the long-term implications of adding a new employee benefit? Can the log cell—which has the great advantage of having no functional ax to grind—take a first cut at these and other difficult issues?

Depending on the types of issues that the log cell is asked to address, it should report to the CEO, the vice president of logistics, or the vice president of strategic planning. This call should also be made on the basis of the relative dynamism of the people involved. I was the CEO-equivalent within my organization, and for most of Desert Shield and Storm, the log cell reported to me. A log cell could easily report to the equivalent of a senior vice president; I have tried it both ways. The trade-off is obvious: it's better to keep the CEO's docket clear. But if the SVP of logistics or planning isn't sufficiently dynamic and farsighted, the log cell may simply wind up doing his staff work.

For these reasons, it's probably smart to think about a solid line from one of the senior vice presidents to the log cell, complemented by a dotted line from the CEO to the log cell. For a whole host of good reasons, I think the CEO should give the log cell at least an occasional assignment firsthand.

I also advocate a corollary to the log cell: Ghostbusters. I had decided early in Desert Shield that I needed a much better sense of what was actually *happening* out there in the field. I recruited a group of bright and politically savvy individuals to serve as my eyes and ears, and report back to me on our progress on specific fronts. Somewhat later, it occurred to me that the log cell and the Ghostbusters were really two pieces of a bigger picture, and that it was possible to train the log cell guys to serve also as Ghostbusters. Stated simply, the same person who dreamed up the plan could be tasked to see if it worked, somewhere down the road.

This would help keep the planning function fully rooted in reality. It would also make the life of the log cell's inhabitants—who would otherwise exist in unsplendid isolation—more varied and interesting, and thereby prolong their tenure on the job.

One management text I've read advocated that the leader create "alter ego employees," who would serve not only as the CEO's eyes and ears, but also as "credible role model[s] to follow in using your vision."[14] I prefer my "Ghostbuster" nickname for this role—it works better on T-shirts—but I like the concept.

Obviously, the log cell–Ghostbuster package is an expensive proposition, and not one that the corner grocery store is going to undertake. But medium-sized firms and bigger (say, with $100 million or more in annual sales) ought to be able to put together some sort of entity. I have run log cells as small as two people, and in the Gulf, as large as thirty, counting Ghostbusters. More is better, but anything is better than nothing.

Learn from History

In the preceding pages, I've been arguing for an integration, professionalization, and upgrading of the logistical function. Lest the reader think that this is just Gus Pagonis idling in neutral, let me point out that there are plenty of historical antecedents for these outcomes.

As far back as 1939, Goodyear's president Paul Litchfield created a logistical coordinating function within his organization. In the early 1950s, H. J. Heinz created a pioneering physical distribution department, which placed a broad range of functional areas under one manager, who reported to Heinz's executive vice president.[15] As noted earlier, however, this trend toward centralization (which I think is a prerequisite to logistical integration, professionalization, and upgrading) has run headlong into opposing corporate trends: disaggregation and decentralization.

"The long-term trend toward decentralization and the creation of autonomous business units," writes one observer, "has led to a fragmentation of logistics resources and facilities. In some cases, this has kept companies from improving overall logistics performance by achieving 'critical mass' in logistics know-how, new logistics-related technologies, and so on. All too often, shared logistics is relegated to a 'traffic council'—essentially a talking shop and focal point for annual price negotiations with transporters."[16]

Some companies have experimented with centralized logistical entities that are intended as profit centers—serving not only their own people, but also outside customers as well. If this is the future of leading-edge logistics, I look forward to it.

LESSONS IN LEADERSHIP

Back when I was a brigadier general in Germany in the late 1980s, I reported to a commanding general who had been in his post for about three years. One day, in the last week of December, the CG called me in and made an unusual request.

"Listen," he said to me. "Every New Year's Day for the past three years, this bunch of Frenchmen in uniforms—some kind of military band—has shown up in front of my house at 8:00 in the morning and started blasting away. I go downstairs, give them coffee, and eventually they go away. I want you to find out who they are, why they're doing it, and how we can get them to stop. I'm going out this New Year's Eve, and I don't want an early wake-up call. Plus, the neighbors have been complaining."

So I started digging into the mystery of the phantom band, and I eventually got hold of the French bandmaster. The bandmaster produced a letter, written some fifteen years earlier, that ordered him to perform at this particular house every New Year's Day. It turned out that my CG's house used to be the French CG's house. The bandmaster was still carrying out those orders, and obviously planned to do so until he was carried from the field.

What conclusions do I draw from this story?

Well, for one thing, nobody likes change. We're creatures of habit, we like the status quo, and we'll take the devil we know over the devil we don't every time.

For another thing, nobody wants to examine assumptions or explore threatening ideas. (This might lead to change.)

Over time, when we fail to examine assumptions or pick up obvious cues—like, how come the general doesn't speak French any more?—disconnects open up between means and ends.

As a result, bad things start to happen (the American general gets a brass reveille), and good things don't happen (the French general, wherever he is, doesn't get his wake-up call).

In my experience, it's leadership that gets new ideas into a system, and gets them accepted by that system. It takes a leader to reforge the ties between means and ends. It takes a leader to put trains back on the right track—to capture the talents and energies of the French band, and redirect them in new and productive directions.

In the next few pages, I'll try and summarize the leadership lessons which I think emerged in the context of the Gulf War.

Keep It Simple

If I had to pick just three words to summarize our experience, it would be these. On the way over to Saudi Arabia, way back in August 1990, we devised a plan that was only slightly more long-winded: reception, onward movement, sustainment. Later, we developed a five-phase scheme that grew directly out of our first plan, and which (with some elaboration) carried us through to the conclusion of Desert Farewell.

On a higher level of abstraction, we also worked hard to develop an organizing *vision* that could sustain our evolving plans. Our first organizationwide slogan, capturing that vision, was "Good Logistics Is Combat Power." Later, after the war was won and safety—rather than combat—was the overriding priority, we adopted General Yeosock's concept of "Not One More Life!"

We used every single tool at our disposal to disseminate and reinforce our plans and visions. Many of those management tools are summarized below (see "Communicate!"). But the first reaction of many first-time visitors to my headquarters in Dhahran was astonishment at our single-minded dedication to getting our message across to the organization. Everything we could squeeze some words onto—from flip charts to pencils to awards to memo pads—reinforced our organizing principle: "Good Logistics Is Combat Power."

In the seventeen months that I was in Saudi Arabia, we went through three sets of commanders and six complete turnovers of staff. Despite this revolving door, we didn't miss a beat. I think this was in large part because we simplified our message, and then communicated that message relentlessly.

Emphasize Training

The other side of this coin is staff development and training. I've already discussed this issue in the last chapter, so I'll simply hit some highlights here. Stated briefly, it's not enough to disseminate the

vision and the plan; the leadership also has to make sure that the
work force has the necessary skills to act on the vision.

Under the crush of circumstances between August 1990 and February 1991, we trained our soldiers on the spot, and as time allowed.
We were extremely fortunate that so many of our people came to us
with good training—and that they were flexible enough to learn on
the job when necessary. As soon as the pressures of Desert Shield
and Desert Storm eased off a bit, we became more systematic in our
training efforts. We actively looked for deficiencies and shortcomings
in the 22d SUPCOM, and implemented training programs to overcome these deficiencies.

In the broad category of "training" I would include orientation.
I think it was our special emphasis on orientation of new personnel
that made the redeployment out of Saudi Arabia possible. If I were
a CEO in the private sector, I'd make sure there was an orientation
session every month, and I'd be sure to be a visible presence at that
session. I'd ask key people to make short presentations—such as the
personnel director and the production manager—but I'd also look
for ways to promote more informal types of dialogue. Question-
and-answer sessions and get-togethers at mealtimes are useful. New
hires might be encouraged to bring in their spouses and/or families
for a day. I'd also make sure that orientation wasn't a one-shot deal.
After some specified period of time had passed, I'd arrange for a
follow-up orientation with a new slant—meanwhile continuing the
original orientation for new employees.

Training sharpens skills, but it also gets all members of the work
force on the same wavelength. People have to know their organization's competitive position, and the steps that are being taken to
improve that position. I would argue that they *want* to know this
information, too. United Parcel Service, certainly a leader in logistics,
runs voluntary workshops for its workers at the end of the day to
discuss just these issues. Four out of five employees, both the manager and the managed, attend these sessions.[17]

Let me conclude this section by emphasizing that the leader has
to take *personal* responsibility for teaching. As Major General Perry
M. Smith, a former commandant at the National War College, once
wrote,

> Teachership and leadership go hand-in-glove. The leader must be will-
> ing to teach skills, to share insights and experiences, and to work very
> closely with people to help them mature and be creative. . . . By

teaching, leaders can inspire, motivate, and influence subordinates at various levels.[18]

Go for Flexibility

It's more than a little unfair to ask the work force to be flexible without making the same demand of your organization. The leader has to ensure that organizational rules and structures don't get in the way of performance. This is especially true in customer-driven and service-driven businesses, which may have to turn on a dime to be responsive to their clients.

The best in-theater example of this was our effort (in cooperation with the Army Materiel Command) to repaint and upgun over 900 tanks on an ad hoc assembly line in the port of Ad Dammam. Our customers (the troops) made an urgent request, and we felt obliged to "customize" our operation in a way that hadn't been done before. We also assumed responsibility for bringing a wholly new class of ammo into the theater on short notice. In both cases, we had to disrupt the already fragile status quo, and find an innovative structure.

Similarly: when it became clear that our reservists would all be going home in the spring of 1991, we had to find a way to bring 6,000 volunteers into our system, and bring them up to speed immediately. To accomplish this formidable job, we organized over sixty provisional, task-specific units, and trained our volunteers within these units.

As noted earlier in this chapter, I think Army doctrine strikes a good balance in this critical area of structure and nonstructure. It provided us with a jumping-off point, and challenged us to do better. We were able to invent and reinvent our logistical systems as time passed, as the mission evolved, and as we got better at what we were doing.

This is as good a place as any to make an obvious point: nothing in what I'm recommending is sacrosanct, or won't be improved by tailoring to fit a specific situation. In fact, business (like war) is so much a moving target that tailoring is an inescapable obligation.

Change is inevitable (the French band notwithstanding); so organizational flexibility and responsiveness have to be built in. It has been pointed out that the Apollo moon missions were on course less than 1 percent of the time. The rest of the time, they were getting or awaiting mid-course corrections from Houston.[19]

Centralize Planning; Decentralize Execution

Everything I've said up to this point should underscore the importance of this, which is a central tenet of my philosophy. It is centralized planning that prevents suboptimization among functional departments—in the logistical field and elsewhere. It is centralized planning that creates the screen through which ideas, good and bad, can be filtered.

Equally important is decentralized execution. It has been said, and I firmly believe, that everybody is an expert within their own twenty-five square feet. In order to draw on that expertise, the organization has to download as much authority as possible. People need to be given a vision and a plan, trained, and then turned loose. Clearly, task-specific planning has to occur at every level of the organization (not just at the top).

One distinction I've made is between goals and objectives. Goals—which operate on the level of visions and plans—should be top-down and nonquantifiable. ("There will be no American presence in Saudi Arabia after January 1992.") Objectives are the collection of concrete, often quantifiable steps that must be taken to implement a goal. ("We will get this much ammo out by this date, and send this many Americans home; then we'll get the remainder out by this date in the following ways.") Objectives get defined and met on every level of a fine-tuned organization.

Communicate!

What makes the contradictory tugs between centralization and decentralization work? What keeps decentralized execution from flying off in every direction? The answer is communication.

My command in Saudi Arabia hinged upon a constant flow of communication: up, down, and sideway. These communications took three forms: 1) bulletins, 2) meetings, and 3) 3 × 5 cards.

My bulletins, issued on specific topics at irregular intervals, have played an important role in all of my commands. They help describe my leadership style and define terms (such as Ghostbusters), as well as set priorities. I'm convinced that semantic confusion is responsible for a large percentage of the problems that plague complex organizations; and as businesses cross borders and incorporate larger numbers of cultures and languages, this challenge will only increase. An inescapable starting point is the definition of terms, which I accomplish in my bulletins. I then use the shared terminology to get a specific message out. This message may be a high-level or relatively low-level one, depending on the needs of the moment.

In the Gulf War, I used a total of ten bulletins, on such topics as cultural orientation, management style, VIP tour procedures, preparation for outside inspections, internal audit reviews, and so on. I regularly asked my officers who had been in the theater for a few months if they had read my bulletins. Word got around. In some cases, new arrivals asked for them before we got around to supplying them.

New arrivals into an organization really want to know what the rules are. They want to have a roadmap, to help them get started in the right direction from Day One. It seems to me that all of us (even leaders) want to be led at first; but once we get our bearings, our needs change. Then we want more latitude, more slack in the reins, more running room. But still, we appreciate strong guidance in that first, difficult period when we're learning the ropes of an organization.

I've already covered my meetings in some depth. Let me say in this context that if I were in the private sector, I'd hold my stand-ups essentially unmodified. I'd start them on time, end them on time, make light of the fact that such senior people were being asked to stand up—and then I'd go right ahead and make 'em stand. Sit-downs would need more tailoring to fit the corporate setting. Absent some major corporate crisis, I'd probably restrict these to once a week, and participation in sit-downs might be done on a rolling basis. Divisions that were separated by distance might be included by teleconference; divisions that were in incompatible time zones would need case-specific solutions.

Again, the point is to surface and share information. Disagreements should be treasured (and resolved). I remember reading about a meeting chaired by Alfred Sloan at General Motors. It seems that everyone in the room agreed with the proposal at hand. "Gentlemen," Sloan allegedly commented, "I take it we are all in complete agreement on the decision here." He looked around the room, and found everyone nodding their assent. "Then," he continued, "I propose we postpone further discussion on this matter until the next meeting to give ourselves time to develop disagreement, and perhaps gain some understanding of what the decision is all about."[20]

Several of my private-sector generals have politely told me that I'm way off base on the meeting issue—that people's time in the corporate world is so valuable that companies can't afford to put all these bigwigs in one room on a regular basis. In response to this criticism I always smile blandly and say, "But what's the alternative?" So far, I haven't gotten a good answer. It's the same argument I use to defend the notion of the log cell: you're either going to plan up front, or you're going to mop up after the fact. Since the latter course usually costs much more, I'll take the former course every time.

Finally, we arrive again at the humble 3 × 5 card. One observer aptly concluded that I use these little white cards to "lubricate the hierarchy."[21] Very true; and this is the string that wraps up my communications package.

So far in these conclusions, I've implicitly respected the chain of command. Now I'll step outside of doctrine for just a minute, and acknowledge that sometimes the hierarchy has to be bypassed. Inevitably, there are times when a lower-level subordinate feels that the hierarchy has missed the point. The 3 x 5 card system is a way to register that complaint—but also to get the information flowing again. If it's the subordinate who has missed the point, then he or she has to hear that. If it's the superior who has missed the point, then a different kind of mid-course correction is called for.

Most issues raised by 3 × 5's are resolved long before they get to the top of the ladder. I think I reviewed only about a tenth of the cards that were generated daily, and most of the ones I reviewed were simply for my information. In some cases, I responded to an open question. In very rare cases, I made an on-the-spot decision to reverse the call that was indicated on the card.

I've used E-mail as a substitute for 3 × 5's, and it works pretty well, especially in small staffs where everybody has a terminal at his or her desk. Having tried them both, I'll admit to a preference for the low-tech approach. I think there's an implied commitment in one's handwriting—a certain vote with your hand and handwriting—that's not there as a result of keyboard pecking. And the physical object, the card which passes through several sets of human hands, acquires its own special impact.

Be Visible; Be Real

I've put these last two points together because I think they're inextricably related. The challenge of the leader is to be real to his organization. Being visible and accessible is a great way to get there.

In the four months before D-Day, General Eisenhower visited twenty-six divisions, twenty-four airfields, five warships, and a variety of other installations.[22] (His subordinates were also circulating constantly during this demanding period.) According to his biographer, Ike talked to literally hundreds of troops in the field, and, "wherever he went, he talked, asked questions, listened, observed. He was patient, clear, and logical in his explanations to his officers and men on an informal basis, got to know them, listened to their gripes, and, when appropriate, did something about them."[23]

Ike was dealing with an exceptionally demanding leadership challenge, but I take note that his response in those extraordinary times was to get out, listen, talk, and be visible. He learned a great deal, but through his presence also conveyed the fact that he was a very human leader. His troops repaid him with great loyalty. I think the identical transaction occurs in less dramatic contexts. If you're real to someone, they perform for you. If you're not, you take your chances.

I circulated constantly during the Gulf War. I personally welcomed every troop into the theater, except when extraordinary circumstances prevented me from doing so. At my wife's urging, we had young soldiers to our house twice a week for many months. (Photos taken with the general help make the general real.) I ate with my soldiers, swam with them, and played basketball with them. All of these gestures combined to make my soldiers feel that I was there for them, and would look out for them.

In my experience, a sense of humor almost always helps in the "reality accounting." It is, as one student of human nature observes, the emotional equivalent of a sense of reality,[24] and inoculates the leader against taking himself or herself too seriously. It also helps break tension in stressful situations, and gives the subordinate an easy way to affiliate emotionally with the leader.

I used to end some of my organizational effectiveness sessions with a homespun and hokey "Karnak the Magnificent" act, borrowed directly from Johnny Carson on the "Tonight" show. After a full day or two of fairly intense interactions, I would come out with a crazy hat on and field written questions from the audience. We were always sure to plant a couple of offbeat questions in with the earnest ones.

But this verges on being too Pagonis-specific. If you're going to be real, you can only be yourself. If you're not a stand-up comic, you can't become one on cue—just as if you're not a scintillating speaker, you can't become one overnight. Instead, the leader has to emphasize those traits in his or her character that will help make genuine contact with subordinates. Through this contact, the leader lends authority, and empowers people throughout the organization.

Chinese poet Lau-tzu, writing in the sixth century B.C., summarized the essence of good leadership:

> *A leader is best*
> *When people barely know he exists,*
> *Not so good when people obey and acclaim him,*
> *Worse when they despise him.*
> *But of a good leader, who talks little,*
> *When his work done, his aim fulfilled,*
> *They will say:*
> *We did it ourselves.*[25]

Andrew Carnegie's tombstone puts it more bluntly: "Here lies one who knew how to get around him men who were cleverer than himself."[26]

A NOTE TO END ON

The last lesson of the Gulf War is the most important of all, and I think it's an appropriate note on which to end this book. It speaks not only to leaders and logisticians, but to all Americans.

More than 560,000 American service members, in all branches of the armed forces, passed through Saudi Arabia and Kuwait during the seventeen months that I was there. The customs and traditions that they encountered in those countries were dramatically different from anything most had ever experienced before. The potential for "Ugly Americanism" seemed great.

And what happened, when these two vastly different cultures came together? Nothing. There was not a single incident of deliberate misconduct on the part of our service members.

Certainly the strict Muslim context helped. (If some of our troops learned that their lives could be lived more happily without the use of drugs or alcohol, then they owe a special debt of thanks to our hosts.) But I think we should keep our eyes on the *character* displayed by our young people. Even toward our "enemy"—and I put the word in quotes here, because the hapless Iraqi conscripts who surrendered by the thousands, scared and starving, were not our enemy—our soldiers show great understanding and compassion.

Our soldiers also demonstrated that they were smart, and talented, and flexible. They operated complex planes, computers, and armaments with ease. In my command, and I'm sure in every other command, they showed an amazing capacity to think on their feet and solve problems.

What's the significance of all this? Easy: these young people are the future of our nation. For all of those who are concerned about the United States and where it is headed; who are concerned about the shortcomings of our educational system, about our work ethic, or about our ability to compete in the work marketplace; I have good news. I know of more than a half-million young Americans who are talented, self-disciplined, and accomplished ambassadors of good will. They have absolutely transformed the way that the Saudis, the Kuwaitis, and even the Iraqis think of us. Less visibly, they have impressed the thousands of third-country nationals—from Bangladesh, India, the Philippines, Egypt, and a dozen other countries—with their fairness and generosity.

They changed the world by force of arms. But down in the trenches, person to person, they also changed the way that the world looks at us. This was a remarkable feat, perhaps even more remarkable and durable than Desert Shield, Desert Storm, and Desert Farewell.

We have a great future ahead of us.

Notes

PREFACE

1. See, for example, *The McKinsey Quarterly,* Issues 3 and 4, 1991.
2. Bryan Perrett, *Desert Warfare* (Wellingborough, England: Patrick Stephens, 1988), p. 109.
3. David Irving, *The Trail of the Fox* (New York: E. P. Dutton, 1977), pp. 70–71.
4. Jack Anderson and Dale Van Atta, *Stormin' Norman: An American Hero* (New York: Kensington Publishing, 1991), p. 182.
5. Excerpt from General Schwarzkopf's February 27, 1991, Central Command Briefing, reprinted in *Military Review* (September 1991), p. 97.

CHAPTER 1

1. *Armed Forces Journal International* (April 1991), p. 5.
2. Statistic cited by Col. Peter C. Langenus, U.S. Army Reserve, commander of the 318th Transportation Agency (Movement Control); in "Moving an Army: Movement Control for Desert Storm," *Military Review* (September 1991), p. 44. See Note 9 on *Military Review.*
3. Hazem Beblawi, *The Arab Gulf Economy in a Turbulent Age* (New York: St. Martin's Press, 1984), p. 150.
4. Ibid.
5. Ray Vicker, *The Kingdom of Oil* (New York: Charles Scribner's Sons, 1974), p. 173.
6. Beblawi, *The Arab Gulf Economy,* p. 150. It is worth noting here that countries to the west of the Gulf—including Iraq, Kuwait, and Saudi Arabia—are Arabic, and speak of the "Arabian Gulf." Iran, to the east of the Gulf, is a Persian nation, and Iranians use the phrase "Persian Gulf." Travelers to the region are well advised to learn and make this distinction.

7. Valerie Yorke and Louis Turner, *European Interests and Gulf Oil* (Brookfield, Vt.: Gower Publishing, 1986), p. 58.

8. I have not sampled EPW [enemy prisoner of war] debriefings in any scientific way; however, these themes occur time and time again in the interrogations I and my colleagues have reviewed.

9. From a transcript of President Bush's address to the nation, entitled "The Deployment of US Armed Forces to Saudi Arabia," August 8, 1990; from *Military Review* (September 1991), p. 83.

10. USMC Lt. Col. Ky L. Thompson's description of Desert Shield, in his February 19, 1991 congressional testimony, as quoted in *Armed Forces Journal International* (April 1991), p. 12.

11. Lieutenant General John J. Yeosock, "Army Operations in the Gulf Theater," *Military Review* (September 1991), p. 3.

12. See "Good Logistics Is Combat Power: The Logistics Sustainment of Operation Desert Storm," by Lieutenant General William G. Pagonis and Major Harold E. Raugh, Jr., in *Military Review* (September 1991), pp. 28–39. All other unattributed statistics concerning Desert Shield and Desert Storm are from my memory of a specific point in time, and may not prove to be the final figures.

13. See "General's Star Feat: Desert Armies Come, and Go," *New York Times*, November 8, 1991.

14. Per a report on National Public Radio's *Morning Edition*, December 13, 1991.

CHAPTER 2

1. Quoted in Michael Maccoby, *The Leader* (New York: Simon & Schuster, 1981), p. 24.

2. Max De Pree, *Leadership Is an Art* (Lansing: Michigan State University Press, 1987), p. 14.

3. Robert L. Taylor and William E. Rosenbach, *Leadership: Challenges for Today's Manager* (New York: Nichols Publishing, 1989), p. 138.

4. As quoted in William A. Cohen, *The Art of the Leader* (Englewood Cliffs, N.J.: Prentice-Hall, 1990), p. 165.

CHAPTER 3

1. Colonel David H. Hackworth, *About Face* (New York: Simon & Schuster, 1989), p. 475.

2. Ibid., p. 551.

CHAPTER 4

1. A specific and detailed description of General John Yeosock's METT-T assessment of the conflict in the Gulf can be found in his article "Army Operations in the Gulf Theater," *Military Review* (September 1991), pp. 2–15.

2. Irving H. Anderson, *Aramco, the United States, and Saudi Arabia* (Princeton, N.J.: Princeton University Press, 1981), p. 9.

3. Hazem Beblawi, *The Arab Gulf Economy in a Turbulent Age* (New York: St. Martin's Press, 1984), p. 114.

4. See, for example, Theodore Draper's survey article, "The True History of the Gulf War," *New York Review of Books,* January 30, 1992, p. 38.

5. Bryan Perrett, *Desert Warfare* (Wellingborough, England: Patrick Stephens, 1988), pp. 10–11.

CHAPTER 5

1. For insight into the *Sharia* in the context of a modern economy, see Ali D. Johany, Michel Berne, and J. Wilson Mixon, Jr., *The Saudi Arabian Economy* (Baltimore: Johns Hopkins University Press, 1986).
2. Jay A. Conger, *The Charismatic Leader* (San Francisco: Jossey-Bass, 1989), p. 42.
3. Quoted in William A. Cohen, *The Art of the Leader* (Englewood Cliffs, N.J.: Prentice-Hall, 1990), p. 158.
4. Ibid., p. 33.
5. Figures taken from the General Accounting Office's report entitled *Operation Desert Storm: Transportation and Distribution of Equipment and Supplies in Southwest Asia*, December 1991, p. 4.
6. "It's a long way from Kansas to Kuwait," *Modern Materials Handling*, July 4, 1991, p. 55. This issue of *Modern Materials Handling* (in which I was named "Materials Handling Man of the Year") includes a 33-page special section devoted to the logistics and materials-handling achievements of Desert Storm.
7. Quoted in Charles C. Manz and Henry P. Sims, Jr., *Superleadership* (New York: Prentice Hall Press, 1989), p. 186.
8. Donald W. Engels, *Alexander the Great and the Logistics of the Macedonian Army* (Berkeley and Los Angeles: University of California Press, 1978), p. 1. It is not too much to say that the publication of van Creveld's *Supplying War* (1977) and this work in the following year marked the beginning of rigorous study in the field of logistics.
9. Ibid., p. 13.
10. Bryant Perrett, *Desert Warfare* (Wellingborough, England: Patrick Stephens, 1988), p. 115.
11. My recollections of the two briefings described on the following pages have been sharpened and augmented by information found in the report "Theater Linehaul Transportation Operations During Desert Shield and Desert Storm," written by Major Paul L. Willis, Transportation Plans Officer, 22d SUPCOM and member of the log cell.

CHAPTER 6

1. Martin van Creveld, *Supplying War* (Cambridge: Cambridge University Press, 1977), p. 200.

CHAPTER 7

1. Sun Tzu, *The Art of War* (London: Oxford University Press, 1977), p. 84.
2. Abraham Zaleznik, *The Managerial Mystique* (New York: Harper & Row, 1989), p. 16.
3. John Keegan, *The Mask of Command* (London: Jonathan Cape, 1987), p. 329.
4. Ibid., p. 138.
5. Ibid., p. 200.

6. Quoted in Robert L. Taylor and William E. Rosenbach, *Leadership: Challenges for Today's Manager* (New York: Nichols Publishing, 1989), p. 109.

7. James A. Belasco, *Teaching the Elephant to Dance* (New York: Crown Publishers, 1990), p. 220.

8. Max De Pree, *Leadership Is an Art* (East Lansing: Michigan State University Press, 1987), p. 11.

9. Keegan, *The Mask of Command,* pp. 301–302.

10. Martin van Creveld, *Technology and War* (New York: Free Press, 1989), p. 239.

11. De Pree, *Leadership Is an Art,* pp. 17–18.

12. Zaleznik, *The Managerial Mystique,* p. 244.

13. Quoted in Charles C. Manz and Henry P. Sims, Jr., *Superleadership* (New York: Prentice Hall Press, 1989), p. 106.

14. Ibid., p. 111.

15. Niccolo Machiavelli, *The Prince* (New York: St. Martin's Press, 1946), p. 185.

16. Belasco, *Teaching the Elephant to Dance,* p. 168.

17. Manz and Sims, *Superleadership,* p. 49.

18. Ibid., p. 163.

19. Zaleznik, *The Managerial Mystique,* p. 38.

20. Taylor and Rosenbach, *Leadership,* p. 64.

CHAPTER 8

1. James L. Heskett, Nicholas A. Glaskowsky, Jr., and Robert M. Ivie, *Business Logistics* (New York: The Ronald Press, 1973), p. 5.

2. These figures and others in this section are taken from a General Accounting Office report entitled "Operation Desert Storm: Transportation and Distribution of Equipment and Supplies in Southwest Asia" (GAO/NSIAD-92-20), published in December 1991.

3. See, for example, Murray Hammick's article on p. 998 of the September 1991 issue of the *International Defense Review.*

4. See Graham Sharman, "Good Logistics Is Business Power," in the *McKinsey Quarterly,* no. 4, (1991), p. 37. The article's title is derived from the 22d SUPCOM's motto: Good Logistics Is Combat Power.

5. See "Top Guns of Desert Storm," in the February 11, 1991 edition of *U. S. News and World Report,* p. 42.

6. Martin van Creveld, *Technology and War* (New York: Free Press, 1989), pp. 316–317.

7. See Sharman, "Good Logistics Is Business Power," p. 35.

8. Quoted in Peter Baily and David Farmer, *Managing Materials in Industry* (New York: John Wiley & Sons, 1973), p. 14.

9. This and following quotes are taken from C. F. H. van Rijn's introductory article in *Logistics: Where Ends Have to Meet* (Oxford: Pergamon Press, 1989), pp. 7–8.

10. Donald J. Bowersox, et al., *Leading Edge Logistics: Competitive Positioning for the 1990s* (Oak Brook, Ill.: Council of Logistics Management, 1989), pp. i–ii.

11. van Rijn, *Logistics: Where Ends Have to Meet,* p. 31.

12. Bowersox et al., *Leading Edge Logistics,* p. 4.
13. Ibid., p. 78.
14. James A. Belasco, *Teaching the Elephant to Dance* (New York: Crown Publishers, 1990), p. 148.
15. For a good historical summary of business logistics through the early 1970s, see Heskett, Glaskowsky, and Ivie, *Business Logistics,* pp. 32–34.
16. Sharman, "Good Logistics Is Business Power," p. 41.
17. Cited in Belasco, *Teaching the Elephant to Dance,* p. 187.
18. Quoted in William A. Cohen, *The Art of the Leader* (Englewood Cliffs, N.J.: Prentice-Hall, 1990), p. 124.
19. Belasco, *Teaching the Elephant to Dance,* p. 38.
20. From Robert L. Taylor and William E. Rosenbach, *Leadership: Challenges for Today's Manager* (New York: Nichols Publishing, 1989), p. 163.
21. Sharman, "Good Logistics Is Business Power," p. 49.
22. Cohen, *The Art of the Leader,* p. 46.
23. Quoted in Charles C. Manz and Henry P. Sims, Jr., *Superleadership* (New York: Prentice Hall Press, 1989), p. 103.
24. Michael Maccoby, *The Leader* (New York: Simon & Schuster, 1981), p. 221.
25. Quoted in Manz and Sims, *Superleadership,* p. 227.
26. Cohen, *The Art of the Leader,* p. 3.

Glossary

APOD	Aerial port of debarkation
ARCENT	Army Central Command, commanded during the Gulf War by Lieutenant General John J. Yeosock
BG	Brigadier General
BOQ	Bachelor officers' quarters
CDC	Combat Development Command
CENTCOM	U.S. Central Command (one of ten unified and specified commands, under which members of the four armed services are placed while in theaters of combat), commanded during the Gulf War by Gen. H. Norman Schwarzkopf
CG	Commanding general
CINC	Commander in Chief
CO	Commanding officer
COSCOM	Corps Support Command; the corps-level logistical structure

CS	Combat support
CSS	Combat service support
DCG	Deputy commanding general
DISCOM	Division Support Command; the division-level logistical structure
DoD	Department of Defense
EAC	Echelon above corps (an Army command structure above the corps level, usually ad hoc)
EPW	Enemy prisoner of war
ER	Evaluation Report, written annually about each officer by his or her two assigned "raters," and the key document in the promotion process
FORSCOM	U.S. Forces Command (one of ten unified and specified commands, under which members of the four armed services are placed while in theaters of combat)
G4	Assistant Chief of Staff, Logistics
HET	Heavy equipment transporter
J4	Director of Logistics
KKMC	King Khalid Military City, a Saudi installation in the northern desert, near Iraq, that served Allied forces as a major supply and transfer center
Log	Logistics
LOTS	Logistics over the shore (an approach to supply that presumes limited or no port facilities)
LSV	Logistics supply vessel
LTG	Lieutenant General
MARCENT	Marine Central Command, commanded during the Gulf War by Lieutenant General Walter E. Boomer
MG	Major General

MHE	Materials handling equipment (e.g., forklifts)
MODA	The Saudi Arabian Ministry of Defense and Aviation
MP	Military police
MRE	Meals, ready to eat
MSR	Main supply route
MWR	Morale, welfare, and recreation
NAVCENT	Navy Central Command, commanded during the Gulf War by Vice Admiral Stanley R. Arthur
NCO	Noncommissioned officer
RA	Regular Army (as opposed to the reserve)
REFORGER	REturn of FORces to GERmany
ROTC	Reserve Officer Training Corps
SITREP	Situation report
SPOD	Seaport of debarkation
SUPCOM	Support Command
TAACOM	Theater Army Area Command (a logistical echelon above corps, used when two or more corps are in a given theater of war)
TPT	Tactical petroleum terminal (a flexible bladder for transport, storage, and distribution of liquids)
TDY	Temporary duty
TPFDL	Time-Phased Force Deployment List (pronounced "tipfiddle"), used to determine sequence of units introduced into a theater of war
USMTM	U.S. Military Training Mission of Saudi Arabia
XO	Executive Officer

Index